Real Estate Appraiser License
State Exam Preparation

Contributors:

Dwight E. Norris

George Hatch

Ashley Crown Systems, Inc.

This publication is designed to provide accurate and current information regarding the subject matter covered. The principles and conclusions presented are subject to local, state and federal laws and regulations, court cases and revisions of the same. If legal advice or other expert assistance is required, the reader is urged to consult with a competent professional in that field.

Project Manager: Brandi Stater
Editor: Marlyss Bird
Cover Design: Dria Kasunich

© 2004 by Ashley Crown Systems, Inc.

Published by Ashley Crown Systems, Inc.
23141 Verdugo Street
Laguna Hills, CA 92653
949-598-0875

All rights reserved. No part of this book may be reproduced or transmitted in any form or by any means, electronic or mechanical, including photocopying, recording or by any information storage or retrieval system, without prior written permission from the publisher.

Printed in the United States of America

ISBN: 0-934-772-81-9

Table of Contents

Introduction 1
Pre-Test 2
   Answer Key 13
Influences on Real Estate Value 17
   Answer Key 21
Legal Considerations in Appraisal 23
   Answer Key 44
Types of Value 53
   Answer Key 59
Economic Principles 61
   Answer Key 71
Real Estate Markets and Analysis 75
   Answer Key 88
Valuation Process 94
   Answer Key 105
Property Description 111
   Answer Key 122
Highest and Best Use Analysis 127
   Answer Key 133
Appraisal Statistical Concepts 136
   Answer Key 149
Sales Comparison Approach 155
   Answer Key 171
Site Value 178
   Answer Key 185
Cost Approach 188
   Answer Key 205
Income Approach 213
   Answer Key 225
Valuation of Partial Interests 231
   Answer Key 234
Appraisal Standards and Ethics 235
   Answer Key 272
Practice Exam 1 289
   Answer Key 310
Practice Exam 2 319
   Answer Key 341
Appendix 1 350

Contributors

Dwight E. Norris

Dwight E. Norris is an AQB Certified USPAP instructor and has been involved in the real estate business since 1979. His experience encompasses many fields with the real estate profession. He has worked as a real estate appraiser, broker, instructor and author. He earned a Bachelor of Arts and a Master of Arts in Communications from Pepperdine University

George Hatch

George Hatch holds a Certified General Appraiser License and is an AQB Certified USPAP Instructor. He has been appraising since 1986 and currently performs commercial appraisals in San Diego County, California. In addition, he has authored and developed a number of ACE-accredited appraisal education courses. He earned a Bachelor of Science in Business from California State University, Long Beach.

Introduction

The purpose of this book is to help you prepare for the real estate appraisal licensing examination. The book is designed to be used after completing the required appraiser license course and is formatted to help you recall material you have learned in your appraisal course.

This book is compromised of the following sections:

1. Pre-Test

    Start with the Pre-Test to determine your readiness for the state examination. Correct your test and mark your results using the Score Chart for the Pre-Test. The Score Chart will allow you to quickly determine your understanding of the material. Before continuing, you should review any of the categories in which you did not score at least 85%.

2. Category Questions

    The fifteen categories parallel the content areas of the Appraisal Qualifications Board (AQB) categories and include all of the topics necessary to prepare for the licensing exam. Answer the category questions, correct them, then, review your answers before starting the next category. Continue the testing process until you are passing each category at 85% or better.

3. Sample Exams

    The mix of questions in the sample exams reflects the mix in the appraisal licensing exam. After completing all of the categories, test your understanding with the first of the two comprehensive sample exams. Take Practice Exam One, correct it and track your results using the Score Chart for Practice Exam One. Review the questions answered incorrectly. If your score is below 85% in any category, thoroughly review that category prior to taking the second practice exam. When you are ready to take Practice Exam Two follow the same procedure.

Although the passing percentage on your state licensing may be lower, we recommend you study until you consistently score above 85%.

This Real Estate Appraiser License Exam Book will help you towards your goal to become a licensed real estate appraiser. By following the steps above and those presented in each section of this book, we believe you will be able to take the state examination with knowledge and confidence, and successfully pass your exam.

Pre-Test

1. You are asked to perform a "condition and marketability report." You are not asked to give a value conclusion as part of the assignment. You:

    a. cannot take this assignment as it violates the ETHICS RULE.
    b. do not have to follow USPAP since there is no conclusion of value requested.
    c. must follow USPAP since this is a valuation service, even though no conclusion of value was requested.
    d. may take this assignment, but may not receive a fee since it is not a complete appraisal as no value conclusion will be given.

2. An appraiser is valuing a single-family residence and observes a foundation that is cracked, has only one bathroom for 4 bedrooms, and has an oversupply of single-family residences for sale in the local market due to a recent local recession. What has the appraiser observed?

    a. Physical deterioration, functional obsolescence, and economic obsolescence
    b. Functional obsolescence, physical deterioration, and economic obsolescence
    c. Economic obsolescence, physical deterioration, and locational obsolescence
    d. Economic obsolescence, functional obsolescence, and locational obsolescence

3. An appraiser considers all of the following when analyzing the physical characteristics of a lot **except**:

    a. whether it is an inside lot or a corner lot.
    b. whether it is a rectangular lot or an odd-shaped lot.
    c. the presence of storm sewers.
    d. the extent of landscaping.

4. Which of the following is often subject to less than adequate market exposure time?

    a. Assessed value
    b. Liquidation value
    c. Insurable value
    d. Value-in-exchange

5. A parcel in a lakefront community with no lake view sells for $100,000, while a parcel in the same community with a lake view sells for 25% more. If you appraised a square lot in this community that measures 10,000 square feet and has a view of the lake, what would be the price of the lot on a front foot basis?

    a. $125
    b. $1,200
    c. $1,250
    d. $1,500

6. Which of the following best describes a complete appraisal?

    a. The act or process of developing an opinion of value without invoking the JURISDICTIONAL EXCEPTION RULE
    b. The act or process of developing an opinion of value without invoking the DEPARTURE RULE
    c. The act or process of developing an opinion of value while invoking the DEPARTURE RULE
    d. The act or process of developing an opinion of value without using a hypothetical condition

7. When a property has a non-conforming use, which of the following is true?

    a. The land is valued on its permissible basis.
    b. The improvements are valued based on the permissible use.
    c. Non-conforming uses cannot be valued because they are illegal.
    d. Non-conforming use value is always less than permissible use value.

8. Which of the following items should be included in a reconstructed statement of net operating income?

    a. Debt service
    b. Management charges
    c. Internal rate of return
    d. Mortgage interest payments

9. Which of the following is calculated using the band-of-investment technique?

    a. Replacement cost
    b. Overall capitalization rate
    c. Net operating income
    d. Return on investment rate

10. When degrees are used in metes and bounds descriptions, all changes in direction are based on which of the following lines?

    a. East West
    b. North South
    c. North East
    d. South West

11. Which of the following is a likely result if development costs rise faster than the prices of existing competitive properties?

    a. The building industry will experience increased competition, resulting in unchecked development.
    b. Supply will outpace demand.
    c. The lack of opportunity for adequate profit will reduce new housing starts, thus limiting supply while demand remains the same.
    d. Prices will go down.

12. 1/4 of a 1/4 section is:

    a. 1/8 of a section.
    b. 1/2 of a section.
    c. 1/16 of a section.
    d. 160 acres.

13. During an appraisal assignment you apply more than one approach to value and derive significant differences in the resulting indications of value. All of the following are appropriate resolutions **except**:

    a. review your math and correct any mistakes.
    b. review the data and consider how you analyzed it.
    c. revise the data to derive one value from all the approaches.
    d. review how you applied the approaches.

14. An appraiser may define or explain a neighborhood in many different ways. All of the following are acceptable ways to define a neighborhood **except**:

    a. subdivision name.
    b. natural boundaries.
    c. race.
    d. district boundaries.

15. An absorption analysis indicates that the residents of a community are capable of purchasing 10 properties per year that cost $150,000 or more. There are currently 40 homes in the area that are available and valued at $250,000. How many years will it take for all these homes to be purchased?

    a. 1 year
    b. 2 years
    c. 4 years
    d. 10 years

16. The economic principle of _____ states that the value of a property is equal to the present value of the property's future income.

    a. contribution
    b. anticipation
    c. supply and demand
    d. substitution

17. Accrued depreciation is estimated using the age-life method by calculating the ratio of a property's effective age to its _____, and applying the ratio to the property's reproduction cost new.

    a. physical age
    b. depreciated age
    c. chronological age
    d. total economic life

18. Some areas in Southern California have been adversely affected by civil disobedience, crime, and illegal immigration. Which of the four forces are these part of?

    a. Environmental
    b. Economic
    c. Governmental
    d. Social

19. An appraiser should consider _____ first when determining market value.

    a. the income approach
    b. land value
    c. highest and best use
    d. current use

20. By definition, market value is the _____ price.

    a. highest price
    b. average price
    c. most probable price
    d. seller's asking

21. An appraiser asks a title company to confirm a sale. The title company confirms the sale as a full value transaction using documentary transfer stamps. The stamps were issued at a rate of $.55 per $500 in value, and they total $308.55. The loan-to-value ratio is 80%, and the buyer didn't assume any pre-existing loans. What was the sales price?

    a. $280,000
    b. $350,000
    c. $561,000
    d. $701,250

22. Which of the following is not a requirement of a written appraisal report?

    a. It must contain a copy of the deed.
    b. It must define the value to be estimated.
    c. It must state the purpose of the appraisal.
    d. It must identify the real estate being appraised.

23. What is the term for representing the cause or interest of another, even if that cause or interest does not necessarily coincide with one's own beliefs, opinions, conclusions, or recommendations?

    a. Activism
    b. Bias
    c. Advocacy
    d. Sponsorship

24. The anticipation of _____ creates value.

    a. future price
    b. cash flow
    c. cost
    d. future benefits

25. An office building sits on a parcel of land. Which of the following statements best describes the parcel's highest and best use?

    a. It cannot be determined.
    b. It is necessarily the current use because the parcel is improved.
    c. It may be different from the current use.
    d. If the building is over five years old, the highest and best use is most likely different from the current use.

26. In a neighborhood full of well maintained homes, a poorly maintained home is an example of:

    a. substitution.
    b. progression.
    c. regression.
    d. competition.

27. What is unique about joint tenancy?

    a. Each owner has equal possession.
    b. Each owner may will their interest.
    c. Each joint tenant has right of survivorship.
    d. Each joint tenant may sell their interest.

28. Excessiveness and inadequacy are both items of:

    a. physical deterioration.
    b. functional inutility.
    c. external obsolescence.
    d. superstructure.

29. A market that has easily produced, readily transferable goods with a large number of buyers and sellers describes a(n):

    a. inefficient market.
    b. monopoly.
    c. efficient market.
    d. effective market.

30. Which process is used to reconcile the adjusted values of comparables?

    a. Average the adjusted results from the appropriate comparables.
    b. Review the comparables and use a median of the adjusted values.
    c. Review the comparables and use the top four values to compare to the subject property.
    d. Review each sale and judge its comparability to the subject property.

31. Which of the following adjustments can not be made using percentage adjustments?

    a. Time
    b. Location
    c. Special conditions
    d. Ownership

32. What is a factor that expresses a relationship between value and a particular property feature?

    a. Element of comparison
    b. Unit of measure
    c. Unit of comparison
    d. Essential element

33. When performing a market analysis, an appraiser must analyze:

    a. mostly the supply factors.
    b. only the demand factors.
    c. supply factors, demand factors, or a combination of both.
    d. supply and finance factors that affect demand.

34. Which of the following conditions is a limitation when using the sales comparison approach?

    a. The approach's reliance on historical data
    b. Comparables that are too similar
    c. An active market
    d. An appraiser using the approach to value residential properties

35. Which of the following statements is correct regarding the sales comparison approach?

    a. When selecting comparable sales, the appraiser does not consider the age of the property.
    b. When using the sales comparison approach, the appraiser adjusts the comparable properties to the subject property.
    c. An appraiser should never use comparable sales that are more than six months old.
    d. The sales prices of comparables are always conclusive evidence of market value in the area.

36. In which of the following circumstances may an appraiser's role be misunderstood?

    a. An appraiser, who is also a real estate broker, acting as a broker
    b. An appraiser when appraising a property
    c. A broker listing a property
    d. When using the DEPARTURE RULE

37. If an appraiser does not develop one of the three approaches to value while performing an appraisal because that approach is not applicable to the appraisal problem, the appraisal is considered:

    a. incomplete.
    b. null and void.
    c. complete.
    d. unreliable.

38. What is the greatest possible interest one can have in real property?

    a. A fee simple
    b. A fee defeasible
    c. A life estate
    d. A reversionary estate

39. The _____ has the burden to disclose in the appraisal report information that is relevant to the assignment.

    a. client
    b. lender
    c. Appraisal Foundation
    d. appraiser

40. A property suffering from superadequacy experiences:

    a. economic obsolescence.
    b. functional obsolescence.
    c. plottage.
    d. progression.

41. If the existing use of a special purpose property is functionally obsolete and no alternatives are feasible, what is its highest and best use?

    a. Its current use
    b. As vacant land
    c. As scrap or salvage
    d. A future use as developed

42. An old, run-down house with a limited economic life stands on a site that is zoned for commercial use. This is an example of:

    a. adverse use.
    b. variance.
    c. interim use.
    d. exception.

43. The income approach would be unreliable if the appraiser uses:

    a. unsupported room adjustments.
    b. unverified age adjustments.
    c. unsupported rent adjustments.
    d. unsupported location adjustments.

44. An example of a governmental force would be:

    a. a trend toward decreasing unemployment rate.
    b. enacting stricter building codes with the city limits.
    c. a higher than average immigration rate.
    d. the building of a new aquatic complex.

45. A _____ depicts topographical features.

    a. plat map
    b. site survey
    c. soil study
    d. contour map

46. What is the length of one side of 1/16th of a square section?

    a. 1/2 mile
    b. 1/4 mile
    c. 1/8th mile
    d. 1/16th mile

47. What form of legal description measures land in terms of townships?

    a. Lot and block system
    b. Topographical survey
    c. Metes and bounds survey
    d. Government survey

48. Which of the following is defined as the study of the supply and demand conditions for a specific product or service in a specific area?

    a. Market analysis
    b. Projection analysis
    c. Economic analysis
    d. Absorption analysis

49. Dollar adjustments may be based on all of the following **except**:

    a. total price of the property.
    b. front foot price.
    c. net sales price.
    d. square foot price.

50. An apartment building contains 260 units, which rent at a rate of 12 per month. How many years will this supply of apartments last?

    a. 5.53 years
    b. 2 years
    c. 1.81 years
    d. 21.67 years

Score Chart

Category	Questions	Score
Influences on Real Estate Value	18, 44	
Legal Considerations in Appraisal	10, 27	
Types of Value	4, 20	
Economic Principles	16, 24, 26	
Real Estate Markets and Analysis	11, 29, 33, 48, 50	
Valuation Process	13, 14, 19, 39	
Property Description	12, 28, 45, 46, 47	
Highest and Best Use Analysis	7, 25, 41, 42	
Appraisal Statistical Concepts	15, 21	
Sales Comparison Approach	5, 30, 31, 34, 35	
Site Value	3, 32, 49	
Cost Approach	2, 17, 40	
Income Approach	8, 9, 43	
Valuation of Partial Interests	38	
Appraisal Standards and Ethics	1, 6, 22, 23, 36, 37	

Answers

1. (c) An appraiser must comply with USPAP any time he or she represents that they are performing a service as an appraiser.

2. (a) Physical deterioration is loss in value due to neglected repairs or maintenance. Functional obsolescence results from defects in a building or structure that detract from its value such as an unworkable design or layout, or features that are outdated. Economic obsolescence is loss in value due to forces outside the property, such as changes in optimum land use, zoning, or the balance of supply and demand.

3. (d) When analyzing the physical characteristics of a lot, the items an appraiser considers include whether it is an inside lot or a corner lot, rectangular lot or an odd-shaped lot, the if there is storm water disposal, and whether it is a flat lot or a sloping lot or one that drops off significantly. However, landscaping is not considered.

4. (b) Liquidation value is a price that an owner is compelled to accept when the property must be sold with less-than-reasonable market exposure.

5. (c) A square lot implies 100 x 100 square feet dimensions (100 x 100 = 10,000 square feet). Therefore, the lot has 100 front feet. Premium parcels sell for $125,000 ($100,000 x 1.25 = $125,000). So $125,000 ÷ 100 = $1,250.

6. (a) A complete appraisal is the act or process of developing an opinion of value without invoking the DEPARTURE RULE.

7. (a) The land value of a non-conforming use is based on the legally permissible use, assuming that the land is vacant and its value can be deducted from the total property value.

8. (b) Management expenses should be included in the net operating income statement. The other expenses are not operating expenses.

9. (b) The band-of-investment technique is commonly used to calculate overall capitalization rate, or overall rate.

10. (b) The north-south line is always the basis changes in direction.

11. (c) Builders will build new housing only if the opportunity for adequate profit exists. If builders do not build new housing, the supply of available housing is limited and the demand is proportionately greater, thus increasing prices of existing housing.

12. (c) ¼ x ¼ = 1/16

13. (c) You should not be correcting any errors in thinking or technique during the reconciliation process. Any corrections that need to be made should be completed during the review process that precedes the final conclusion of value.

14. (c) An appraiser must never consider race when defining a specific neighborhood or rendering an opinion of value.

15. (c) Simply divide the number of available homes by the rate at which the residents can purchase them. $40 \div 10 = 4$.

16. (b) The principle of anticipation states that the value of a property is based on the expectation of future benefits, such as its projected income.

17. (d) Accrued depreciation = effective age/total economic life.

18. (d) By definition.

19. (c) The steps in the appraisal process are: 1) state the problem; 2) list the data needed and their sources; 3) gather, record, and verify the necessary data; 4) determine the highest and best use; 5) estimate the land value; 6) estimate the value by each of the three approaches; 7) reconcile the estimated values for the final value estimate; and 8) report the final value estimate.

20. (c) By definition.

21. (a) The stamps are calculated as $0.55 per $500 of new money. 561 x 0.55 = $280,000. It represents the entire transaction amount and not just the loan amount- there were no loans assumed.

22. (a) According to Standards Rule 2-2, each style of written appraisal report must define the value to be estimated, and state the purpose of the appraisal (SR 2-2 a, b, and c [v]). All written appraisal reports must also identify the real estate being appraised (SR 2-2 a, b, and c [iii]).

23. (c) Advocacy is representing the cause or interest of another, even if that cause or interest is not necessarily in line with one's own beliefs, opinions, conclusions, or recommendations.

24. (d) Value is created by the anticipation of future benefits. This is the concept of the principle of anticipation, which is the basis of the income capitalization approach.

25. (c) A property's highest and best use may not be its current use. Many factors may change over time, including zoning ordinances, local economics, and local land use.

26. (b) A home that is poorly maintained will benefit from its location in a neighborhood of well-maintained homes. Conversely, a well maintained home that suffers from its location in a neighborhood of poorly-maintained homes is an example of regression.

27. (c) The most important and unique quality of joint tenancy is the right of survivorship. A joint tenant cannot transfer title to his or her share through a will.

28. (b) By definition. Gold faucets in the bathroom or too few bathrooms in the house could both be examples of functional inutility.

29. (c) By definition.

30. (d) The process to reconcile the adjusted values of comparables is to review each sale and judge its comparability to the property being appraised.

31. (d) Percentages are often used to express the differences between a subject property and a comparable sale. This is especially true for time, special conditions, and location adjustments. Residential appraisals use sales price as the unit of comparison, and the adjustments are made in dollars, not percentages.

32. (c) By definition.

33. (c) When conducting a residential market analysis, an appraiser should analyze the supply factors, demand factors, or a combination of both.

34. (a) You may have to adjust historical data of comparable sales to reflect the current market. All of the other choices are advantages to the sales comparison approach.

35. (b) Comparable properties are always adjusted to the subject property, never the subject property to the comparables.

36. (a) An appraiser who is also a real estate broker must be careful not to mislead clients. The appraiser must make clear to clients in what capacity he or she is performing.

37. (c) The definition of a complete appraisal is one in which the appraiser did not invoke the DEPARTURE RULE. An appraiser is not required to use all three approaches to value, only the approach(es) that are most appropriate to the assignment.

38. (a) A fee simple estate is the greatest possible interest one can have in real property. It is unqualified, indefinite in duration, freely transferable, and inheritable.

39. (d) USPAP requires appraisers to disclose information that is applicable to the appraisal assignment.

40. (b) Superadequacy exists within the property lines, therefore it is functional obsolescence.

41. (c) If the existing use of a special purpose property is physically or functionally obsolete and no alternative uses are feasible, the highest and best use of the property as improved may be scrap or salvage.

42. (c) Interim use is a temporary use of a property while it awaits transition to its highest and best use. Since the current use is not legally permitted due to the zoning classification, it cannot qualify as the property's highest and best use. Once the home is demolished, a commercial property must be constructed there.

43. (c) The income approach may be unreliable if the appraiser uses unsupported market rent adjustments.

44. (b) By definition. Employment and construction of a new aquatic complex are examples of an economic force, and population (immigration rate) is a social force.

45. (d) Plat maps and most site surveys include linear dimensions, not topography. A soil study includes verbal descriptions of soil composition and topography, but generally doesn't depict topography. A contour map specifically depicts topography.

46. (d) A section is a mile square; ¼ mile x ¼ mile = 1/16 mile

47. (d) The government survey form of legal land description measures land in units called townships that measure 6 miles by 6 miles.

48. (a) Market analysis is the study of real estate market conditions for a specific type of property in a specific area.

49. (c) If dollar adjustments are used, they may be based on either the total price of the whole property, or on the other units of comparison, such as price per square foot, price per front foot, price per acre, or per dwelling unit permitted by zoning on the site. Net sales price is the result of all the adjustments, not an adjustment by itself.

50. (c) The total supply is divided by the number of units rented per year. 260 ÷ (12x12).

Influences on Real Estate Value

1. Which of the following impacts the appraised value?

    a. Assessed value
    b. Original cost
    c. Loan amount
    d. None of the above

2. Which of the following is likely to result in an increase in value?

    a. Increase in supply
    b. Decrease in demand
    c. Downzoning
    d. Decrease in interent rates

3. Which of the following is an economic factor that influences value?

    a. Employment trends
    b. Birth rates
    c. Attitudes towards education
    d. Population change

4. Which of the following factors influences price?

    a. Supply
    b. Demand
    c. Favorable financing
    d. Purchasing power

5. Which principle of value best describes the affect an industrial plant would have on property values in a surrounding neighborhood?

    a. Highest and best use
    b. Externalities
    c. Contribution
    d. Supply and demand

6. Corner influence is:

    a. the use of unfair advantage to reach agreement in a negotiation of a contract.
    b. a form of functional obsolescence caused by uneven corners.
    c. the effect on value produced by a corner lot location.
    d. a form of functional obsolescence caused by building a house in the corner of a square parcel of land.

7. For a commercial business, a corner lot provides:

    a. more sunlight.
    b. greater privacy.
    c. better access and exposure.
    d. increased site depth.

8. An example of an economic force would be:

    a. a trend toward larger household sizes.
    b. the area is known for its good weather.
    c. the county increasing the property tax rate.
    d. a new bio-tech company locating in the city.

9. An example of a social force would be:

    a. higher interest rates.
    b. lower residential construction costs.
    c. the trend towards an aging population.
    d. increased unemployment rate.

10. An example of a governmental force would be:

    a. a trend toward decreasing unemployment rate.
    b. enacting stricter building codes with the city limits.
    c. a higher than average immigration rate.
    d. the building of a new aquatic complex.

11. Which of the following is **not** a governmental influence?

    a. Closure of a large chemical manufacturing plant
    b. City bonds financing the construction of a new aquatic complex
    c. An increase in the sales tax
    d. Restricting signage in downtown areas

12. If an area is known to have a high crime rate, it is an example of a(n):

    a. social force.
    b. governmental force.
    c. economic force.
    d. environmental force.

13. An area has excellent mountain vistas. Which force would it exhibit?

    a. Physical
    b. Social
    c. Economic
    d. Governmental

14. A city enforces thirty foot set backs in residential neighborhoods. This is an example of which kind of force?

    a. Physical
    b. Social
    c. Economic
    d. Governmental

15. San Diego is known for its mild climate and beautiful beaches on the Pacific Coast. Which of the four forces are these part of?

    a. Environmental
    b. Economic
    c. Governmental
    d. Social

16. Some areas in Southern California have been adversely affected by civil disobedience, crime, and illegal immigration. Which of the four forces are these part of?

    a. Environmental
    b. Economic
    c. Governmental
    d. Social

17. Annually, tornados cause severe damage in the midwest. Which of the four forces does this represent?

    a. Environmental
    b. Economic
    c. Governmental
    d. Social

18. The Sea World resorts in Orlando, FL and San Diego, CA have had a significant impact on uses and value of the land surrounding the resorts. Which of the four forces does this represent?

    a. Environmental
    b. Economic
    c. Governmental
    d. Social

19. The Department of Defense developed the King's Bay Submarine Base in southeastern Georgia to build nuclear submarines. Which of the four forces does this represent?

    a. Environmental
    b. Economic
    c. Governmental
    d. Social

20. In 1986, the Tax Reform Act eliminated many of the tax advantages for passive real estate investors. Which of the four forces does this represent?

    a. Environmental
    b. Economic
    c. Governmental
    d. Social

21. A real estate investor plans to purchase some wooded acreage with gently rolling hills in order to develop a single-family subdivision with homes priced from $500,000 to $650,000. After completing his market analysis he discovers that the prevalent purchaser in the area has a gross income level in the $60,000 to $75,000 per year range and decides not to buy the land. Which of the four forces does this represent?

    a. Environmental
    b. Economic
    c. Governmental
    d. Social

22. More people recycle their bottles, aluminum cans, and paper than ever before. Which of the four forces does this represent?

    a. Environmental
    b. Economic
    c. Governmental
    d. Social

Answers

1. (d) None of these should have impact on an appraised value.

2. (d) Reduction in interest rates lowers payments and enables more debt service, which in turn enables higher prices at the same payment cost.

3. (a) While employment trends are economic factors that influence value, all of the others are social factors that influence value.

4. (c) All of the others influence value.

5. (b) Influences from outside a property's boundaries that may affect its value are called externalities.

6. (c) Corner influence is the effect on property value produced by a corner lot location. The value may be greater or less than inside lots, depending on the perceived benefits of being located on a corner.

7. (c) Corner locations are exposed to more automobile and pedestrian traffic than interior lots.

8. (d) By definition. Household size is a social force, climate and weather are environmental forces, and taxes are definitely a governmental force.

9. (c) By definition. Interest rates are a governmental force, construction costs and employment rates are economic forces.

10. (b) By definition. Employment and construction of a new aquatic complex are examples of an economic force, and population (immigration rate) is a social force.

11. (a) Plant closure is an example of an economic force. Choices b, c, and d are all examples of governmental influence.

12. (a) By definition.

13. (a) By definition.

14. (d) By definition.

15. (a) By definition.

16. (d) By definition.

17. (a) By definition.

18. (b) By definition.

19. (c) By definition.

20. (c) By definition.

21. (d) The inadequate income level will not translate into purchasing power.

22. (d) By definition.

Legal Considerations in Appraisal

1. Which of the following is not a legal description of real property?

    a. Assessor's parcel number
    b. Address
    c. Mailing address
    d. All of the above

2. Before selling his property, Joe places a deed restriction on the property that states it must never be used for anything but a Little League field, which is its current use. Bob buys the property, and due to the deed restriction, has a:

    a. leasehold interest.
    b. fee simple defeasible.
    c. life estate
    d. fee simple absolute.

3. A life estate can never be based on the life of:

    a. the original grantor.
    b. the life tenant
    c. any third person.
    d. a corporation.

4. Suppose Erin grants a life estate to Jill for the life of Kim. Erin does not identify a third party to have an estate in remainder. If Jill dies before Kim, which of the following is true?

    a. Erin would maintain an estate in reversion.
    b. Jill's heirs would not acquire the life estate.
    c. Kim still maintains an estate in remainder.
    d. None of the above.

5. Allison grants a life estate to Sam for the life of Kim, and after Kim's death, the estate will pass to Peter. Which of the following is true?

    a. Allison maintains an estate in reversion.
    b. If Peter dies before Kim, then Peter loses the estate in remainder.
    c. Kim automatically acquires the estate in remainder.
    d. Allison retained no interest in the property.

6. Which of the following is shown on a plat map?

    a. The layout of the sites in a neighborhood
    b. The way dwelling is situated on a lot
    c. The additional value that results from owning the adjoining property
    d. The tract of land to be subdivided

7. Which is true regarding a trade fixture?

    a. It is always personal property.
    b. It is always real property.
    c. It is included in the appraised value.
    d. It depends on the use and manner of affixing.

8. Which of the following is always considered personal property?

    a. Trade fixture
    b. Mortgage
    c. A portable spa
    d. All of the above

9. An appraiser may be asked to appraise which of the following?

    a. Ownership in severalty
    b. Ownership in joint tenancy
    c. Community property
    d. All of the above

10. Which of the following is not a leasehold estate?

    a. Estate of periodic tenancy
    b. Life estate
    c. Estate for years
    d. Estate for will

11. Which of the following is an example of a riparian right?

    a. Reasonable use of water from a river
    b. Reasonable use of water from a lake
    c. Reasonable use of water from a sea
    d. Reasonable use of water from a ocean

12. Which of the following is an example of a littoral right?

    a. Reasonable use of water from a lake
    b. Reasonable use of water from a river
    c. Reasonable use of water from a stream
    d. Reasonable use of water from a watercourse

13. Which of the following is not true of personal property?

    a. It can be alienated.
    b. It is generally immovable.
    c. It can be hypothecated.
    d. It can become real property.

14. Which of the following is true concerning the grantor in a life estate?

    a. The grantor is no longer the owner.
    b. The grantor may not collect rent.
    c. The grantor has exclusive possession.
    d. The grantor has a reversionary interest.

15. Which of the following is **not** true regarding joint tenancy?

    a. All owners must have equal interest.
    b. All owners must have equal rights.
    c. All owners must have possession.
    d. If there are only two owners, they must be married.

16. A husband and wife may have which of the following type(s) of ownership?

    a. Severalty
    b. Tenants in common
    c. Joint tenancy
    d. Both b an c

17. A husband and wife each have a child from a previous marriage. Each spouse wants to ensure that their child is heir to their interest in the residence they currently own. To accomplish this, they should not take ownership:

    a. as tenants in common.
    b. as joint tenants.
    c. as a fee simple absolute.
    d. in severalty.

18. What is the only unity required for tenancy in common?

    a. Time
    b. Title
    c. Interest
    d. Possession

19. What is unique about joint tenancy?

    a. Each owner has equal possession.
    b. Each owner may will their interest.
    c. Each joint tenant has right of survivorship.
    d. Each joint tenant may sell their interest.

20. Which of the following terms means that the title reverts to the state when a person dies without a will and leaves no heirs?

    a. Inverse condemnation
    b. Police power
    c. Eminent Domain
    d. Escheat

21. Which of the following is **not** true regarding eminent domain?

    a. A property owner may not sue for severance damage.
    b. A property owner may not sue for inverse condemnation.
    c. It may be exercised by states, counties or cities.
    d. Fair market value must be compensated.

22. Which of the government's powers allows it to establish zoning ordinances and building codes to protect the safety and health of the public?

    a. Eminent domain
    b. Police power
    c. Escheat
    d. Condemnation

23. The process of acquiring an interest in property by prescription is very similar to acquiring title to property through adverse possession. What is the distinguishing requirement?

    a. The acquisition must be hostile.
    b. The possessor must occupy the property for 5 consecutive years.
    c. The possessor must have some claim to the property.
    d. The possessor must pay the property taxes.

24. Easements may be terminated in all of the following ways **except**:

    a. at will by the servient tenement.
    b. destruction of the servient tenement.
    c. excessive use.
    d. merger of the two properties.

25. Which of the following is a unique feature of an easement in gross?

    a. The easement runs with the owner.
    b. There is no servient tenement.
    c. There is no dominant tenement.
    d. It can belong to a legal or natural person.

26. Surfers do not have access to the local beach, so they begin walking across Joe's property to get to the beach. Assuming they meet all of the requirements for use, they are attempting to gain which of the following types of easements?

    a. Easement by prescription
    b. Easement in gross
    c. Appurtenant easement
    d. Easement by adverse possession

27. CC&R's are usually placed in which kind of document?

    a. By-laws
    b. Declaration of Homestead
    c. Declaration of Conditions
    d. Declaration of Restrictions

28. A homeowner wants to add a room to his house, but the current zoning does not permit the future use. The homeowner should apply for which of the following?

    a. A variance
    b. Re-zoning
    c. A building permit
    d. A partition appeal

29. Joe and Bill are neighbors. Joe realizes that the wall Bill built last year is actually on Joe's property. This is:

    a. an easement.
    b. an encroachment.
    c. a zoning violation.
    d. allowed as long as Bill properly notifies Joe.

30. Within how many years can a homeowner bring action against a neighbor who has encroached on his property?

    a. 4 years
    b. 2 years
    c. 5 years
    d. 3 years

31. Which of the following is true regarding life insurance companies?

    a. They prefer to make long-term loans.
    b. They like to make loans on large single-family residences.
    c. They like to make short-term loans.
    d. None of the above.

32. Which of the followng entities purchase FHA, VA, and conventional loans?

    a. Insurance companies
    b. Mutual Savings banks
    c. FNMA
    d. Both a and c

33. Which legal description(s) would be used to create a subdivision?

    a. Metes and bounds
    b. Rectangular survey
    c. Lot, block, and track
    d. Both a and b

34. How many acres does Township 2 North, Range 2 East, San Bernardino Base, and Meridian contain, assuming it is a standard township?

    a. 640
    b. 36
    c. 23,040
    d. 43,560

35. All standard townships lack which of the following?

    a. Same number of acres
    b. Same number of sections
    c. Same square footage
    d. Both a and c

36. What is the distance between section 2 and section 23 in any township?

   a. 1 miles
   b. 2 miles
   c. 3 miles
   d. 4 miles

37. What is the distance between section 2 and 16 in any township?

   a. 1.4 miles
   b. 2 miles
   c. 4 miles
   d. 36 miles

38. How big is a township?

   a. 1 mile square
   b. 4 miles square
   c. 36 miles square
   d. None of the above

39. How big is a section?

   a. 1 mile square
   b. 1 square mile
   c. Both a and b
   d. None of the above

40. Which of the following townships is furthest north?

   a. T2NR2E
   b. T1NR4E
   c. T4SR1E
   d. T3SR3S

41. North 60 degrees East is an example of which legal description?

   a. Metes and bounds
   b. U.S. Government Rectangular Survey
   c. Lot and Block
   d. Assessor's

42. When degrees are used in metes and bounds descriptions, all changes in direction are based on which of the following lines?

    a. East West
    b. North South
    c. North East
    d. South West

43. The builder of a new single-family neighborhood restricts the owner from installing a wood fence. This is an example of which of the following?

    a. Public restriction
    b. Zoning restriction
    c. Condition
    d. Covenant

44. John grants a life estate to Greg for Greg's life. If Greg dies, the estate goes to Carl. If Carl dies before Greg, which of the following is **not** true?

    a. Greg may encumber the estate.
    b. Carl's heirs will subsequently get title when Greg dies.
    c. John retains nothing.
    d. John retains an estate in reversion upon Carl's death.

45. All of the following are used in a metes and bounds legal property description **except**:

    a. Monuments.
    b. Degrees, minutes, and seconds.
    c. Meridians.
    d. Point of beginning.

46. Pet Paradise pet store leases space in Northcoast Mall. Under its lease, Pet Paradise must pay a base rent of $2,000 per month. If sales revenue exceeds $50,000 per month, Pet Paradise must pay 5% of the extra sales. If Pet Paradise's total sales are $60,000 this month, how much total rent do they have to pay?

    a. $2,500
    b. $3,000
    c. $3,500
    d. $5,500

47. One acre of land costs $20,000. What is the price of the N ½ of the SW ¼ of the SW ¼ of one section?

    a. $ 10,000
    b. $ 20,000
    c. $400,000
    d. $400,500

48. A tenant installs wall-to-wall carpeting in her individual unit without the landlord's permission. What legal right gives the landlord ownership of the carpet when the lease ends?

    a. Allocation
    b. Accession
    c. Accretion
    d. Assemblage

49. Which of the following statements about local zoning ordinances is **incorrect**?

    a. zoning prevents decline in property values within a certain zoning district.
    b. zoning determines what types of structures may be built in certain areas.
    c. zoning limits the height, size, and placement of structures.
    d. zoning may allow the same area to have multiple uses.

50. Which of the following is the definition of a *leased fee estate*?

    a. The rights enjoyed by the owner of a leased property
    b. The reversionary interest retained by the tenant
    c. The interest held by the owner of a vacant property
    d. The rights of the tenant under a percentage lease

51. Peterson Custom Homes paid $480,000 for the E ½ of the N ½ of the SW ¼ of Section 13. What was the price per acre?

    a. $ 6,000
    b. $ 8,000
    c. $12,000
    d. $48,000

52. A local tax is levied against a property owner to pay for the paving of a road directly in front of her property. What is this tax called?

    a. Implied easement tax
    b. Special assessment tax
    c. Road improvement tax
    d. Homeowners' tax

53. Which of the following statements is **incorrect**?

    a. One square mile contains 640 acres.
    b. One acre contains 46,360 square feet.
    c. One tract contains 16 townships.
    d. One township is 36 miles square.

54. Property taxes are calculated by:

    a. dividing the tax rate by the assessed value.
    b. multiplying the tax rate by the assessed value.
    c. dividing the tax rate by the most probable sales price.
    d. multiplying the tax rate by the most probable sales price.

55. The two legal interests created by a lease are the:

    a. freehold estate and the fee simple estate.
    b. leased fee estate and the leasehold estate.
    c. leased fee estate and the fee simple estate.
    d. market rent and the contract rent.

56. A lease creates two interests, one of which is the leased fee estate. Which party to the lease holds the leased fee estate?

    a. Lessor
    b. Lessee
    c. Mortgagee
    d. Fiduciary

57. In the rectangular survey method of legal land description, what is the name for an area of land measuring one mile by one mile?

    a. Range
    b. Township
    c. Section
    d. Tract

58. What distinguishes an easement in gross from other types of easements?

    a. An easement in gross requires recording of the easement in the public land records.
    b. There is no servient estate with an easement in gross.
    c. There is no dominant estate with an easement in gross.
    d. An easement in gross requires at least two parcels of land, the dominant and servient estates.

59. Which method of legal land description describes a property's boundaries in terms of courses and distances?

    a. U.S. government survey system
    b. Site analysis
    c. Metes and bounds method
    d. Lot and block system

60. What is the difference between real and personal property?

    a. Real property includes land and physical structures affixed to the land, as well as all the interest, benefits, and rights associated with ownership; personal property includes movable items.
    b. Real property is the physical structure affixed to the land; personal property includes movable items.
    c. Real property is the property affixed to a structure; personal property includes the physical structure that is affixed to the land.
    d. Real property includes all interests, benefits, and rights from the ownership of real estate; personal property includes the financial assets.

61. Which of the following is defined as the land and anything permanently attached to the land?

    a. Real property
    b. Real estate
    c. Personal property
    d. Fixtures

62. Who benefits directly if a property's market rent exceeds its contract rent?

    a. Landlord
    b. Leaseholder
    c. Leased fee holder
    d. Management

63. All of the following are powers of government **except**:

    a. escheat.
    b. eminent domain.
    c. police power.
    d. deed restrictions.

64. All of the following properties are subject to ad valorem taxes **except**:

    a. an office building.
    b. office machinery.
    c. a warehouse.
    d. a retail center.

65. All of the following are true **except**:

    a. An easement is created to allow access to property.
    b. An easement may be vertical or horizontal.
    c. An easement may be called a right-of-way.
    d. An easement benefits the servient tenement.

66. The owner of a parcel of land has the right to:

    a. charge taxes on the property.
    b. rezone the property as commercial.
    c. lease a part of the property.
    d. exercise the right of escheat.

67. A property owner's rights may be limited by all of the following **except**:

    a. a license.
    b. police power.
    c. eminent domain.
    d. ad valorem taxation.

68. Which of the following is voluntary?

    a. Property tax lien
    b. Mortgage lien
    c. Mechanic's lien
    d. Judgment lien

69. Which of the following is an example of an involuntary conveyance of title?

    a. A will
    b. An encumbrance
    c. A mortgage
    d. A condemnation

70. A/An _____ is a personal right to use the land of another that does not encumber the title.

    a. license
    b. mineral right
    c. easement
    d. lease

71. According to current law, how high do air rights go?

    a. 200 feet
    b. 1 mile
    c. As high as can be used
    d. An unlimited height

72. An owner's right to recover the use of his property at the end of a lease is called:

    a. right of survivorship.
    b. reversionary right.
    c. remainder interest.
    d. eminent domain.

73. All of the following have the right of eminent domain **except**:

    a. the county government.
    b. the city council.
    c. the county housing authority.
    d. a private developer.

74. Which of the following is not part of an appraiser's concept of land?

    a. Ethnic
    b. Social
    c. Geographic
    d. Legal

75. Land is affected by ongoing:

    a. industrial processes.
    b. commercial processes.
    c. socio-economic processes.
    d. psychological processes.

76. Which of the following does not influence the social concept of real estate?

    a. Building ordinances
    b. Subdivision regulations
    c. Environmental controls
    d. Financial policies

77. Which form of legal description is based on a recorded map or survey?

    a. government survey
    b. metes and bounds
    c. lot and block system
    d. geodetic survey

78. An appraiser would not consider littoral rights when valuing a/an:

    a. marina at a large lake.
    b. house whose lot borders a river.
    c. townhouse on the bay.
    d. ocean-front restaurant.

79. The definition of allodial is:

    a. a system of land ownership in which the king holds title to all lands and others are merely tenants.
    b. the system of free and full land ownership by individuals.
    c. soil that builds up as a result of accretion in a river.
    d. according to value.

80. Bulk zoning is:

    a. zoning that controls density and avoids overcrowding by regulating setbacks, building heights, and open space requirements.
    b. zoning that requires new buildings to conform to specific architectural styles.
    c. zoning that requires the street floors of office buildings be used for retail establishments.
    d. zoning that permits higher uses to exist on land zoned for lower uses, but not vice versa.

81. Spot zoning is:

    a. zoning that controls density and avoids overcrowding by regulating setbacks, building heights, and open space requirements.
    b. a change in the local zoning ordinance permitting a particular use that is inconsistent with the zoning classification of the area.
    c. zoning that requires the street-level floors of office buildings be used for retail establishments.
    d. zoning that permits higher uses to exist on land zoned for lower uses, but not vice versa.

82. Directive zoning:

    a. controls density and avoids overcrowding by regulating setbacks, building heights, and open space requirements.
    b. is a change in the local zoning ordinance permitting a particular use that is inconsistent with the zoning classification of the area.
    c. is used as a planning tool to ensure that land is used at its highest and best use.
    d. permits higher uses to exist on land zoned for lower uses, but not vice versa.

83. Incentive zoning:

    a. controls density and avoids overcrowding by regulating setbacks, building heights, and open space requirements.
    b. permits higher uses to exist on land zoned for lower uses, but not vice versa.
    c. is used as a planning tool to ensure that land is used at its highest and best use.
    d. requires the street-level floors of office buildings to be used for retail establishments.

84. Cumulative zoning:

    a. controls density and avoids overcrowding by regulating setbacks, building heights, and open space requirements.
    b. permits higher uses to exist on land zoned for lower uses, but not vice versa.
    c. is used as a planning tool to ensure that land is used at its highest and best use.
    d. requires the street-level floors of office buildings to be used for retail establishments.

85. Aesthetic zoning:

    a. controls density and avoids overcrowding by regulating setbacks, building heights, and open space requirements
    b. requires new buildings to conform to specific architectural styles
    c. requires the street-level floors of office buildings to be used for retail establishments
    d. permits higher uses to exist on land zoned for lower uses, but not vice versa

86. A setback is:

    a. a zoning restriction that specifies the required distance between a house or building and the lot line.
    b. the unlawful intrusion of one property owner's permanent improvement on the adjacent property owned by another.
    c. a claim or liability that attaches to a property and limits the value or negatively affects that property's title or use.
    d. a zoning restriction requiring street-level floors of office buildings to be used for retail establishments.

87. An avigation easement is an easement:

    a. that is not specific to any one parcel
    b. that runs with the land
    c. on land that borders a flowing body of water such as a stream or river
    d. that permits aircraft approaching an airport to fly at low elevations above private property

88. Riparian rights are:

    a. the rights of an landowner whose land borders a lake, ocean, sea, or other non-flowing body of water.
    b. the rights of a landowner whose land borders a river, stream, or other watercourse.
    c. the right to use or pass over a certain portion of another's property.
    d. the right to seize private property for a public use.

89. Which kind of deed offers a buyer the least protection?

    a. Warranty deed
    b. Quitclaim deed
    c. Tax deed
    d. Bargain and sale deed

90. Mark leases a property to Don, who then subleases the property to Tracy. What is Mark's ownership interest in the property?

    a. Leased fee
    b. Leasehold
    c. Fee simple defeasible
    d. Sandwich lease

91. Under a triple net lease, which of the following does the lessee **not** pay?

    a. Maintenance expenses
    b. Property taxes
    c. Debt service
    d. Rent

92. All of the following are types of easements **except**:

    a. avigation.
    b. utility.
    c. setback.
    d. conservation.

93. A private property is taken by the state for public use and the owner is paid just compensation. This is an example of:

    a. escheat.
    b. seizure.
    c. eminent domain.
    d. a zoning change.

94. Which of the following types of zoning is used as a planning tool?

    a. Bulk
    b. Directive
    c. Incentive
    d. Aesthetic

95. If the term real estate means the physical land and structures attached to it, what does the term real property refer to?

    a. the personal items attached to the land and physical structures
    b. tangible property such as homes, cars, and crops
    c. the bundle of rights inherent in the ownership of real estate
    d. the fee simple estate held by the owner of real estate

96. An appraiser would include a neighboring property on a subject property's sketch:

    a. to show the relative size of the subject property's lot.
    b. if there is an encroachment.
    c. to show the subject property's boundaries.
    d. if he is using the neighboring property as a comparable.

97. When a deed of trust is used to finance real estate, the _____ hypothecates the property to be held as security for the debt.

    a. mortgagee
    b. trustor
    c. trustee
    d. beneficiary

98. The _____ would not be included in a sketch of the subject property, unless it adversely affects the property.

    a. property size
    b. property dimensions
    c. surrounding property
    d. distance from the nearest busy street

99. How many acres does the S ½ of the NW ¼ of the SE ¼ of a section of land contain?

    a. 20 acres
    b. 60 acres
    c. 140 acres
    d. 640 acres

100. Who are the three parties involved in a deed of trust?

    a. Trustee, trustor, and beneficiary
    b. Trustee, beneficiary, and principal
    c. Beneficiary, principal, and broker
    d. Trustee, trustor, and broker

101. Which type of easement consists of a servient estate, but no dominant estate?

    a. Easement by prescription
    b. Easement in service
    c. Public easement
    d. Easement in gross

102. The owners of a vacant lot of land owe property taxes of $2.10/$100 of assessed value. What is the tax rate in mills?

    a. 0.21 mills
    b. 20.1 mills
    c. 21 mills
    d. 210 mills

103. What is the term for a mortgage that is secured by two or more separate properties?

    a. wraparound mortgage
    b. leveraged mortgage
    c. blanket mortgage
    d. secured mortgage

104. Several people own shares in a corporation, which in turn owns a piece of real estate. What type of ownership is this?

    a. Real Estate Investment Trust
    b. Timeshare
    c. Cooperative
    d. Ownership in severalty

105. All of the following are methods of legal land description **except**:

    a. metes-and-bounds system.
    b. rectangular survey system.
    c. lock and block system.
    d. lot-and-block system.

106. Which of the following is a right or responsibility associated with a *leasehold estate*?

    a. The right of the owner of a property that has been leased to use the property
    b. The right of a tenant who is leasing property to use and occupy the property
    c. The right of the owner of a property that is not currently leased to locate a tenant
    d. The responsibility of a trustee who holds the lease to perform maintenance on the leased property

107. What is the term for someone who rents property to another under a lease agreement?

    a. Lessee
    b. Lessor
    c. Tenant
    d. Mortgagee

108. Who holds the leased fee interest in a property being leased?

    a. Lessor
    b. Lessee
    c. Tenant
    d. Trustee

109. In a net lease, the lessee is normally not responsible for:

   a. property taxes.
   b. insurance.
   c. regular maintenance expenses.
   d. mortgage debt service.

110. Which of the following parties to a lease has a leasehold estate?

   a. Lessor
   b. Lessee
   c. Trustee
   d. Landlord

111. In which type of lease does the lessor pay the property taxes, property insurance, and maintenance expenses?

   a. Gross lease
   b. Net lease
   c. Net net lease
   d. Concurrent lease

112. The tenant pays all expenses in a:

   a. gross lease.
   b. modified gross lease.
   c. standard lease.
   d. net lease.

113. A property's _____ is estimated for property tax purposes.

   a. investment value
   b. tax value
   c. return value
   d. assessed value

114. Which legal doctrine assumes a potential purchaser would take note of a worn path that crosses a property, indicating the presence of an unrecorded prescriptive easement against the property?

    a. Actual notice
    b. Constructive notice
    c. Caveat emptor
    d. Lis pendens

115. What is the wall located between two condominium units normally considered?

    a. Personal element
    b. Limited common element
    c. Public element
    d. Unrestricted common element

Answers

1. (d) None of these are legal ways to describe real property.

2. (b) A fee simple defeasible form of ownership is subject to conditions.

3. (d) The death of the stockholders or officers of the corporation does not terminate the corporation.

4. (a) Since a third party was not identified to have an estate in remainder, the original grantor maintains an estate in reversion.

5. (d) Once a third party is identified to receive the property upon death of identified person, the grantor retains no interest. Also, even if Peter dies prior to Kim, Peter's heirs would then receive the estate in remainder.

6. (a) A plat map is "A map representing a parcel of land subdivided into lots, showing streets and other details or a single site."

7. (a) Trade fixtures are always personal property.

8. (d) Personal property includes any movable or intangible thing that is not classified as real property.

9. (d) Appraisers appraise property interests rather than merely the physical elements.

10. (b) A life estate is a freehold estate.

11. (a) All of the other choices are examples of littoral rights.

12. (a) All of the other choices are examples of riparian rights.

13. (b) Personal property is defined as any movable or intangible thing that is not classified as real property.

14. (d) The grantor is the owner, may collect rent, does not have exclusive possession and has a reversionary interest.

15. (d) Joint tenants are not required to be married.

16. (d) A tenancy in common is created when two or more people take a title. They must have unity of possession. A joint tenancy is ownership by two or more parties. Joint tenants must have unity of time, unity of possession, the parties must have equal undivided interest, and they all must take title on the same deed. Severalty is ownership by one person only.

17. (b) Joint tenancy has right of survivorship. The surviving spouse would acquire the property.

18. (d) Tenants in common have unity in possession. Each tenant has the right to possession of the entire property and cannot be excluded by the other tenants.

19. (c) The most important and unique quality of joint tenancy is the right of survivorship. A joint tenant cannot transfer title to his or her share through a will.

20. (d) Escheat is defined as the reversion of property to the state or county if the owner dies intestate (without a will) or without heirs.

21. (a) Property owners can sue for severance.

22. (b) The government's police powers allow it to establish laws and enforce them for the public good.

23. (d) Adverse possession requires the payment of taxes in most states.

24. (a) The servient tenement cannot terminate the easement.

25. (c) An easement in gross belongs to an individual person or business and does not run with any specific parcel of land. Therefore, there is no dominant tenant.

26. (a) Easement by prescription is acquired by continuous, open, and hostile use of the property for the period of time prescribed by state law.

27. (d) Conditions, covenants, and restrictions (CC&R's) are found in the Declaration of Restrictions filed by the subdivision developer and incorporated by reference in the deed to each subdivision lot.

28. (a) A variance is an allowable deviation to the zoning ordinance for a structure or land use.

29. (b) An encroachment is the unlawful intrusion of one property owner's permanent improvement on the adjacent property owned by another.

30. (d) In most states, a homeowner has 3 years to bring action against a neighbor who has encroached on his property.

31. (a) Life insurance companies like long-term investments.

32. (d) Insurance companies and FNMA are part of the secondary market. Savings banks usually originate loans and then sell them to the secondaries, such as insurance companies and FNMA.

33. (d) They are usually created using either metes and bounds or rectangular survey, but sold by lot, block and tract.

34. (c) There are 36 sections in one township, and 640 acres per section. 640 x 36 = 23,040

35. (d) Because of the curvature of the earth, not all townships are standard, and do not contain the same land area.

36. (b) Each section is 1 mile from its northern boundary to its southern boundary. There are two sections, 11 and 14, between section 2 and 23.

37. (a) The distance from the southwest corner of section 2 to the northeast corner of section 16 is the diagonal of section 10. To find the length of the diagonal, use the formula $a^2 + b^2 = c^2$, where a and b are the sides of the section and c is the diagonal of the section. $1 + 1 = c^2$; $2 = c^2$; $\sqrt{2} = c$; $\sqrt{2} = 1.4 = c$.

38. (d) A township is 6 miles square and 36 square miles.

39. (c) One square mile means that each side is 1 mile high in length. One square mile means that the total area is 1 mile square. In this instance, they are the same.

40. (a) Townships are numbered sequentially north or south from the Base Line. Township 2N is the furthest north of the answer options.

41. (a) Metes and bounds land description uses compass readings to mark the boundaries of a property, starting at a point of beginning.

42. (b) The north-south line is always the base of changes in direction.

43. (d) A covenant is a promise or agreement to do or not do something, or stipulating certain uses or nonuses of property.

44. (a) The estate is granted to Carl as a remainderman. If Carl dies, his heirs inherit his rights. John retains nothing unless the estate is specifically set up that way. Greg can't encumber because he never takes title to the estate-he's basically a tenant without the rent.

45. (c) Meridians are the north–south imaginary lines used in the rectangular survey system of legal land description.

46. (a) Base rent = $2,000. Sales exceeded the $50,000 mark by $10,000. 5% of $10,000 is $500. $2,000 + $500 = $2,500.

Legal Considerations in Appraisal - Answers

47. (c) One section = 640 acres.
    ¼ of one section = 160 acres
    ¼ of ¼ of one section = 40 acres
    ½ of ¼ of ¼ of one section = 20 acres
    20 acres x $20,000 = $400,000

48. (b) Accession is the transfer of ownership of fixtures or land when those fixtures or land are attached to another's property.

49. (a) Zoning ordinances perform all of the other functions; however, they do not guarantee that property values will not decline.

50. (a) A leased fee estate is the set of rights enjoyed by the owner of a leased property.

51. (c) One section equals 640 acres. ½ of ½ of ¼ of one section = 40 acres. $480,000/40 = $12,000.

52. (b) A special assessment tax is imposed only against those parcels of property that will benefit from a proposed public improvement.

53. (b) One acre of land contains 43,560 square feet.

54. (b) Property taxes are calculated by multiplying the tax rate, or millage rate, by the assessed value of the property.

55. (b) A lease creates a leased fee estate and a leasehold estate.

56. (a) The lessor, or owner, holds the leased fee estate and conveys the leasehold estate to the tenant.

57. (c) The rectangular survey system of legal land description divides land into townships, which contain 36 sections. Each section measures one square mile.

58. (c) An easement in gross does not run with any parcel of land. It provides access to many different parcels of land. They are used frequently by public utilities.

59. (c) A metes and bounds description starts at a point of beginning and continues around the boundaries of a property, which are described in terms of courses and distances.

60. (a) Personal property includes tangible, movable items. Real property refers to land and physical structures affixed to the land, as well as the interests, benefits, and rights associated with ownership.

61. (b) Real estate includes land and the things that are permanently attached to the land such as buildings and other improvements to the land. Real property includes the bundle of rights associated with the ownership of real estate. Personal property is not permanently attached to the land, such as furniture and personal belongings.

62. (b) If the market rent is greater than the contract rent, the tenant benefits.

63. (d) Deed restrictions are private limitations placed on land. All the others are powers of government.

64. (b) Ad valorem taxes are based on the assessed value of property. They are based on real property, not on personal property or trade fixtures. Office machinery is not considered real property.

65. (d) Easements allow a person to use or cross another's land for a specific purpose. They may be horizontal, such as a driveway across another's property, or vertical, such as underground utility easements. They may also be called a right-of-way. Easements benefit the dominant tenement, not the servient tenement.

66. (c) The bundle of rights that accompany ownership of real property include the right to occupy and to use the property, to sell it in whole or in part, to bequeath it, to lease it, or to do nothing at all with it. However, the owner may not charge taxes on the property, rezone the property as commercial, or exercise the right of escheat – these are all governmental rights.

67. (a) A license is a personal right given by a contract to go onto the land of another and does not encumber the title to real property. All the other choices are limits on a property owner's bundle of rights.

68. (b) Liens may be voluntary or involuntary. Voluntary liens are given freely by the property owner, such as a mortgage lien. Involuntary liens are created by operation of law and include mechanic's liens, property tax liens, and judgment liens.

69. (d) The government has the right to force an involuntary conveyance or take title of private land for public benefit. This process is called condemnation. Just compensation is due to the property owner. All of the other choices are voluntary conveyances.

70. (a) A license is a personal right given by a contract to go onto the land of another and does not encumber the title to real property.

71. (c) The useful height or depth of land ownership is limited only by the practicalities of engineering, economics, and zoning.

Legal Considerations in Appraisal - Answers

72. (b) An owner who leases real estate relinquishes his right to occupy the property. However, he retains the title, subject to the lease, and the right to recover use at the end of the lease. This is known as reversionary right.

73. (d) Eminent domain is the government's right to take private lands for the public's benefit. A private developer is not a part of the government.

74. (a) An appraiser recognizes the geographic, legal, social, and economic concepts of land.

75. (c) Land is affected by ongoing physical, chemical, biological, and socioeconomic processes which all influence land's capability and use.

76. (d) The social concept of real estate is influenced by building ordinances, subdivision regulations, and environmental controls.

77. (c) The lot and block system is based on a recorded map or survey. The rectangular survey is based on townships, sections, ranges, and acres. The metes and bounds system measures property by describing the property's boundaries.

78. (b) Littoral rights apply to land that borders large bodies of water such as a lake or a sea, and allows the owners to use and enjoy the body of water. Riparian rights apply to property bordering flowing bodies of water such as rivers and streams, such as the house on the river.

79. (b) The allodial system is our current system of free and full land ownership by individuals, as opposed to the feudal system in which the king owned all the land and his tenants could only use the land.

80. (a) Bulk zoning is used to control density and avoid overcrowding by establishing requirements for setbacks, building height, and open areas.

81. (b) Spot zoning is a change in a specific zoning area that allows a use which is inconsistent with the zoning classification. Also called a variance.

82. (c) Directive zoning is used as a planning tool to ensure property is used at its highest and best use.

83. (d) Incentive zoning requires the street-level floors of office buildings to be used for retail establishments. It often allows a developer to exceed zoning restrictions in exchange for the additional retail space.

84. (b) Cumulative zoning permits higher uses to exist on land zoned for lower uses, but not vice versa.

85. (b) Aesthetic zoning requires new buildings to conform to specific architectural styles.

86. (a) A setback is established by bulk zoning and specifies the minimum distance between the lot line and a building.

87. (d) An avigation easement affects land near airports. It allows aircraft to fly at low elevations over private property, and prevents property owners from making improvements or allowing trees to grow above a certain height. The extent of restriction depends on the glide angle required for safe landing and take-off.

88. (b) Riparian rights are the rights of a landowner whose land borders a stream, river, or other flowing watercourse, including the right of use, access, flow, and drainage. In contrast, littoral rights are associated with land bordering non-flowing water such as a lake, ocean, or sea.

89. (b) A quitclaim deed offers a buyer the least protection of any deed. Quitclaim deeds do not guarantee good title. The grantor of the deed does not make any claim of ownership interest in the property being conveyed.

90. (a) Mark has a leased fee ownership interest in the property. His interest remains unchanged despite the fact that Don has subleased the property.

91. (c) Under a triple net lease, a tenant pays a fixed rent plus operating and other expenses such as taxes, assessments, insurance, and maintenance. However, the tenant does not pay the debt service on the mortgage.

92. (c) Avigation, utility, and conservation are all types of easements. A setback is a zoning restriction.

93. (c) Escheat is the right to take intestate property. Seizure is the taking of property where illicit or illegal activities occur. Zoning is a regulatory power.

94. (b) Bulk zoning controls density by regulating setbacks, building heights, and percentage of open area. Incentive zoning requires that street floors of office buildings be used for retail establishments. Aesthetic zoning requires buildings to conform to certain types of architecture.

95. (c) In some states, real estate and real property are used interchangeably. Technically, the definition of real property is the rights inherent in the ownership of land, also known as the bundle of rights.

96. (b) Neighboring property is included in a property sketch only if the surrounding property adversely affects the subject property, as in the case of an encroachment.

97. (b) The trustor is the borrower and pledges the property to be used as security for repayment of the debt. The lender, or mortgagee, is the beneficiary, and the person who represents the lender is the trustee.

98. (c) A property sketch doesn't usually include surrounding property, unless the adjacent property adversely affects the subject property.

99. (a) There are 640 acres in one section of land. Multiply the total number of acres by each fraction of the section. 640 x 0.5 x 0.25 x 0.25 = 20 acres.

100. (a) The three parties who are involved in a deed of trust are the trustee, the trustor, and the beneficiary.

101. (d) An easement in gross affects only one parcel of land, which is the servient estate. There is no dominant estate. Utility companies often use easements in gross.

102. (c) One mill equals 1/10 of one cent. So $2.10/$100 = 0.021 or 21 mills.

103. (c) A blanket mortgage is secured by two ore more properties. Developers often use blanket mortgages to cover several parcels of land.

104. (c) A cooperative is an indirect form of property ownership in which individuals own shares of a trust or corporation that in turn holds the legal title to the real estate. This form of ownership is often used with residential properties.

105. (c) The lock and block system does not exist.

106. (b) A leasehold estate is the right of a tenant who has leased a property to use and occupy the property for a finite period of time. The property owner holds a leased-fee estate.

107. (c) The lessor, or landlord, rents property to a lessee, or tenant.

108. (a) The landlord, or lessor, holds a leased fee interest in a leased property. The tenant, or lessee, holds a leasehold interest.

109. (d) Under a net lease, the lessee is usually not responsible for the mortgage debt service. The landlord usually pays this.

110. (c) The tenant, or lessee, holds a leasehold interest in the property. The landlord, or lessor, holds a leased fee interest in the property.

111. (a) A gross lease requires the lessor, or landlord, to pay the property taxes, property insurance, and maintenance expenses.

112. (d) A net lease requires the tenant to pay rent plus all expenses.

113. (d) Assessed value is determined for property tax purposes. It is a property's value according to the tax rolls. It may be related to market value but does not necessarily equal market value.

114. (b) Constructive notice is knowledge that the law assumes a person has about a fact. The law would assume a buyer would notice the worn path and the prescriptive easement. Actual notice is if the person was specifically told about the path and prescriptive easement.

115. (b) The wall between two adjoining condominium units is normally considered a limited common element. It is jointly owned by all the unit owners but is under the exclusive control or possession of only some of the owners.

Types of Value

1. The definition of market value includes which of the following?

    a. The highest price
    b. The lowest price
    c. The average price
    d. The most probable price

2. Market value is synonymous with which of the following?

    a. Subjective value
    b. Objective value
    c. Assessor's value
    d. Insurable value

3. Which of the following terms is defined as the most probable price for which property should sell to a knowledgeable buyer in a competitive market?

    a. Market value
    b. Value in use
    c. Assessment value
    d. Investment value

4. In appraisal, _____ is defined as the ratio of exchange of one commodity for another.

    a. price
    b. value
    c. cost
    d. profit

5. Appraisers most commonly seek:

    a. insurable value.
    b. assessed value.
    c. inheritance value.
    d. market value.

6. What element(s) must be present for value to exist?

    a. Utility alone
    b. Scarcity alone
    c. Both utility and scarcity
    d. None of the above

7. Value-in-exchange means the same as:
   a. assessed value.
   b. purchase value.
   c. market value.
   d. financing value.

8. Which of the following is often subject to less than adequate market exposure time?
   a. Assessed value
   b. Liquidation value
   c. Insurable value
   d. Value-in-exchange

9. Which type of value is used for tax appraisals?
   a. Assessed value
   b. Investment value
   c. Insurable value
   d. Liquidation value

10. Which of the following is based on the replacement cost of physical items that are subject to loss?
    a. Value-in-use
    b. Insurable value
    c. Liquidation value
    d. Assessed value

11. An appraiser should include a definition of value in an appraisal because:
    a. the definition of market value changes over time.
    b. different definitions never result in the same estimated value.
    c. different definitions may produce different estimated values.
    d. none of the above

12. Insurable value is based on:
    a. replacement or reproduction cost.
    b. tax potential.
    c. market behavior.
    d. investment potential.

13. A forced sale, such as a foreclosure, results in which form of value?

    a. Value-in-exchange
    b. Liquidation value
    c. Taxable value
    d. Assessed value

14. A property's value to a specific user is called:

    a. assessed value.
    b. value-in-use.
    c. insurable value.
    d. value-in-exchange.

15. Value-in-use would estimate market value when:

    a. there is a significant amount of depreciation to deduct.
    b. there are a significant number of buyers.
    c. there are only a few buyers.
    d. the market is inactive.

16. In most definitions of market value, adjustments must be made to comparable properties for:

    a. special types of financing.
    b. closing fees paid by the buyer.
    c. costs the seller is required to pay.
    d. all of the above

17. Which type of value does a museum have?

    a. Investment value
    b. Value in use
    c. Assessed value
    d. Market value

18. A house burns down and you must determine the replacement cost for the physical items that were lost. What type of value do you need to find?

    a. Salvage value
    b. Value in exchange
    c. Market value
    d. Insurance value

19. A written instrument that conveys property to a trustee and creates a lien on the real estate that is used as security for the repayment of a debt is called a:

    a. deed of trust.
    b. mortgage.
    c. grant.
    d. easement.

20. Which of the following refers to property taxes that are based on assessed value?

    a. Investment tax
    b. Ad valorem tax
    c. Assessed tax
    d. Market tax

21. *Market value* refers to:

    a. the most probable price real estate should sell for under normal market conditions.
    b. the value of goods and services in exchange for other goods and services in the marketplace.
    c. the price a property would bring on the open market.
    d. the market rent that could reasonably be charged for the property.

22. What does the term *ad valorem* mean?

    a. Additional value
    b. According to value
    c. According to sales price
    d. Additional tax

23. When appraising a single-family residence, the most common value estimate provided would be:

    a. market value.
    b. value in use.
    c. going concern value.
    d. insurable value.

24. When appraising an established business, the value estimate sought would be:

    a. market value.
    b. value in use.
    c. going concern value.
    d. insurable value.

25. Which valuation estimate might be based on a limited marketing period?

    a. Assessed value
    b. Market value
    c. Going concern value
    d. Liquidation value

26. Which value estimate provides the basis for real property taxes?

    a. Assessed value
    b. Market value
    c. Going concern value
    d. Liquidation value

27. In the definition of market value, which of the following is considered a condition?

    a. Buyer and seller are typically motivated
    b. Credit is available
    c. Buyer and seller are equally informed of every detail of the transaction
    d. Buyer and seller are not related

28. A reasonable marketing period for a single-family residence is:

    a. 30 days.
    b. 60 days.
    c. 180 days or until the seller gets his asking price.
    d. Unknown; each market is different.

29. By definition, market value is:

    a. the highest price.
    b. the average price.
    c. the most probable price.
    d. the seller's asking price.

30. What is the value to a specific owner or occupant?

    a. Value in use
    b. Market value
    c. Going concern value
    d. Liquidation value

31. The value to a particular investor is known as:
    a. assessed value.
    b. investment value.
    c. going concern value.
    d. liquidation value.

Answers

1. (d) Market value is defined as the most probable price that real estate should bring in a sale occurring under normal market conditions.

2. (b) Market value is assumed to be based on an open and competitive market and as such, is considered to be the objective value.

3. (a) Market value is the most probable price which a property should bring in a competitive and open market under normal conditions, with a knowledgeable buyer and seller acting at arm's length.

4. (b) In appraisal, value is the ratio of exchange of one commodity for another.

5. (d) The value most commonly sought in an appraisal is market value.

6. (c) Utility is basic to value, but it does not establish value by itself. Scarcity must also be present. No object can have value unless it possesses some degree of utility as well as scarcity.

7. (c) Market value and value-in-exchange both mean the highest price a property would bring in an open market under normal conditions, with an informed buyer and informed seller.

8. (b) Liquidation value is a price that an owner is compelled to accept when the property must be sold with less-than-reasonable market exposure.

9. (a) Assessed value is based on a uniform schedule for tax rolls.

10. (b) Insurable value is based on the replacement and/or reproduction cost of physical items subject to destruction or loss.

11. (c) Different definitions of value can result in different value estimates. Therefore, appraisers should be careful to state the definition they use in each appraisal.

12. (a) Insurable value is based on the replacement or reproduction cost of physical items that are subject to destruction or loss.

13. (b) Liquidation value is the price that an owner is compelled to accept when the property must be sold with less-than-reasonable market exposure.

14. (b) Value-in-use is the value of a good to a specific user, based on its productivity (in the form of income, utility or amenity).

15. (b) Value-in-use does not necessarily represent market value, unless there are a significant number of buyers/users active in the market place who are willing and able to purchase the commodity or service.

16. (a) Adjustments to comparables must be made for special or creative financing or sales concessions.

17. (b) A special purpose building such as a museum has value in use. Value in use is based on a particular use, and is often part of a broader operation or process.

18. (d) The insurance carrier will pay whatever the insurable value (amount on the policy) is, regardless of the market value.

19. (a) A deed of trust legally conveys property to a trustee who holds it as security for the repayment of a debt.

20. (b) Ad valorem taxes are property taxes and are calculated according to the value of the property being taxed.

21. (a) Market value is the most probable price real estate should sell for under normal market conditions.

22. (b) Ad valorem is Latin for "according to value."

23. (a) Market value is the most common value estimated by appraisers.

24. (c) By definition.

25. (d) Liquidation results from a short marketing period such as a bank foreclosure or an auction.

26. (a) By definition

27. (a) Market value occurs under conditions where both buyer and seller are typically motivated.

28. (d) Each local market is different. In some markets, 60 days may be reasonable, and in others it could be as little as 30 days.

29. (c) By definition.

30. (a) By definition

31. (b) By definition

Economic Principles

1. Which of the following is true regarding supply and demand in the real estate market?

    a. Supply is relatively elastic.
    b. Demand changes faster than supply.
    c. Supply never responds to demand.
    d. None of the above

2. Which of the four agents of production is the last agent to be satisfied?

    a. Land
    b. Labor
    c. Coordination
    d. Capital

3. When there are several listings in a neighborhood, what principle suggests that the least expensive listing will sell first, assuming all else is equal?

    a. Change
    b. Supply and Demand
    c. Substitution
    d. Contribution

4. Which appraisal principle suggests that the appraiser should analyze the cost of new structures as well as the market values of existing structures?

    a. Contribution
    b. Substitution
    c. Anticipation
    d. Supply and demand

5. Which of the following economic principles explains why, when several parcels of property with virtually the same utility are offered on the open market, the one with the lowest listing price will attract the greatest demand?

    a. Competition
    b. Balance
    c. Conformity
    d. Substitution

6. Which element of value requires the presence of financial ability as well as the need or desire for a product or service?

    a. Demand
    b. Competition
    c. Increasing and decreasing returns
    d. Balance

7. Value is determined by an individual's anticipation of:

    a. market rent.
    b. gross rent.
    c. current benefits.
    d. future benefits.

8. An appraiser needs to determine the optimal building-to-land ratio for a site that will be improved with an office building. Which of the following economic principles will she use?

    a. Conformity
    b. Balance
    c. Contribution
    d. Change

9. The economic principle of _____ states that land and improvements should not be valued on the basis of different uses.

    a. change
    b. conformity
    c. consistent use
    d. contribution

10. Which economic principle states that there is a point of equilibrium where a property will produce its greatest return?

    a. Conformity
    b. Balance
    c. Anticipation
    d. Contribution

11. What does profit tend to result in?

    a. Change
    b. Surplus productivity
    c. Competition
    d. Balance

12. What is another name for the principle of contribution?

    a. Principle of marginal productivity
    b. Principle of conformity
    c. Principle of surplus productivity
    d. Principle of anticipation

13. When applied to the cost approach, the principle of substitution states that:

    a. when there are alternate choices of similar properties, value equals the price to acquire an equally desirable property.
    b. a property's value is related to its competitive position among alternative investment choices that produce the same net income.
    c. a property's value is indicated by the actions of informed buyers in the market toward comparable properties.
    d. no one will pay much more for a property than the cost of acquiring a comparable site and constructing a comparable improvement.

14. The principle of external economics is applied when:

    a. several commodities or services with virtually identical utility or benefit are available.
    b. the current land use is considered a superadequacy.
    c. there is a high degree of homogeneity in the marketplace.
    d. inconveniences are imposed on others.

15. The valuation of parcels of land with varying depths would be directly influenced by which of the following principles?

    a. Substitution
    b. Contribution
    c. Conformity
    d. Balance

16. Which of the following may prevent a site from reaching its highest and best use?

    a. Deed restrictions, government regulations, and zoning
    b. Easements, zoning, and license
    c. Deed restrictions, easements, and license
    d. Government regulations, license, and right-of-ways

17. Which of the following will decrease as a result of excess competition?

    a. Market interest
    b. Utility
    c. Profit
    d. Demand

18. The demand for a commodity is created by its:

    a. conformity.
    b. utility.
    c. balance.
    d. anticipation.

19. The principle of substitution states that, all other things being equal:

    a. the highest price indicates the best product.
    b. the highest price attracts the greatest demand.
    c. the lowest price is undervalued.
    d. the lowest price attracts the greatest demand.

20. Which of the following is a physical force that affects value?

    a. The price level
    b. The geographic distribution of social groups
    c. A zoning regulation
    d. The climate

21. What will happen to the price of a product if demand is strong and purchasing power is increasing faster than the supply?

    a. Increase slightly
    b. Decrease slightly
    c. Increase greatly
    d. No change

22. *Surplus productivity* is:

    a. an individual's total income for spending or investment, after deductions for taxes.
    b. the total annual income produced by a property before expenses are deducted.
    c. an individual or company's total assets, less their total liabilities, often used to determine creditworthiness.
    d. the net income that remains after the costs of labor, capital, and coordination have been deducted from total income.

23. In a neighborhood full of well maintained homes, a poorly maintained home is an example of:

    a. substitution.
    b. progression.
    c. regression.
    d. competition.

24. The economic principle that is associated with receiving future benefits from owning or leasing land is:

    a. anticipation.
    b. contribution.
    c. change.
    d. competition.

25. Lot A has a front footage of 70 feet and is 210 feet deep. Lot B has the same frontage as Lot A, but is 150 feet deep. Lot A sells for $25,000, while Lot B sells for $21,500. The difference in price describes which economic principle?

    a. Contribution
    b. Anticipation
    c. Substitution
    d. Balance

26. The degree to which a subject property and other properties in the real estate market are similar is associated with the economic principle of:

    a. comparison.
    b. contribution.
    c. conformity.
    d. progression and regression.

27. *Surplus productivity* refers to:

    a. the income that is generated above the current market rate for a specific type of property.
    b. the income that remains after costs for labor, capital, and coordination have been deducted.
    c. the income attributable to land rent that remains after operating expenses, taxes, and debt service have been deducted.
    d. the income generated in excess of the average level of productivity.

28. What is the fundamental economic principle that underlies the sales comparison approach?

    a. Contribution
    b. Balance
    c. Surplus productivity
    d. Substitution

29. What is the fundamental economic principle that underlies the sales comparison approach?

    a. Contribution
    b. Balance
    c. Surplus productivity
    d. Substitution

30. What is the fundamental economic principle that underlies the sales comparison approach?

    a. Contribution
    b. Balance
    c. Surplus productivity
    d. Substitution

31. A developer plans to build a retail center on a parcel of land and you are asked to determine the highest and best use of the parcel. To do this, you calculate the optimal land-to-building ratio of the parcel. This practice illustrates which economic principle?

    a. Conformity
    b. Balance
    c. Change
    d. Anticipation

32. Several houses with virtually the same utility are for sale. Which economic principle explains why the one with the lowest price will attract the greatest demand?

    a. Conformity
    b. Contribution
    c. Substitution
    d. Balance

33. On which economic principle is estimated accrued depreciation based?

    a. Conformity
    b. Increasing and decreasing returns
    c. Contribution
    d. Balance

34. The anticipation of _____ creates value.

    a. future price
    b. cash flow
    c. cost
    d. future benefits

35. The principle of _____ states that the maximum value of a property generally cannot exceed the cost of its replacement.

    a. conformity
    b. substitution
    c. supply and demand
    d. contribution

36. The economic principle of _____ states that the value of property is created and maintained when there is equilibrium in the supply, demand, and location of real estate.

    a. balance
    b. conformity
    c. contribution
    d. anticipation

37. The economic principle of _____ states that the value of a property is equal to the present value of the property's future income.

    a. contribution
    b. anticipation
    c. supply and demand
    d. substitution

38. Which economic principle normally influences how an improvement, such as a house, should be placed on a site?

    a. Conformity
    b. Allocation
    c. Anticipation
    d. Substitution

39. The four agents of production are:

    a. scarcity, utility, desire and purchasing power.
    b. land, labor, capital, and entrepreneurship.
    c. land, labor, materials, and cost.
    d. desire, labor, utility, and entrepreneurship.

40. What characteristics must an item have to have value?

    a. Scarcity, utility, desirability, and transferability
    b. Scarcity, utility, desirability, and entrepreneurship
    c. Scarcity, utility, desirability, and effective purchasing power
    d. Desirability, labor, utility, and entrepreneurship

41. What two items comprise effective demand?

    a. Cost and value
    b. Desire and value
    c. Desire and effective purchasing power
    d. Desire and satisfaction

42. The value of a component is a function of its contribution to the whole rather than as a separate component defines the principle of:

    a. conformity.
    b. contribution.
    c. surplus productivity.
    d. anticipation.

43. If an appraiser values the improvements as one use, but the site as another use, he has violated the theory of:

    a. supply and demand.
    b. agents of production.
    c. caveat emptor.
    d. consistent use.

44. A site's physical possibilities, legal permissibility, financial feasibility, and maximally productive uses relate to:

    a. agents of production.
    b. highest and best use.
    c. supply and demand.
    d. factors that create value.

45. Scarcity, utility, effective purchasing power, and desire relate to:

    a. agents of production.
    b. highest and best use.
    c. supply and demand.
    d. factors that create value.

46. If cost increases, but yield decreases, it is called:

    a. decreasing returns.
    b. highest and best use.
    c. supply and demand.
    d. change.

47. If a swimming pool cost $12,000 to install, but the increase in market value to the property is only $4,000, which principle of value is illustrated?

    a. Decreasing returns
    b. Contribution
    c. Supply and demand
    d. Change

48. Of the following, which is one of the four criteria of highest and best use?

    a. Cost
    b. Functionally feasible
    c. Effective purchasing power
    d. Financially feasible

49. Substitution is the primary basis of which approach to value?

    a. Sales comparison approach
    b. Cost approach
    c. Income approach
    d. All of the above

50. Entrepreneurial incentive means the same as:

    a. contribution.
    b. anticipation.
    c. competition.
    d. profit.

51. All of the following are economic characteristics of value, **except**:

    a. desirability.
    b. effective purchasing power.
    c. financial feasibility.
    d. utility.

52. The combination of desirability and effective purchasing power is called:

    a. supply unit.
    b. demand unit.
    c. scarcity.
    d. competition.

53. The theory that each incremental item becomes less expensive as the volume is increased is called:

   a. profit.
   b. desirability.
   c. economies of scale.
   d. highest and best use.

Answers

1. (b) Real estate is relatively non-liquid, therefore supply cannot change as quickly as demand.

2. (c) Coordination, or management, is the last of the four agents of production to be satisfied. The order is capital, labor, land, and management.

3. (c) The principle of substitution states that the price someone is willing to pay for a property is influenced by the cost of acquiring a substitute or comparable property.

4. (b) The principle of substitution holds that value is indicated by the prices of similar properties in the marketplace. There are times when an investor can purchase a property for less than the cost to construct new a similar property.

5. (d) The principle of substitution states that the price someone is willing to pay for a property is influenced by the cost of acquiring a substitute or comparable property. If the asking price for one property is $250,000, and nearby a very similar property is asking $210,000, the property listed for $210,000 will receive the greatest demand.

6. (a) Demand is defined as the desire for a good or service, accompanied by the financial ability to purchase it.

7. (d) The principle of anticipation states that property value may be affected by expectation of a future benefit.

8. (b) The principle of balance states that there is an ideal equilibrium in assembling and using the factors of production. In this example, the appraiser needs to determine the balance between the land and the building.

9. (c) The principle of consistent use states that land may not be valued on the basis of one use while the improvements are valued on the basis of a different use.

10. (b) The economic principle states there is a theoretical point of equilibrium in each property that will produce the greatest net return.

11. (c) Profit tends to breed competition. However, excess profit tends to encourage ruinous competition.

12. (a) The principle of contribution is also known as the principle of marginal productivity.

13. (d) No rational person will pay more for a property than the amount required to purchase a site and construct a building of equal desirability and utility.

14. (d) External economics occur when costs or inconveniences are imposed on other people by an individual or a company.

15. (b) The principle of contribution states that the value of any individual agent in production depends on how much it contributes to value by its presence or detracts by its absence.

16. (a) Deed restrictions, zoning, and government regulations may not conform to current market requirements, so the site may remain undeveloped to its highest and best use.

17. (c) Reasonable competition stimulates further creative contribution, but in excess it can destroy profits.

18. (b) Demand for a commodity is created by its utility and scarcity, and is limited by the financial ability of people to purchase it.

19. (d) The principle of substitution states that, when several products or services with virtually the same utility or benefit are available, the one with the lowest price will attract the greatest demand.

20. (d) Physical or environmental forces created either by nature or society that affect value include climate and topography, natural resources, soil fertility, mineral resources, and technological advances that affect land use.

21. (c) If demand is very strong and purchasing power is increasing faster than the ability of the supply to satisfy the increased need, sales prices will rise.

22. (d) Surplus productivity is the net income that is left after the costs for various agents of production have been paid. It is used with the income approach.

23. (b) A home that is poorly maintained will benefit from its location in a neighborhood of well-maintained homes. Conversely, a well maintained home that suffers from its location in a neighborhood of poorly-maintained homes is an example of regression.

24. (a) According to the principle of anticipation, value is created by the expectation of benefits to be derived in the future.

25. (a) Lot A's larger size is the determining factor in its higher price. If both properties sold for the same price, the principle of substitution would apply.

Economic Principles - Answers

26. (c) The economic principle of conformity states that buildings should be similar in design, age, construction, condition, and market appeal to other buildings in the neighborhood. Non-conformity may work to the advantage or disadvantage of the nonconforming property.

27. (b) Surplus income is the remainder after the costs of labor, capital, and coordination have been deducted from the total income. Residual valuation techniques are based on the concept of surplus productivity.

28. (d) According to the principle of substitution, the maximum value of an item is established by determining the cost of acquiring an equally desirable substitute. This is the basis for the sales comparison approach.

29. (d) According to the principle of substitution, the maximum value of an item is established by determining the cost of acquiring an equally desirable substitute. This is the basis for the sales comparison approach.

30. (d) According to the principle of substitution, the maximum value of an item is established by determining the cost of acquiring an equally desirable substitute. This is the basis for the sales comparison approach.

31. (b) According to the principle of balance, there is an ideal balance in the assembly and use of the factors of production. In this case, the equilibrium of land and building.

32. (c) The principle of substitution explains that the maximum value of a parcel of real estate is established by determining the cost to acquire an equally desirable substitute. The lowest priced home among a number with equal utility will attract the greatest demand.

33. (c) According to the principle of contribution, the value of a component part of a piece of property is equal to what that component adds to the total value, less any costs incurred. When using the cost approach, accrued depreciation is subtracted from replacement or reproduction cost.

34. (d) Value is created by the anticipation of future benefits. This is the concept of the principle of anticipation, which is the basis of the income capitalization approach.

35. (b) To replace a property would be to substitute another identical property.

36. (a) The principle of balance explains the concept of equilibrium in the marketplace. A property will achieve its greatest value when the four factors of production (land, labor, capital, and management) are in balance.

37. (b) The principle of anticipation states that the value of a property is based on the expectation of future benefits, such as its projected income.

38. (a) The principle of conformity states that residential houses should be similar in design, construction, age, condition, and market appeal. A property's conformity influences its value. Non-conformity may be an advantage or disadvantage to the property owner.

39. (b) By definition.

40. (c) By definition.

41. (c) Demand is simply the combination of desirability and effective purchasing power.

42. (b) By definition.

43. (d) Consistent use theory states that land cannot be valued under one highest and best use while the improvement are valued based on another highest and best use.

44. (b) By definition.

45. (d) By definition.

46. (a) This principles states that as capital units are added, a certain point is reached where the added units do not contribute value equal with their costs.

47. (b) The value of a component is a function of its contribution to the whole rather than as a separate component.

48. (d) The four criteria are: physically possible, legally permissible, financially feasible, and maximally productive.

49. (d) Substitution is important to all 3 approaches to value.

50. (d) Profit is the reward for the entrepreneur's risk and efforts.

51. (d) The four characteristics are scarcity, utility, desirability, and effective purchasing power.

52. (b) By definition.

53. (c) By definition.

Real Estate Markets and Analysis

1. Which of the following might the Federal Reserve Board do to stimulate the economy?

    a. Decrease the reserve requirement
    b. Sell bonds
    c. Raise the discount rate
    d. Raise the prime rate

2. Which of the following is not one of the four essential elements of value?

    a. Scarcity
    b. Demand
    c. Appreciation
    d. Transferability

3. An apartment building contains 260 units, which rent at a rate of 12 per month. How many years will this supply of apartments last?

    a. 5.53 years
    b. 2 years
    c. 1.81 years
    d. 21.67 years

4. An apartment building contains 260 units, which rent out at a rate of 10 per month. What is the annual absorption rate?

    a. 2.17%
    b. 46.15%
    c. 3.85%
    d. 26%

5. Which of the following is not a typical participant in the secondary mortgage market?

    a. FNMA
    b. Life insurance companies
    c. GNMA
    d. FHLMC

6. The real estate market is not a perfect market. Which of the following is a characteristic of an imperfect market?

   a. Unstable prices
   b. Little intervention by the government
   c. Price is determined exclusively by supply and demand
   d. Many buyers and many sellers

7. Which of the following is **not** a source of demand for money?

   a. Commercial bank
   b. FNMA
   c. Insurance company
   d. Mortgage banker

8. Which of the following is likely to create a seller's market?

   a. Lowering the reserve requirement
   b. Bond selling by the government
   c. An increase in the discount rate
   d. An inflationary period

9. The process of compounding interest is the opposite of the process of:

   a. calculating simple interest.
   b. discounting interest.
   c. adjusting interest.
   d. annualizing interest.

10. How are costs of construction and the principle of supply and demand related?

    a. They are not.
    b. The value of an existing property may increase or decrease depending on the cost to produce a similar property.
    c. If the cost to produce a similar property is high, the value of an existing property decreases.
    d. If the cost to produce a similar property is low, the value of an existing property increases.

11. Which of the following is a likely result if development costs rise faster than the prices of existing competitive properties?

    a. The building industry will experience increased competition, resulting in unchecked development.
    b. Supply will outpace demand.
    c. The lack of opportunity for adequate profit will reduce new housing starts, thus limiting supply while demand remains the same.
    d. Prices will go down.

12. Which of the following is a likely result if construction costs fall faster than the values of existing properties?

    a. New properties will be developed and the prices of existing properties will fall.
    b. Prices of all homes in the market area will rise.
    c. Demand will outpace supply.
    d. Developers will abandon starting new projects because of slimmer profit margins.

13. How does the principle of balance relate to the cost approach to value?

    a. The principle of balance suggests that the factors of production can be assembled in an optimal combination to result in highest value and utility for a given location.
    b. The principle of balance suggests that builder cost and consumer expense will always balance out.
    c. The principle of balance suggests that cap rates and gross rent multipliers will be inversely proportional.
    d. The principle of balance has nothing to do with the cost approach.

14. What is the difference between *market price* and *market value*?

    a. Market price is the average price similar properties are selling for, and market value is the same as assessed value.
    b. Market price is what the property actually sells for, and market value is what the sales price should be in a normal marketplace.
    c. There is no difference because market price and market value are the same thing.
    d. Market price is what the property is currently worth, and market value is what is actually paid for the property.

15. A $100,000 loan has monthly payments of $908.70. The first month's interest totals $833.33 and the principal is $75.37. What is the annual mortgage constant?

    a. 0.03
    b. 0.09
    c. 0.11
    d. 0.13

16. Which of the following is the greatest possible interest one can have in real property?

    a. A fee simple
    b. A fee determinable
    c. A life estate
    d. A reversionary estate

17. Which of the following is defined as the study of the supply and demand conditions for a specific product or service in a specific area?

    a. Market analysis
    b. Projection analysis
    c. Economic analysis
    d. Absorption analysis

18. The ratio of the loan payment divided by the _____ equals the mortgage loan constant.

    a. loan term
    b. loan amount
    c. interest rate
    d. appraised property value

19. A lender who grants a _____ makes payments on a first loan while giving the borrower a second, larger loan that is subordinate to the first.

    a. direct reduction mortgage
    b. participation mortgage
    c. wrap around mortgage
    d. shared appreciation mortgage

20. What is the government agency that influences the secondary mortgage market principally through the mortgage-backed security program?

    a. Federal Deposit Insurance Corporation (FDIC)
    b. Federal Home Loan Mortgage Corporation (FHLMC)
    c. Government National Mortgage Association (GNMA)
    d. Housing Finance Board

21. The normal definition of *market value* assumes which of the following conditions?

    a. A property's value will increase the longer it is on the market.
    b. A property's value will decrease the longer it is on the market.
    c. Payment for a property will be made in cash or its equivalent.
    d. A property's current use is its highest and best.

22. One important characteristic of land that adds to its value is its:

    a. mobility.
    b. divisibility.
    c. diversity.
    d. stability.

23. Prices and market values decrease when there is an oversupply of real estate. This creates:

    a. a buyer's market.
    b. a seller's market.
    c. an change in the real estate market.
    d. an interest in the real estate market.

24. Which of the following is **not** considered general data?

    a. Comparable sales
    b. Environmental regulations
    c. Zoning ordinances
    d. Consumer price index

25. Which of the following will most affect the marketability of a property?

    a. Economic potential of the community
    b. Income potential of the property
    c. Economic history of the community
    d. Financing available to the property owner

26. Which of the following is **not** a major factor in real estate market activity?

    a. Supply
    b. Price
    c. Demand
    d. Original cost

27. The main regulatory force in real estate market activity is:

    a. anticipation.
    b. competition.
    c. substitution.
    d. supply and demand.

28. All of the following external factors **except**_____ may affect the local real estate market.

    a. seasonal activity
    b. availability of financing
    c. government regulation
    d. weather variations

29. In general, the real estate market:

    a. possesses efficient market characteristics.
    b. does not possess efficient market characteristics.
    c. is a free, open, and unregulated market.
    d. is not subject to seasonal activity.

30. For competition to be effective:

    a. there must be a limited number of buyers and sellers.
    b. the actions of a single buyer must greatly influence the market.
    c. buyers and sellers must be free from compulsion.
    d. buyers and sellers must be uninformed.

31. All of the following economic characteristics of single-family residences **except** _____ make them distinct from most other economic goods.

    a. their long life
    b. their liquidity
    c. they are large economic units
    d. the fixity of their location

32. A single-family residence has a typical economic life of:

    a. 15 to 30 years.
    b. 30 to 50 years.
    c. 50 to 70 years.
    d. more than 120 years.

33. What economic characteristic determines the usability of a house?

    a. Accessibility
    b. Age
    c. Size
    d. Deterioration

34. What economic characteristic results in an increase in rent and selling prices?

    a. An increase in supply
    b. An increase in demand
    c. An increase in cost
    d. A decrease in demand

35. A seller's market may:

    a. decrease market interest.
    b. stimulate new construction.
    c. decrease the absorption rate.
    d. all of the above

36. It is profitable for developers to begin building new units when:

    a. supply exceeds demand.
    b. prices drop dramatically.
    c. demand exceeds supply.
    d. costs rise dramatically.

37. Which of the following is a combined supply and demand factor used in market analysis?

    a. Absorption rate
    b. Depreciation rate
    c. Raw land development cost
    d. Financing conditions

38. When performing a market analysis, an appraiser must analyze:

    a. mostly the supply factors.
    b. only the demand factors.
    c. supply factors, demand factors, or a combination of both.
    d. supply and finance factors that affect demand.

39. When performing a market analysis, what is the first step the appraiser should take?

    a. Collect data from the residential real estate market.
    b. Calculate the current absorption rate.
    c. Determine whether the market is currently a seller's or buyer's market.
    d. State the purpose of the analysis.

40. The Gramm-Leach-Bliley Act (GLB):

    a. made illegal lender discrimination based on age, gender, national origin, marital status, religion, and race.
    b. guaranteed a worker's right to be paid fairly by establishing a 40-hour work week, minimum wage, and restrictions on child labor.
    c. established the Office of Thrift Supervision to ensure another savings and loan disaster does not happen.
    d. ensured consumer privacy is protected, and prohibited financial institutions from releasing non-public and personal consumer information.

41. A money market fund consists of:

    a. short-term financing instruments.
    b. long-term financing instruments.
    c. mutual funds.
    d. a mixture of short and long-term financing instruments.

42. The most profitable interest rate is:

    a. 1% monthly.
    b. 4% quarterly.
    c. 8% semiannually.
    d. 10% annually.

43. When _____, then market value, price, and cost are more likely to be equal.

    a. supply exceeds demand
    b. demand exceeds supply
    c. supply and demand are in equilibrium
    d. supply increases conversely to demand

44. Which of the following affect market value most?

    a. Land, labor, capital, and management
    b. Progression, regression, conformity, and contribution
    c. Supply and demand, substitution, surplus, and highest and best use
    d. Government, escheat, eminent domain, and police power

45. Real estate is dependent on local conditions because of its:

    a. immobility.
    b. homogeneity.
    c. productivity.
    d. durability.

46. What is the term for the estimated rate at which a specific type of property will be sold or leased each year?

    a. Absorption rate
    b. Saturation rate
    c. Market rate
    d. Occupancy rate

47. What is the term for the financial device that is used to maximize cash flow by using other people's money?

    a. Finance
    b. Loan
    c. Leverage
    d. Tax shelter

48. Which of the following terms refers to the *mortgagor*?

    a. Trustor
    b. Trustee
    c. Broker
    d. Borrower

49. What does the term *amortization* refer to?

    a. The periodic repayment of debt
    b. The accumulation of interest
    c. The increase in value of real estate over time
    d. The decrease in value of real estate over time

50. Which of the following is most similar to the concept of return on capital?

    a. Exchange rate
    b. Interest rate
    c. Capitalization rate
    d. Amortization rate

51. Which term refers to the lump sum that an investor receives at the termination of an investment?

    a. Return
    b. Reversion
    c. Rate
    d. Capital

52. Which statement is **incorrect** regarding the adjustments made to the sales prices of comparables when using the sales comparison approach?

    a. Adjustments affecting the overall property value should be made first.
    b. Usually the first two adjustments categories are for financing and time.
    c. The order in which the adjustments are made does not affect property value.
    d. Adjustments methods include both percentage and dollar valuations.

53. What is the term for a series of equal periodic payments or receipts on an investment?

    a. Debt service
    b. Annuity
    c. Interest
    d. Capitalization

54. A borrower pays an amount to the lender at the time the loan is created. The payment accounts for the difference between the market interest rate and the lower face rate of the loan. This amount is called the:

    a. loan fee.
    b. discount points.
    c. discount rate.
    d. interest rate fee.

55. Which of the following conditions most directly affects demand in the marketplace?

    a. Purchasing power
    b. Interest rates
    c. Building codes
    d. Construction rates

56. What is the term for a single mortgage that is obtained for more than one parcel of real estate?

    a. Blanket mortgage
    b. Dual mortgage
    c. Wraparound mortgage
    d. Transferable mortgage

57. *Primary data* is data:

   a. about the property when it was first constructed.
   b. collected by the appraiser that is not available in published sources.
   c. that the appraiser relies on most.
   d. found in publications and other sources.

58. A group of complementary land uses defines a(n):

   a. area.
   b. district.
   c. neighborhood.
   d. region.

59. Occupancy and absorption of a particular product in a defined area relates to:

   a. demand.
   b. supply.
   c. market boundaries.
   d. linkage.

60. The Federal Reserve Board uses all of the following **except** _____ to regulate credit.

   a. Reserve requirements.
   b. Federal Open Market Committee.
   c. Federal discount rate.
   d. Fiscal policy.

61. Of the following, a capital market instrument is a:

   a. mortgage.
   b. treasury bill.
   c. commercial paper.
   d. federal fund.

62. The systematic reduction of debt over time defines:

   a. points.
   b. amortization.
   c. leverage.
   d. hypothecation.

63. A point is calculated as:

    a. 1% of the loan amount.
    b. 1% of the purchase price.
    c. 1% of the market value.
    d. 1% of the interest.

64. A market that has easily produced, readily transferable goods with a large number of buyers and sellers describes a(n):

    a. inefficient market.
    b. monopoly.
    c. efficient market.
    d. effective market.

65. Which study examines the profitability of a proposed property?

    a. Feasibility study
    b. Market study
    c. Marketability study
    d. Trade area analysis

66. Which study examines an environment of buyers/sellers or landlords/tenants?

    a. Feasibility study
    b. Market study
    c. Marketability study
    d. Trade area analysis

67. Which study examines the time required to absorb a particular product?

    a. Feasibility study
    b. Market study
    c. Marketability study
    d. Trade area analysis

68. Which of the following is **not** a component of supply?

    a. Existing inventory
    b. Properties under construction
    c. Planned properties
    d. Absorption

69. A mortgage in which the interest rate moves with an indexed rate is called a(n):

    a. package mortgage.
    b. adjustable rate mortgage.
    c. fixed rate mortgage.
    d. reverse mortgage.

70. The data collected for an appraisal that encompasses all of the four forces would be:

    a. general data.
    b. specific data.
    c. secondary data.
    d. primary data.

71. What is the data collected in the analysis of a specific property?

    a. General data
    b. Specific data
    c. Secondary data
    d. Primary data

72. Data that the appraiser personally gathers is called:

    a. general data.
    b. specific data.
    c. secondary data.
    d. primary data.

Answers

1. (a) Decreasing the reserve requirement increases the money supply.

2. (c) The four essential elements of value are scarcity, demand, transferability, and utility.

3. (c) The total supply is divided by the number of units rented per year. 260 ÷ (12x12).

4. (b) The annual rental rate is divided by the total supply: (10x12) ÷ 260.

5. (b) On the secondary mortgage market, individual mortgages are sold to investors. Insurance companies do not participate in this market.

6. (a) The other choices are criteria for a perfect market.

7. (b) Fannie Mae is a participant in the secondary mortgage market, which is not a source of demand for money.

8. (a) Lowering the reserve requirement increases the money available to loan. This would likely drive the price of money down and create a higher demand for money.

9. (b) The process of compounding interest increases the amount of money. The process of discounting decreases the amount of money. Future value = principal + interest (compounding); present value = principal – discount (discounting).

10. (b) If the cost to produce a competitive property is high, the value of existing properties tends to increase. If the cost to produce a competitive property is low, the value of existing properties tends to decrease. Conversely, if the value of competitive properties is high and there is scarcity, the market may allow for an increase in costs of materials, labor, land, and entrepreneurial profits.

11. (c) Builders will build new housing only if the opportunity for adequate profit exists. If builders do not build new housing, the supply of available housing is limited and the demand is proportionately greater, thus increasing prices of existing housing.

12. (a) New properties will be developed because it is cheaper and more profitable to do so. Also the new development will offset supply and demand, causing values of existing properties to fall.

13. (a) A less than optimal combination will result in less than optimal utility and lower value in the marketplace.

14. (b) Market price is what the property actually sells for, while market value is what a typical buyer should be willing to pay under normal market conditions.

15. (c) The annual debt service is $10,904.40 ($908.70 x 12 months). Divide the annual debt service by $100,000 = 0.109 rounded to 0.11. The principal and interest figures are irrelevant.

16. (a) The highest and most complete form of ownership is the fee simple estate. Fee simple ownership includes the right to use the land now and for an indefinite period of time in the future.

17. (a) Market analysis is the study of real estate market conditions for a specific type of property in a specific area.

18. (b) The mortgage loan constant, or mortgage capitalization rate, is the ratio of the first-year debt payment divided by the beginning loan balance.

19. (c) In a wrap around mortgage the lender takes over payments of the borrower's previous mortgage and provides the borrower with a new mortgage in the amount of the previous mortgage plus an additional amount.

20. (c) GNMA is a government organization that receives funding from the U.S. Treasury. The agency is responsible for providing assistance to mortgage programs that require extraordinary support. In the mortgage-backed security program, mortgage payments are passed to the holder of the security. Mortgages are grouped in amounts of $1 million or more, issued as securities, and guaranteed by GNMA.

21. (c) Market value is the most probable price which a property should bring in a competitive and open market under normal conditions, with a knowledgeable buyer and seller acting at arm's length, with payment made in cash or its equivalent.

22. (b) Since real estate includes legal rights and interests that may be divided and sold separately, different users, such as tenants, may have legal interests in real estate without ownership. Therefore, different legal interests may result in different values being placed on the property.

23. (a) In a buyer's market there are more sellers than buyers.

24. (a) General data helps an appraiser understand the influence of the four forces of value (social, economic, governmental, and environmental) on a property's value. The forces all originate outside the property. Comparable sales fall under specific data, which includes details about the property being appraised, comparable sales and rental properties, and relevant local market characteristics.

25. (a) A major limiting factor affecting the market value of real estate is the economic potential of the community where it is located.

26. (d) Supply, demand, and price are all major factors in market activity. Original cost is not a factor.

27. (b) Competition is the main regulative force in the real estate market.

28. (d) The real estate market is subject to many outside factors such as seasonal activity, general and local economic activity, the availability of financing, and government regulations.

29. (b) The real estate market does not possess features essential for maximum efficiency, such as a central marketplace, simplicity of financing, minimal legal requirements and restrictions, and standardized products.

30. (c) If competition is to be effective, buyers and sellers must be free from compulsion, financing must not be difficult or time consuming, there must be a minimum of legal requirements, and few (if any) government regulations or restrictions.

31. (b) Single-family residences have four special economic characteristics that distinguish them from most other economic goods: their location is fixed, they have a long life, they are large economic units, and they are interdependent on public and private property.

32. (c) Most houses have an economic life of 50 to 70 years.

33. (a) A house's usability depends upon its accessibility.

34. (b) An increase in rents and selling prices is normally the result of an increase in the demand for space.

35. (b) In a seller's market, prices may rise to a level high enough to stimulate new construction.

36. (c) When the vacancy rate decreases, demand increases relative to the static supply, and prices begin to rise. As a result, building profits begin to rise, and it becomes profitable for builders to construct new units again.

37. (d) The combined supply and demand factors that are used in market analysis include business, employment, income, and financing conditions.

38. (c) When conducting a residential market analysis, an appraiser should analyze the supply factors, demand factors, or a combination of both.

39. (d) The first step in a market analysis is to state the objective or purpose of the analysis.

40. (d) The Gramm-Leach-Bliley Act implemented the most sweeping overhaul of financial services regulation in the United States in over 60 years. Also known as The Financial Modernization Act of 1999, it includes privacy provisions to protect consumer information held by financial institutions.

41. (a) A money market fund is composed of short-term financing instruments such as US Treasury bills, notes, certificates of deposit, commercial paper, and Eurodollars. Long-term financing instruments, such as mortgages, bonds, and stocks, are traded on the capital market.

42. (a) The more frequently interest is compounded, the greater the interest and profit earned. For example, if you invest $1000 and receive 12% interest compounded annually, you'll receive $120 in interest after one year. However, if you invest the same amount at 1% interest compounded monthly, you will receive $127 in interest after one year.

43. (c) Answer A describes a supply shortage, which leads to price reductions. Answers B and D describe a demand shortage, which leads to price increases. Only Answer C leads to a stable market. Costs tend to respond to prices rather than lead them, and generally lag behind the sales market trends.

44. (c) Supply and demand, substitution, surplus, and highest and best use are all basic principles of value. Land, labor, capital, and management are the four agents of production, not value. Progression, regression, conformity, and contribution have to do with how the type and quality of a surrounding neighborhood can affect the value of a house. Government, escheat, eminent domain, and police power are all types or aspects of the government's right to take land.

45. (a) The marketplace for other goods or services may move. However, land is immobile, and therefore dependent on local conditions.

46. (a) The absorption rate refers to the rate at which new property that comes on the market will be leased or sold. It is usually expressed in square feet per year or units per year.

47. (c) Leverage is the use of borrowed money to finance all or part of the purchase price of an item.

48. (d) The person or company who takes out the loan is the mortgagor.

49. (a) Amortization is the periodic repayment of a debt, such as a mortgage, over time.

50. (b) Return on capital is most like an interest rate. It is the rate of return on the amount of money that has been invested in a project.

51. (b) Reversion is the lump sum an investor receives at the termination of an investment.

52. (c) Adjustments should be made in sequence, with those affecting the property value being made first, followed by those affecting individual property features.

53. (b) An annuity is a series of equal payments or receipts on an investment. Annuity tables calculate present and future values of annuities.

54. (b) Discount points are fees paid to a lender to compensate for the difference between the market interest rate and the contract or face rate of a loan.

55. (a) Purchasing power most directly affects demand in the marketplace. When purchasing power increases or decreases, so does effective demand.

56. (a) A blanket mortgage covers more than one parcel of real estate. It is often used for subdivisions and condominiums.

57. (b) Primary data is any data the appraiser collects or compiles himself, even if the data does not directly affect the property's value. Data that was prepared by someone other than the appraiser, such as information in publications and other sources, is called secondary data.

58. (c) By definition.

59. (b) By definition.

60. (d) Fiscal policy is the government's management of revenues and expenses.

61. (a) Choices a, b, and c are examples of money market instruments.

62. (b) By definition.

63. (a) By definition.

64. (c) By definition.

65. (a) By definition.

66. (b) By definition.

67. (c) By definition.

68. (d) Absorption is described as the change of occupied units over a specified period of time.

69. (b) By definition.

70. (a) By definition.

71. (b) By definition.

72. (d) By definition.

Valuation Process

1. An appraiser always _____ when determining final value.

    a. averages
    b. uses the adjusted value of the best comparable
    c. reconciles
    d. disregards listings

2. Which of the following approaches to value must an appraiser always complete, unless the appraiser documents a reason for its exclusion?

    a. Market approach
    b. Cost approach
    c. Income approach
    d. All of the above

3. An appraisal is valid for what period of time?

    a. The escrow period
    b. The effective date only
    c. Until the loan is funded
    d. Until an update is necessary

4. If an appraiser describes the process of collecting, confirming, and reporting data, he is completing which of the following?

    a. A restricted appraisal report
    b. A self-contained appraisal report
    c. A summary appraisal report
    d. None of the above

5. When an appraiser describes his opinion of the highest and best use of the real estate he is completing which of the following?

    a. A restricted appraisal report
    b. A self-contained appraisal report
    c. A summary appraisal report
    d. A letter report

6. The systematic, orderly procedure to address a valuation problem and convey the findings describe:

    a. the purpose of the valued addressed.
    b. the valuation process.
    c. the identification of the real property.
    d. the highest and best use analysis

7. If an appraiser states the exclusion of any of the three valuation approaches, he or she is completing which type of report?

    a. Self-Contained appraisal report
    b. Restricted Use appraisal report
    c. Summary appraisal report
    d. All of the above

8. If an appraiser makes his appraisal as is but recommends that the subject property be inspected by an expert because of some observed cracks in the foundation, the appraiser's value is which of the following?

    a. Valid if the appraiser bases the value on an extraordinary assumption
    b. Valid only if it is inspected by an expert and no problems exist
    c. Valid on the day that the appraiser inspected the subject property
    d. Not valid until the appraiser re-visits the subject property to verify correction of the problem

9. When appraising a new house based on plans provided by the builder, what should the appraiser do regarding upgrades such as flooring and security systems?

    a. Ask the salesperson how much the buyer paid for the upgrades and use that figure as the adjustment for those items.
    b. Not consider the upgrades because upgrades do not impact market value.
    c. Note the upgrades but not adjust for them because all of the comparables should be new homes from the same development.
    d. Reconcile these upgrades in the identifiable market and determine the impact, if any, on value.

10. When measuring a single-family residence, the appraiser should make sure that the house squares. What does this refer to?

    a. All the exterior corners form right angles.
    b. When cutouts are included the house forms a square.
    c. The total length of the back of the house equals the total length of the front of the house.
    d. All the interior angles are right angles.

11. When appraising an office building occupied primarily by doctors and dentists, the appraiser should:

    a. exclude all movable equipment used in the normal course of the doctor or dentist's business.
    b. always appraise this property exclusively using the income approach.
    c. assume all equipment to stay in the sale and include in value.
    d. base the inclusion or exclusion of such items on size.

12. Which approach to value would be affected by the negative impact of traffic?

    a. The sales comparison approach
    b. The cost approach
    c. The income approach
    d. All of the above

13. Which of the following is **correct** regarding the reconciliation process?

    a. The appraiser should average all the approaches to value to reach his conclusion of value.
    b. The appraiser should only use the results from the approaches that provide the most favorable conclusions of value.
    c. The appraiser should consider the relationship between the final value estimate and market expectations.
    d. The appraiser should consider the relationship between the market data and market perceptions.

14. Which of the following steps in the valuation process occurs last?

    a. Application of the three approaches to value.
    b. Determine the highest and best use.
    c. Define the purpose of the appraisal.
    d. Reconciliation of the results of each approach.

15. An appraiser must analyze many features of a residential neighborhood when considering its attributes. These include physical features, governmental controls, economic data, and:

    a. total number of residential properties.
    b. population characteristics.
    c. number of amenities each dwelling contains.
    d. all of the above

16. What is the key difference between the sales comparison approach and the market data approach?

    a. None, they refer to the same approach.
    b. The sales comparison approach is used for personal property, and the market data approach is used for real property.
    c. Adjustments must be made when using the sales comparison approach but not when using the market data approach.
    d. The sales comparison approach is used to value residential property and the market data approach is used to value income-producing property.

17. Which of the following has an affect on neighborhood quality ratings?

    a. The type of residential property in the area
    b. The type of churches in the area
    c. Racial makeup of the residents
    d. None of the above

18. What is the principal reason an appraiser may analyze a neighborhood?

    a. To identify the area on a zoning map
    b. To identify and evaluate factors that may influence property values
    c. To satisfy requirements of the FHA/VA
    d. To determine assessed value for tax purposes

19. Which of the following factors does an appraiser rely on most when deciding which approach(es) should be given the most weight during the reconciliation step of the appraisal process?

    a. The time it took to finish the assignment and the quantity of data available
    b. The compensation paid by the client and the client's overall importance
    c. The definition of value sought and the quality of available data
    d. The amount of outstanding debt against the property and the value of the surrounding properties

20. Which approach to value should be used when appraising excess land?

    a. Cost approach only
    b. Sales comparison and income approach
    c. Sales comparison and income approach
    d. None of the approaches are appropriate for determining the value of excess land

21. If applicable, during which step of the appraisal process is income capitalization performed?

    a. Scope of work
    b. Data collection
    c. Application of approaches to value
    d. Reconciliation

22. What is the first step in the appraisal process?

    a. Collect and analyze data
    b. Define the problem
    c. Apply the approaches to value
    d. Reconcile the approaches and make a value estimate

23. A feasibility study is used to determine:

    a. cost of construction.
    b. economic viability.
    c. depreciation.
    d. rate of capitalization.

24. An appraiser should review the appraisal objective and the legal interests being appraised during reconciliation because:

    a. the three approaches may result in greatly varying conclusions, which indicates an error in the appraisal process.
    b. the market value will vary depending on the investor.
    c. the value may vary greatly depending on the interest being appraised or the definition of use.
    d. the appraiser should tailor the conclusion of value on the financing needs of the client.

25. During an appraisal assignment you apply more than one approach to value and derive significant differences in the resulting indications of value. All of the following **except** to _____ are appropriate resolutions.

    a. review your math and correct any mistakes
    b. review the data and consider how you analyzed it
    c. revise the data to derive one value from all the approaches
    d. review how you applied the approaches

26. One condition of _____ is that the property must be exposed to the marketplace for a reasonable period of time.

    a. value in exchange
    b. value-in-use
    c. market value
    d. taxable value

27. Locational data collected during the valuation process would include information on which of the following?

    a. Interest rates
    b. Neighborhood
    c. Deed restrictions
    d. Listings

28. Which of the following steps would an appraiser not perform when defining the problem during an appraisal?

    a. Identify the property rights to be appraised.
    b. State any limiting conditions.
    c. Determine how long the appraisal will take.
    d. State the effective date of value.

29. Which of the following is general data that an appraiser should consider when performing an appraisal?

    a. Economic influences
    b. Gross potential income
    c. Comparable sales
    d. Building cost history

30. Which of the following should an appraiser include in a topographical description of a site?

    a. Deed restrictions
    b. Lot size
    c. Contour and grade
    d. Easements

31. All of the following are steps in stating the problem **except** to:

    a. define the value sought.
    b. identify the property.
    c. identify the property rights to be appraised.
    d. describe the financing terms.

32. An appraiser should include a complete legal description of the property in which of the following sections of an appraisal report?

    a. Addenda
    b. Definition of the problem
    c. Highest and best use analysis
    d. Site identification

33. During which step of the appraisal process is the fee established?

    a. Definition of the problem
    b. Preliminary survey
    c. Site valuation
    d. Reconciliation

34. An appraiser is using the sales comparison approach to value a residential property. He has completed his initial reconciliation and determines that the quantity and quality of the comparable sales are insufficient to develop the sales comparison approach. To solve this problem, the appraiser should seek data from all of the following **except**:

    a. a greater geographic area.
    b. a longer time frame.
    c. a wider price range.
    d. a different property type.

35. The final step in the reconciliation process is:

    a. calculate the estimate of value.
    b. choose the most appropriate value.
    c. check all data and analysis for accuracy.
    d. select the most appropriate approach to value.

36. If an appraiser does not use all of the approaches to value, what must he do?

    a. Report the reason for their elimination.
    b. Make sure the data from the other(s) is absolutely correct.
    c. Use the narrative appraisal report.
    d. The appraiser must always use all three approaches to value.

37. All of the following steps are part of the preliminary survey and appraisal plan phase of the appraisal process **except** to:

    a. determine what data is needed.
    b. make a flow chart.
    c. present a fee proposal.
    d. collect and analyze data.

38. What process does an appraiser use to value a large number of properties using standard methods and common data?

   a. Market feasibility analysis
   b. Mass appraisal
   c. Appraisal consulting
   d. Investment analysis

39. When developing an appraisal, an appraiser must consider all of the following **except** the:

   a. existing land use.
   b. reasonable probability that the land use could change.
   c. effective age.
   d. physical adaptability of the real estate.

40. Land should be appraised:

   a. as though fully developed.
   b. as if available for development to its highest and best use.
   c. such that any improvements are valued based on their contribution to the site.
   d. both b and c

41. If an appraiser must develop an opinion of highest and best use, the opinion must:

   a. provide evidence to support the conclusion(s).
   b. include assumptions about the market area trends.
   c. be developed in accordance with the current property use.
   d. disclose the current use of the property if different than its highest and best.

42. An appraiser does all of the following in the certification section of an appraisal report **except**:

   a. discloses any present or prospective interest in the property.
   b. discloses his bias toward the property or the parties involved.
   c. states that a personal inspection of the subject property was or was not made.
   d. states that compensation is not contingent upon the estimate of value.

43. An appraisal is prepared by one appraiser and reviewed by another. Who is responsible for the report?

   a. The appraiser who did the appraisal
   b. The appraiser who signed the appraisal
   c. Both a and b
   d. Neither a nor b

44. All of the following are functions of an appraiser who reviews appraisals **except**:

    a. form an opinion about the competency of the original appraiser.
    b. provide an opinion on the data and adjustments.
    c. identify the property being reviewed.
    d. identify the type of review being done.

45. If an appraiser is hired for an appraisal in an unfamiliar area, which of the following should she **not** do?

    a. Disclose her lack of knowledge about the market before taking the assignment.
    b. Take necessary steps to complete the assignment competently.
    c. Accept the assignment and complete it to the best of her current ability.
    d. Describe in the report any lack of knowledge about the market and the steps she took to complete the report competently.

46. The primary purpose of an appraisal is to:

    a. estimate some kind of value
    b. estimate the highest price a property will sell for in the open market
    c. estimate future market trends in a specific area
    d. all of the above

47. Which of the following do not perform appraisals?

    a. Lender's staff appraisers
    b. Brokers
    c. Fee appraisers
    d. Staff appraisers of government agencies

48. The data used in an appraisal report must be:

    a. collected, verified, analyzed, and reconciled.
    b. identified, filtered, analyzed, and averaged.
    c. collected, filtered, analyzed, and judged.
    d. identified, collected, compared, and reconciled.

49. What are mass appraisals generally used for?

    a. Ad valorem taxation
    b. Foreclosure valuation
    c. Sale of a business
    d. Valuing bare land

50. Which of the following economic bases is usually the strongest?

    a. A local business serving the local community
    b. A diverse local base that exports local products
    c. An economic base that is dominated by one large corporation
    d. A strong local base with a limited amount of imports

51. The URAR is most appropriately used for which of the following?

    a. An individual condo in an urban area
    b. A school in an inner-city area
    c. An office complex in a suburban area
    d. A museum

52. An appraiser should consider _____ first when determining market value.

    a. the income approach
    b. land value
    c. highest and best use
    d. current use

53. In a narrative style appraisal report, the subject property's functional utility is stated in the:

    a. comparison grid.
    b. description of improvements.
    c. utilities.
    d. neighborhood data.

54. Which of the following is considered general data?

    a. property boundaries and topography
    b. community economic and demographic statistics
    c. legal description
    d. sales history

55. What is primary data?

    a. Data about the property when it was first constructed
    b. Data collected by the appraiser that is not available in published sources
    c. Data that the appraiser relies on most
    d. Data found in publications and other sources

56. An appraiser defines *neighborhood* as:

    a. a political and social group of residential properties within a single tax district having similar architectural design.
    b. a zoning district.
    c. a section of similar land uses within a single school district.
    d. a geographic area identified by geographic or political boundaries and characterized by having complementary land uses.

57. Which of the following factors is most influential in determining which approach(es) to value should be given the greatest weight during the reconciliation step of the appraisal process?

    a. The approach the appraiser is most familiar with
    b. The quantity of primary and secondary data gathered by the appraiser
    c. The nature of the assignment and the quality of available data
    d. The type of property being appraised and the quantity of available data

58. An appraiser may define or explain a neighborhood in many different ways. All of the following are acceptable ways to define a neighborhood **except**:

    a. subdivision name.
    b. natural boundaries.
    c. race.
    d. district boundaries.

59. The _____ has the burden to disclose in the appraisal report information that is relevant to the assignment.

    a. client
    b. lender
    c. Appraisal Foundation
    d. appraiser

Answers

1. (c) The appraiser never averages. Although the appraiser may sometimes select the adjusted value of a comparable, he or she always reconciles.

2. (d) Every approach to value must be part of the appraisal unless the appraiser excludes the approach for valid reasons, which must be stated in the appraisal report.

3. (b) An appraisal is valid on the effective date of appraisal only.

4. (b) According to USPAP, the operative word in a restricted appraisal report is state (Standards Rule 2-2 (c) ix); the operative word in a summary appraisal report is summarize (Standards Rule 2-2 (b) ix); and the operative work in a self-contained appraisal report is describe (Standards Rule 2-2 (a) ix).

5. (b) In USPAP, Standards Rule 2-2 (a) (x), requires the appraiser to describe the support and rationale for the appraiser's opinion of the highest and best use of the real estate as part of a self-contained appraisal report.

6. (b) The valuation process is s systematic orderly procedure to address valuation problem and convey the findings. Choices (a), (c) and (d) refer to steps in the valuation process.

7. (d) All three types of report format require the appraiser to state and explain departure from specific requirements, such as the exclusion of any of the valuation approaches. See Standards Rule 2-2 (a,b,c) xi.

8. (a) The appraiser should use an extraordinary assumption in case the inspection turns up information that would affect the valuation.

9. (d) "A" assumes that cost equals value; "B" ignores upgrades; "C" assumes all comps have upgrades; "D" searches for the contributory value, if any.

10. (c) Square means that the lengths of the parallel walls equal each other, regardless of the number of right angles. Starting at point "a" and measuring all the way around the structure should "close" the diagram by returning point "z" to point "a."

11. (a) Portable equipment used in the normal course of a business is personal property. Dental offices use extra plumbing and gas lines, often with affixed pumps and regulators. These types of equipment often remain with the real property because they are built in.

12. (d) All approaches to value would be affected.

13. (d) The appraiser should always consider market data and perceptions. The appraiser will need to use subjective judgments when reconciling alternate conclusions, since some differences in value will occur between the approaches.

14. (d) Reconciliation of the results of each approach is completed prior to submitting the report to the client. Choices (a), (b) and (c) refer to earlier steps in the valuation process.

15. (b) There are four factors that influence value: social, economic, physical/environmental, and governmental. Population characteristics fall into the social category.

16. (a) The sales comparison approach is also called the market data approach. However, the term market data approach is rarely used.

17. (a) There are four factors that influence value: governmental, physical/environmental, economic, and social. The type of residential property in the area falls into the social category. Single-family houses may be favored in some areas, while condominiums or townhouses may be favored in others.

18. (b) Most factors that influence value occur outside of the actual real estate, and may be present in the surrounding neighborhood.

19. (c) When reconciling, the appraiser reviews his or her work and considers at least four factors: 1) the definition of value sought, 2) the amount and reliability of the data collected in each approach, 3) the inherent strengths and weaknesses of each approach, and 4) the relevance of each approach to the subject property and market behavior.

20. (b) Both the sales comparison approach and the income approach can be used for considering the value of excess land. The cost approach cannot be used to obtain a value for land.

21. (c) Capitalizing income is part of the income approach to value. It is performed as part of the approaches to value.

22. (b) The first step in the appraisal process is to define the problem. Defining the problem includes: identify and state the location of the real estate; identify the property rights to be appraised; define the value to be estimated; state the purpose or intended use of the appraisal; state the effective date; and state any limiting conditions.

23. (b) A feasibility study is a detailed analysis of a real estate project to determine the most feasible use, including its economic viability.

24. (c) The interest being appraised and the definition of use can influence the final conclusion of value. The value will probably vary slightly depending on which approach was used, due to the natural variations in data.

25. (c) You should not be correcting any errors in thinking or technique during the reconciliation process. Any corrections that need to be made should be completed during the review process that precedes the final conclusion of value.

26. (c) Market value is defined as the most probable price that a property should bring in a competitive and open market. One of the conditions of market value is that the property is exposed to the open market for a reasonable time.

27. (b) Locational data includes information about the region, community, and neighborhood. This includes information on population characteristics, price levels, and employment opportunities.

28. (c) Defining the problem to be solved involves six steps: identification of the real estate (site, improvements, and personal property), identification of the property rights to be valued, the date of the value estimate, the intended use of the appraisal, the definition of value, and other limiting conditions.

29. (a) General data includes the social, economic, governmental, and environmental influences that affect property values in the region.

30. (c) A topographic description should include information about the contour, grades, drainage, soil conditions, view, and general physical usability of the land.

31. (d) The first step in the appraisal process, defining the problem, involves six steps: identification of the real estate (site, improvements, and personal property), identification of the property rights to be valued, the date of the value estimate, the intended use of the appraisal, the definition of value, and other limiting conditions.

32. (a) A complete legal description of the property should be included in the addenda.

33. (b) The preliminary survey and appraisal plan contains six steps: decide which data is needed; identify the sources of the necessary data; determine what personnel are needed; make a time schedule; make a flow chart; and present a fee proposal, agree upon a fee, and sign a contract.

34. (d) The appraiser should review the data over a longer period of time, over a wider price range, and from a greater geographic area to ensure that more appropriate comparables are not available.

35. (b) The final step of the reconciliation process is to choose the most appropriate value.

36. (a) When an appraiser does not use one or two of the three approaches to value, the reason for their elimination should be included in the appraisal report.

37. (d) The preliminary survey and appraisal plan contains six steps: decide which data is needed; identify the sources of the needed data; determine what personnel are needed; make a time schedule; make a flow chart; and present a fee proposal, agree upon a fee, and sign a contract.

38. (b) A mass appraisal is the process of valuing a large number of properties as of a given date using standard methodology, employing common data, and allowing for statistical testing.

39. (c) According to Standards Rule 1-3(a), when developing an appraisal, an appraiser must identify and analyze the effect on use and value of existing land use regulations, reasonably probable modifications of such land use regulations, economic demand, the physical adaptability of the real estate, and market area trends.

40. (d) According to Standards Rule 1-3 (b), an appraiser must develop an opinion of highest and best use of the real estate. He or she must appraise the property as though vacant and available for development to its highest and best use, and that the appraisal of improvements is based on their actual contribution to the site.

41. (a) According to Standards Rule 1-3 (b), an appraiser must analyze the relevant legal, physical, and economic factors to the extent necessary to support the appraiser's highest and best use conclusion(s).

42. (b) Standards Rule 2-3 requires an appraiser to disclose any present or prospective interest in the property being appraised. It also requires the appraiser to state that a personal inspection was made of the property and that his or her compensation is not contingent upon any predetermined value. SR 2-3 also requires the appraiser to state that he or she has no bias with respect to the property or the parties involved, not to disclose whether or not a bias exists.

43. (c) An appraiser who signs an appraisal report prepared by another in any capacity accepts full responsibility for the appraisal and the contents of the appraisal report.

44. (a) According to Standards Rule 3-1, a reviewer may form an opinion of the completeness of the report, the quality of work, and the adequacy of the report, but not on the competency of the appraiser.

45. (c) The COMPETENCY RULE requires an appraiser to be competent in the market in which he or she is performing an appraisal. If he or she is not competent, they must disclose the lack of knowledge and/or experience to the client before accepting the assignment, take steps to become competent, and describe the lack of knowledge and the steps taken to perform the appraisal competently in the appraisal report.

46. (a) The fundamental purpose of an appraisal is to develop an opinion of some kind of value.

47. (b) Real estate appraisals are generally made by staff appraisers of organizations requiring such appraisals or by fee appraisers who are independent contractors. Brokers do not perform appraisals.

48. (a) According to Standards Rule 1-4, an appraiser must collect, verify, analyze, and reconcile all the information that is applicable to the appraisal.

49. (a) A mass appraisal's primary application is for ad valorem property tax purposes.

50. (b) The strongest economic base is one that is stable and provides a tax base for services that contribute to values. Answers a and d are examples of a limited economic base that is oriented only to local services and attracts no employment. Answer c has exporting but is not diverse, so it is an example of an economic base that can collapse if the single company leaves. Only answer b indicates the strengths of local and export markets as well as diversity.

51. (a) The URAR is most appropriate for residential properties.

52. (c) The steps in the appraisal process are: 1) state the problem; 2) list the data needed and their sources; 3) gather, record, and verify the necessary data; 4) determine the highest and best use; 5) estimate the land value; 6) estimate the value by each of the three approaches; 7) reconcile the estimated values for the final value estimate; and 8) report the final value estimate.

53. (b) The description of improvements section should contain information on the functional utility of the improvements such as construction, features, any necessary maintenance, and any physical deterioration or functional obsolescence.

54. (b) General data is information that can apply to many properties. It usually includes the four value forces: social, economic, environmental/physical, and governmental. Specific data generally can apply only to a particular property. Community economic and demographic statistics is general data.

55. (b) Primary data is any data the appraiser collects or compiles himself, even if the data does not directly affect the property's value. Data that was prepared by someone other than the appraiser, such as information in publications and other sources, is called secondary data.

56. (d) A neighborhood is a geographic area identified by geographic or political boundaries that is characterized by having complementary land uses.

57. (c) An appraiser must consider both the nature of the assignment and the quality of the available data when determining which approach or approaches to value must be given the greatest weight.

58. (c) An appraiser must never consider race when defining a specific neighborhood or rendering an opinion of value.

59. (d) USPAP requires appraisers to disclose information that is applicable to the appraisal assignment.

Property Description

1. 1/4 of a 1/4 section is:

    a. 1/8 of a section.
    b. 1/2 of a section.
    c. 1/16 of a section.
    d. 160 acres.

2. Which of the following measurements is closest to one acre?

    a. 512' x 85'
    b. 45,000 square feet
    c. 640 sections
    d. 1 square mile

3. What is the length of one side of 1/16th of a square section?

    a. 1/2 mile
    b. 1/4 mile
    c. 1/8th mile
    d. 1/16th mile

4. Which of the following is always **true** concerning townships?

    a. They all have the same number of sections.
    b. They all have the same number of acres.
    c. They all have the same number of footage.
    d. Section 36 is in the southwest corner.

5. How many acres are in the NE 1/4 of the SE 1/4 of the NE 1/4 of a section?

    a. 10 acres
    b. 20 acres
    c. 32 acres
    d. 64 acres

6. How many acres are in one section?

    a. 1 acre
    b. 43,560 acres
    c. 640 acres
    d. 36 acres

7. 250,000 square feet is equivalent to:

   a. 390.63 acres
   b. 5.74 acres
   c. 25,000 square yards
   d. 1 section

8. Which of the following roof types slopes on four sides?

   a. gable
   b. gambrel
   c. hip
   d. mansard

9. Which of the following roof types is double pitched on two sides?

   a. gable
   b. gambrel
   c. hip
   d. mansard

10. Which of the following roof types slopes on two sides?

    a. gable
    b. gambrel
    c. hip
    d. mansard

11. How many sections are in 36 miles square?

    a. 36 sections
    b. 640 sections
    c. 1,296 sections
    d. 23,040 sections

12. Reinforced concrete is concrete that:

    a. contains additional mortar.
    b. contains less water.
    c. contains steel.
    d. is thicker.

13. Two vacant lots have the same width. Lot A is 300 feet deep and Lot B is 750 feet deep. If Lot A is 12 acres, how many acres is Lot B?

    a. 4 acres
    b. 15 acres
    c. 20 acres
    d. 30 acres

14. Which term is defined as land that is not necessary for the principal improvements on a parcel of land?

    a. Excess land
    b. Superadequacy
    c. Residual land
    d. Plottage

15. What does the term *site* refer to?

    a. Land that is raw, undeveloped, and ready to be improved
    b. Land and any improvements
    c. Land that is developed to its highest and best use
    d. Land that is currently being improved

16. Which of the following may be used to privately control the use of land?

    a. Eminent domain
    b. Zoning ordinances
    c. Deed restrictions
    d. Easements

17. The term for improvements to a site that extend over the site's property line onto an adjacent property is a(n):

    a. license
    b. encumbrance
    c. easement
    d. encroachment

18. What is the term for the length of a boundary that borders a thoroughfare?

    a. Zoning
    b. Building setback
    c. Frontage
    d. Depth

19. What is the effective area of a lot?

    a. The excess land
    b. The front 25% of the lot area
    c. The area of the entire lot minus the unimproved portion
    d. The usable area of the lot

20. Which of the following statements about drainage is **true**?

    a. A swale may be used to channel surface water into a natural drainage area.
    b. Drainage is not necessary if the lot has no slope.
    c. A swale can only be used with homes that are built on hillsides, as swales keep the surface water near the sides of the house to control the flow of water better.
    d. All of the above

21. The economic principle of _____ states that a site's improvements obtain maximum value if they reasonably match the surrounding buildings.

    a. competition
    b. contribution
    c. conformity
    d. balance

22. The economic principle of _____ applies when situating improvements on a lot in relation to the adjacent lots.

    a. conformity
    b. contribution
    c. substitution
    d. balance

23. Public regulations determine what types of materials may be used to construct improvements. These regulations are:

    a. easements.
    b. building codes.
    c. setback requirements.
    d. zoning ordinances.

24. A comparable property was sold subject to a special assessment. The subject property is not subject to such an assessment. What should the appraiser do?

    a. Make no adjustment.
    b. Make an adjustment to the comparable property.
    c. Make an adjustment if the assessment is greater than $5,000.
    d. Make an adjustment if the assessment is greater than $10,000.

25. What form of legal description measures land in terms of townships?

    a. Lot and block system
    b. Topographical survey
    c. Metes and bounds survey
    d. Government survey

26. Zoning is an example of which of the following?

    a. Eminent domain
    b. Government's police power
    c. Taxation
    d. Condemnation

27. The value of a site might be reduced by all of the following **except**:

    a. its location near a fire station.
    b. its location in a flood area.
    c. its location near a freeway.
    d. its location near an environmental conservation area.

28. The only access to a parcel of land is through a back alley. This will most likely cause the property value to:

    a. increase.
    b. decrease.
    c. increase or decrease, depending on the market.
    d. the value would not be impacted by this sort of information.

29. All of the following economic factors affect the value of a property **except**:

    a. the prices of nearby lots.
    b. its tax burden compared to comparable properties.
    c. its utility costs.
    d. easements on the property.

30. An appraiser might include all of the following as part of a site's cost **except**:

    a. cost of grading.
    b. cost of maintenance.
    c. cost of utility connections.
    d. cost of landscaping.

31. An appraiser should _____ to determine the effect of a corner lot location on property value.

    a. measure the lot and its frontage
    b. examine market data
    c. examine the tax records
    d. review the zoning and building codes

32. What is an elevation sheet?

    a. Drawings that provide a building's precise elevation, relative to sea level
    b. The page on the blue prints that depicts a house or room as if a vertical plane were passed through the structure
    c. Another name for a blueprint
    d. None of the above

33. *Fenestration* is:

    a. the design and placement of windows in a building.
    b. a window that has no moving parts, such as a picture window.
    c. the base or bottom of a foundation pier, wall, or column.
    d. a method of painting on wet plaster on a wall.

34. Which type of utility would require an assessment of soil, percolation, and mid-soil absorption?

    a. Natural gas
    b. Septic tank
    c. Storm water containment
    d. Underground electricity

35. Which of the following would be found on the elevation page in a set of building plans?

    a. Width of the footing
    b. Height of dividing walls or other interior structures
    c. Number of feet the roof fascia is above sea level
    d. Total height of the structure

36. What are the three types of framing construction?

    a. Ridge, platform, and pier and beam
    b. Platform, balloon, and post and beam
    c. Gambrel, flat, and beam
    d. Monolithic, floating, and pier and beam

37. An appraiser would include a topographic map of a subject property in his appraisal report:

    a. to show flood zones.
    b. to show the contour of the land.
    c. when a feature of the land has an affect on value.
    d. all of the above

38. What is the term for a quality or feature of a property that brings its owner satisfaction and non-monetary benefits?

    a. Amenity
    b. Improvement
    c. Asset
    d. Annuity

39. A _____ depicts topographical features.

    a. plat map
    b. site survey
    c. soil study
    d. contour map

40. What is the primary support for the flooring in a building?

    a. Joists
    b. Sub-flooring
    c. Footings
    d. Studs

41. Which of the following is considered an off-site improvement?

    a. A detached garage
    b. A swimming pool off the back deck
    c. Landscaping, grading, and paving
    d. Curbs, gutters, and storm sewer drains

42. Which of the following is considered an on-site improvement?

    a. The sidewalk
    b. Landscaping
    c. The street
    d. A connecting utility line

43. Which standard measurement of land is applied at the frontage of the street line or waterfront?

    a. Acre
    b. Front foot
    c. Setback
    d. Front yard

44. What is the term for a plot of land that has been prepared for, or underlies, a structure or development?

    a. Site
    b. Lot
    c. Parcel
    d. Plot

45. What does the term *frontage* refer to?

    a. The area of a site
    b. The width of a site
    c. The linear distance of a piece of land along a lake, river, street, or highway
    d. The linear distance between the front of a site and the back of a site

46. An appraiser's knowledge of construction should be:

    a. equal to a high school student's.
    b. less than a real estate broker's.
    c. more than an engineer's.
    d. less than a builder's, but more than a high school student's.

47. Which of the following is true of construction materials and techniques?

    a. They change over the years.
    b. They vary based on the builder's mood.
    c. They remain the same.
    d. They don't impact the value of the property.

48. A *site* is:

    a. unimproved land.
    b. a plot of land that is suitable to be built on.
    c. the location of a government building or airfield.
    d. a structure constructed on a property to facilitate its use.

49. The relationship between frontage and property value is determined by:

    a. the appraiser's report.
    b. the developer.
    c. buyers and sellers.
    d. the width of the road.

50. An appraiser must measure and report the exact size of a land parcel:

    a. when the client requests it.
    b. when the appraiser can't find it in the legal description.
    c. always.
    d. never.

51. For commercial use, which of the following types of typography is most desirable?

    a. Level, at street grade
    b. Gently rolling, elevated
    c. Sloping, elevated
    d. Hilly, at street grade

52. Determining if a property is located within a floodplain should be done by:

    a. an appraiser.
    b. a broker or lawyer.
    c. an engineer or surveyor.
    d. an environmentalist.

53. If a land tract is located in a floodplain, this means that it:

    a. always floods.
    b. sometimes floods.
    c. is designated as such by FEMA.
    d. cannot be built on.

54. A land tract is designated as wetlands if:

    a. it is always under water.
    b. it is occasionally under water.
    c. it is located in a floodplain.
    d. it possesses the hydraulic, soil type, or vegetation influences that lead the government to designate it as wetlands.

55. An appraiser should check for available utilities by:

    a. asking an engineer or surveyor.
    b. asking the owner.
    c. consulting the local municipality or body responsible for installing the lines.
    d. carefully digging up the lines.

56. The term *"substructure"* refers to:

    a. floor joists.
    b. vacant land.
    c. construction components below ground.
    d. a building that did not pass it's building inspection.

57. Footings are:

    a. part of the substructure.
    b. part of the superstructure.
    c. connected to the floor joists.
    d. only used in buildings more than two stories high.

58. Studs are:

    a. a specific type of nail.
    b. used in masonry buildings only.
    c. environmental hazards.
    d. vertical framing members.

59. Roof trusses are:

    a. the portion of the roof that hangs over the exterior wall.
    b. the exterior facing of a structure.
    c. factory-built systems that support the roof.
    d. classified as either flat, gable, mansard, gambrel, or hip.

60. Since the 1950's, most interior walls and ceilings have been made of:

    a. drywall.
    b. plaster over wood lath.
    c. tongue-in-groove planks.
    d. sheathing.

61. Compared with those in older homes, modern kitchens and bathrooms tend to have:

    a. fewer built-in components.
    b. more built-in components.
    c. less functional utility.
    d. more frontage.

62. Which of the following is a list of the four basic sections of a house?

    a. Superstructure, substructure, foundation, and framing
    b. Gable, mansard, joists, and roofing
    c. Mechanical equipment, foundation, roofing, and exterior walls
    d. Bathroom quarters, living quarters, sleeping quarters, and food preparation/dining quarters

63. Functional utility is:

    a. the ability of a component or item to perform its intended task.
    b. the test of a shower's water pressure.
    c. more of an issue in dining rooms than in bathrooms.
    d. increased if more expensive equipment is used.

64. Excessiveness and inadequacy are both items of:

    a. physical deterioration.
    b. functional inutility.
    c. external obsolescence.
    d. superstructure.

65. Compared with older homes, modern _____ tend to suffer the greatest amount of functional inutility.

    a. dining rooms and bedrooms
    b. bedrooms and bathrooms
    c. kitchens and bathrooms
    d. ceilings and dining rooms

Answers

1. (c) ¼ x ¼ = 1/16

2. (a) One acre is 43,560 square feet regardless of the dimensions, and 512' x 85' equals 43,520 square feet.

3. (d) A section is a mile square; ¼ mile x ¼ mile = 1/16 mile

4. (a) Although not all sections are the same size due to the curvature of the earth, all townships have 36 sections.

5. (a) This represents 1/64th of a section. 1/64th of 640 acres is 10 acres.

6. (c) One section contains 640 acres.

7. (b) 250,000 divided by the number of square feet in 1 acre (43,560) = 5.74 acres.

8. (c) A hip roof slopes evenly on all four sides.

9. (b) A gambrel roof is double pitched on two sides and is most often seen on barns.

10. (a) A gable roof slopes evenly on two sides.

11. (c) 36 miles square is 36 townships (36 miles on each side). So 36 townships x 36 sections per township = 1,296 sections.

12. (c) Reinforced concrete is structural concrete reinforced with steel.

13. (d) 750 is 2.5 times larger than 300. Given that the lots have the same width, their depth determines their relative sizes. Since Lot B is 2.5 times deeper than Lot A, it is 2.5 times as many acres. 12 acres x 2.5 = 30 acres.

14. (a) When a building site is larger than is necessary for the improvements, the extra land is called excess land. Vacant sites may also have excess land if the area is larger than is necessary for its highest and best use.

15. (b) Site is the land and improvements that make it ready for use, including streets, sewer systems, and utility connections.

16. (c) A property owner may place deed restrictions on the use of his or her land that will run with the title to the land as it passes on to future owners.

17. (d) An encroachment is an improvement that extends over the property line onto an adjacent property.

18. (c) Frontage is the length of a boundary that borders a road or waterway.

19. (d) The area of a lot may be divided into its effective area and its excess land. The effective area of a lot is its usable area. The excess land is usually worth substantially less than the effective area.

20. (a) Surface and storm water must be drained from property in some way. A swale that channels water off the surface of the lot to the street or into some natural drainage is a common and effective solution.

21. (c) The principle of conformity states that to obtain maximum value, the improvements of the property being appraised should reasonably conform to those on surrounding lots.

22. (a) The principle of conformity applies to the placement of improvements on a lot.

23. (b) Building codes control the design of permitted buildings and the types of materials that may be used.

24. (b) An appraiser must always adjust the comparable(s), never the subject property.

25. (d) The government survey form of legal land description measures land in units called townships that measure 6 miles by 6 miles.

26. (b) Zoning is part of the government's police power.

27. (d) Hazards and nuisances that are located adjacent to a property may reduce its value. Such hazards include flood areas, potential slides, earthquakes, dangerous ravines and bodies of water, and unusual fire danger. Nuisances include noisy highways, firehouses, gas stations, utility poles and high-tension wires, motels and hotels, and funeral parlors.

28. (c) Access via a back alley or a special service road may add to or detract from value, depending on the market.

29. (d) The value of a property might be affected by prices of nearby properties, its tax burden compared to comparable lots, its utility costs, and service costs. Easements may impact the property value, but they are not an economic factor.

30. (b) Appraisers include such items as the cost of clearing a site, grading, and landscaping, drainage, water and sewer connections, electric and gas service, private access streets, alleys, drives, and sidewalks as part of the site analysis.

31. (b) The appraiser must determine the influence a corner lot location has on property value. The decision should be made based on the specific lot and the market where it is located. While a corner lot may provide more light, air, and prominence, it may also be subject to more road noise, higher taxation, and less privacy.

32. (b) An elevation sheet is a page on the blue prints that depicts a house or room as if a vertical plane were passed through the structure. It shows the interior wall construction as it will appear when complete.

33. (a) Fenestration is the decorative manner or plan of placing doors or windows in a structure.

34. (b) When considering installing a septic tank, it's important to understand the surrounding soil.

35. (c) An elevation sheet is found in the blue prints and depicts the house or room as if a vertical plane were passed through the structure. It shows the elevation of the structure in relation to sea level.

36. (b) Platform framing is the most widely used type of construction for one and two-story residential buildings. Balloon framing is usually used when the exterior will be constructed of brick, stone veneer, or stucco. Post and beam framing is used mainly with contemporary buildings.

37. (d) An appraiser might include a topographic map of a subject property in his appraisal report to show flood zones, the contour of the land, or when a feature of the land has an affect on value.

38. (a) An amenity is a quality of a property, which may be tangible or intangible, that brings the owner satisfaction and non-monetary benefits, such as a view, location, or recreational facilities.

39. (d) Plat maps and most site surveys include linear dimensions, not topography. A soil study includes verbal descriptions of soil composition and topography, but generally doesn't depict topography. A contour map specifically depicts topography.

40. (a) Roof and floor joists are the primary support for their respective structures.

41. (d) Off-site improvements are located outside the confines of the site and include streets, curbs, gutters, sidewalks, storm sewer drains, and connecting utility lines. On-site improvements include landscaping, paving, utility lines, grading, etc.

42. (b) Off-site improvements are located outside the confines of the site and include streets, curbs, gutters, sidewalks, storm sewer drains, and connecting utility lines. On-site improvements include landscaping, paving, utility lines, grading, etc.

43. (b) The front foot is a measurement of a property's frontage. Each foot extends the depth of the property. A property's value may be quoted per front foot.

44. (a) A site is land that has been prepared or improved for a specific purpose.

45. (c) Frontage is the footage of a site along a lake, river, street, or other facility.

46. (d) An appraiser needs to recognize different construction techniques and materials. He also should know how different styles and designs are valued in the market. However, he does not need to know all the details that a builder or engineer would deal with.

47. (a) Construction materials and techniques change along with new discoveries and technology. They are also affected by changing consumer preferences.

48. (b) A site is vacant land that has been improved sufficiently to be able to support buildings. This means that utilities such as gas, electricity, water, sewer, and telephones are available, and roads have been built.

49. (c) Buyers and sellers determine the value by what they are willing to pay. Frontage on a lake or ocean may be highly valued in some areas. In other areas, frontage on a golf course might be considered more valuable.

50. (d) The appraiser never needs to measure the land parcel. That is a surveyor's role.

51. (a) Level, street grade topography is most desirable for commercial use. However for residential use, gently rolling, elevated topography is most desirable.

52. (c) Nationwide floodplain studies have been prepared by the Federal Emergency Management Agency (FEMA), and floodplain areas have been documented on FEMA maps. However, because of the scale, it is often difficult to relate the FEMA maps to a specific property. A surveyor or engineer is often needed to make the final determination.

53. (c) Nationwide floodplain studies have been prepared by the Federal Emergency Management Agency (FEMA), and floodplain areas have been documented on FEMA maps. This designation alerts consumers to a potential hazard even if the land never floods.

54. (d) Wetlands are generally protected from development, and land must be given the wetlands designation by the federal government. Land can be given that designation because of the hydraulic (water) influences, but both soil type and vegetation are important factors as well.

55. (c) The appraiser should check with public officials to verify the presence and accessibility of public utilities.

56. (c) Substructure refers to construction components below ground. The substructure supports the visible parts of the building, the superstructure.

57. (a) Footings and foundation walls make up the substructure.

58. (d) By definition.

59. (c) By definition.

60. (a) Prior to the 1950's, plaster over wood lath was the most common. However, skilled workmen were required for the difficult construction process. During the 1950's, drywall started to replace plaster, and the installation process is much simpler.

61. (b) Older homes typically had only a few built-in cabinets, and the stove and refrigerator were both freestanding. In today's homes, there are often many more cabinets and other built-in appliances.

62. (d) By definition.

63. (a) By definition.

64. (b) By definition. Gold faucets in the bathroom or too few bathrooms in the house could both be examples of functional inutility.

65. (c) Market standards for kitchens and bathrooms have changed significantly over the years. Consequently, they are the rooms that are most likely to suffer from functional inutility.

Highest and Best Use Analysis

1. In considering the highest and best use of a property, the appraiser:

   a. chooses among the different uses determined through his analysis.
   b. selects only one general use that meets the criteria for highest and best use.
   c. never considers the highest and best use of the property as if vacant if there is a structure on the land.
   d. both a and b

2. Which of the following is a consideration when determining highest and best use?

   a. Physically possible
   b. Legally permissible
   c. Financially feasible
   d. All of the above

3. In order for a use to be considered highest and best, it must:

   a. reduce ad valorem taxes.
   b. use the largest percentage of the available land.
   c. be a profitable and legal use.
   d. result in a high gross potential income.

4. When _____, an alternative use will usually become the highest and best use of a property.

   a. the improvements represent a negative value to the property
   b. the improvements reach a specified chronological age
   c. the alternate provides a greater return on the investment
   d. the alternative uses a greater percentage of the usable land

5. All of the following are benefits of residential owner-occupied real estate **except**:

   a. prestige.
   b. enjoyment.
   c. earning potential.
   d. security.

6. The primary potential benefit of speculative land is:

   a. it has lower development costs.
   b. its resale profit.
   c. it has a better tax rate.
   d. it is raw and undeveloped.

7. If the existing use of a special purpose property is functionally obsolete and no alternatives are feasible, what is its highest and best use?

    a. Its current use
    b. As vacant land
    c. As scrap or salvage
    d. A future use as developed

8. In an economic sense, _____ creates the highest and best use of a property.

    a. market supply
    b. market demand
    c. tax base
    d. property profitability

9. In a highest and best use analysis, the economic principle of _____ would influence the most profitable use of a property.

    a. substitution
    b. supply and demand
    c. change
    d. anticipation

10. The economic principle that sets the parameters for the ideal use of a property is:

    a. change.
    b. substitution.
    c. competition.
    d. conformity.

11. A highest and best use analysis should include both as vacant and as improved statements of value when:

    a. the purpose of the appraisal is highest and best use analysis.
    b. there are two or more possible uses.
    c. the land is valued separately from the improvements.
    d. zoning will change in the future.

12. Which of the following statements about highest and best use is **true**?

    a. Highest and best use is only one of the ways a property should be analyzed in an appraisal.
    b. The appraisal report should include the highest and best uses of the comparable properties.
    c. The property should be analyzed for highest and best use as if improved.
    d. Only commercial and income-producing properties require a highest and best use analysis.

13. What is the name for the temporary use of a property until it can be utilized at its highest and best use?

    a. An interim use
    b. An alternate use
    c. A non-conforming use
    d. A secondary use

14. Any increase in value that results from a legal non-conforming use is:

    a. directly related to the improvements.
    b. directly related to the marketplace in which the property is located.
    c. directly related to the zoning ordinances.
    d. not considered in a valuation since it does not conform.

15. A special purpose property's highest and best use is probably:

    a. a projected future use.
    b. as developed.
    c. its present use.
    d. a different zoning classification.

16. The highest and best use of _____ is a future use.

    a. non-conforming land
    b. subdivided land
    c. special purpose property
    d. commercial property

17. When a property has a non-conforming use, which of the following is **true**?

    a. The land is valued on its permissible basis
    b. The improvements are valued based on the permissible use
    c. Non-conforming uses cannot be valued because they are illegal
    d. Non-conforming use value is always less than permissible use value

18. All of the following are tests to determine a property's highest and best use **except**:

    a. economically feasible.
    b. legally permitted.
    c. environmentally sound.
    d. physically possible.

19. All of the following are used to analyze a property's highest and best use **except**:

    a. direct zoning.
    b. aesthetic value.
    c. incentive.
    d. bulk zoning.

20. What does interim use refer to?

    a. The original land use
    b. The highest and best use
    c. A temporary use until the property transitions to its highest and best use
    d. A change in a specific zoning area that allows a use that is inconsistent with the zoning classification

21. What is the definition of highest and best use?

    a. The legally permissible, physically possible, economically feasible, and maximally productive use
    b. The legally permissible, environmentally sound, maximally productive, and most profitable use
    c. The current use
    d. The future, fully developed use of the property

22. An old, run-down house with a limited economic life stands on a site that is zoned for commercial use. This is an example of:

    a. adverse use.
    b. variance.
    c. interim use.
    d. exception.

23. All of the following are associated with a property's highest and best use **except**:

    a. building codes.
    b. available utility.
    c. rate of return.
    d. depreciation.

24. When an appraiser is determining a property's highest and best use, which of the following would he consider first?

    a. Legally permissible
    b. Physically possible
    c. Economically feasible
    d. Maximally productive

25. A downtown corner lot is zoned light industrial. The surrounding lots are zoned commercial. What is the corner lot's highest and best use?

    a. Duplex
    b. Pet store
    c. Dental office
    d. Warehouse

26. What is the term for the legally and physically possible use that, at the time of appraisal, is most likely to produce the greatest land value?

    a. Highest and best use
    b. Vacant
    c. Improved use
    d. Fully developed

27. A land use must meet certain criteria to be considered highest and best. All of the following are criteria used to determine highest and best use **except**:

    a. physically possible.
    b. legally permissible.
    c. financially feasible.
    d. aesthetically viable.

28. An office building sits on a parcel of land. Which of the following statements best describes the parcel's highest and best use?

    a. It cannot be determined.
    b. It is necessarily the current use because the parcel is improved.
    c. It may be different from the current use.
    d. If the building is over five years old, the highest and best use is most likely different from the current use.

29. The concept of consistent use means:

    a. land cannot be used for more than one use.
    b. land must be valued using the values of similar land types.
    c. land cannot be valued based on a use that is different from the improvements.
    d. improvements must be built in a manner that is consistent with those of the surrounding sites.

30. Special purpose properties should be valued based on which two highest and best uses?

    a. Value in use and value in exchange
    b. Value in use and investment value
    c. Value in exchange and investment value
    d. Interim use and speculative use

Answers

1. (d) There may be more than one highest and best use that yields a similar net return.

2. (d) The four tests used to determine highest and best use are: physically possible, legally permitted, economically feasible, and maximally productive.

3. (c) Highest and best use is defined as the physically possible, legally permissible, economically feasible, and maximally productive use.

4. (a) When no value may be attributed to a property's improvements or they represent a negative value to the property, an alternative use will usually become the highest and best use.

5. (c) Potential buyers of real estate for personal use or occupancy are motivated primarily by benefits such as enjoyment, prestige, or security.

6. (b) The principal potential benefit of speculative land is resale profit.

7. (c) If the existing use of a special purpose property is physically or functionally obsolete and no alternative uses are feasible, the highest and best use of the property as improved may be scrap or salvage.

8. (b) Market demand creates highest and best use.

9. (c) Change impacts the most profitable use of a property because land use is constantly changing.

10. (d) The principle of conformity tends to set the size, price range, and other characteristics of the ideal improvement since houses that are similar to others in the neighborhood will normally have the highest ratio of value to cost.

11. (c) Each parcel of real estate may have one highest and best use of the land or site as though vacant and a different highest and best use of the property as improved.

12. (b) The report should identify the highest and best uses, both vacant and improved, of the comparable sales.

13. (a) An interim use is a temporary use of a property until the time when its highest and best use can be attained.

14. (a) Usually, any benefit that a non-conforming use may bring to a property's value is directly related to the improvements.

15. (c) The highest and best use of a special purpose property as improved is probably its current use.

16. (b) Subdivided land is awaiting development and its highest and best use is its future, fully developed use.

17. (a) The land value of a non-conforming use is based on the legally permissible use, assuming that the land is vacant and its value can be deducted from the total property value.

18. (c) The four tests to determine a property's highest and best use are: legally permissible, physically possible, economically feasible, and maximally productive.

19. (c) Direct, aesthetic value, and bulk are all types of zoning. Zoning is one of the primary considerations in determining if a property's use is legally permitted, the second requirement for a highest and best use.

20. (c) Interim use refers to a temporary use of a property until that property transitions to its highest and best use. A good example is vacant land that is awaiting development.

21. (a) A property's highest and best use is determined using four tests. In order for a use to be highest and best, it must be legally permissible, physically possible, economically feasible, and maximally productive.

22. (c) Interim use is a temporary use of a property while it awaits transition to its highest and best use. Since the current use is not legally permitted due to the zoning classification, it cannot qualify as the property's highest and best use. Once the home is demolished, a commercial property must be constructed there.

23. (d) The four tests to determine a property's highest and best use are: legally permissible, physically possible, maximally productive, and economically feasible. Building codes refer to legal permission, available utility refers to maximum production, and rate of return refers to economic feasibility. Depreciation does not affect a property's highest and best use.

24. (b) An appraiser would consider whether a project is physically possible, meaning possible within the laws of nature and physics, before considering if it meets legal codes and the other tests of highest and best use.

25. (d) A pet store and a dental office are both commercial properties. Because the lot is zoned light industrial, these two uses would not be legally permitted, one of the requirements of a highest and best use of the land. A duplex is a residential use. Only the warehouse is industrial and passes the legally permitted use test.

26. (a) The highest and best use of land is the physically possible, legally permitted, economically feasible, and maximally productive use.

27. (d) In order for a use to be considered highest and best, it must be physically possible, legally permissible, financially feasible, and maximally productive. Aesthetically viable is not a criterion.

28. (c) A property's highest and best use may not be its current use. Many factors may change over time, including zoning ordinances, local economics, and local land use.

29. (c) According to the concept of consistent use, land cannot be valued based on a use that is different from its improvements. When an appraiser is analyzing a property's highest and best use, the improvements must contribute to the land value in order to have a value themselves. Improvements that do not contribute to land value may have an interim use or a negative value.

30. (a) Special use properties should be valued on the basis of their value in use and value in exchange. Value in use is based on the current use of the property. Value in exchange is based on an alternative use. Because special use properties may have a limited number of uses or only one use, the appraiser may have to value them based on an alternative use.

Appraisal Statistical Concepts

1. If a borrower takes out a loan that has an annual interest rate of 9%, an original amortization period of 30 years, and monthly payments of $900, what was the original loan balance?

    a. $72,000
    b. $144,282
    c. $324,400
    d. $720,000

2. If the sales price of the subject property is $280,000, and the buyer takes out a 30-year loan with an interest rate of 8% and a loan-to-value ratio of 75%, what would the monthly payments be?

    a. $1,400.00
    b. $1,540.98
    c. $1,866.67
    d. $2,054.64

3. What was the original purchase price of a home if the buyer took out an 80% loan-to-value loan with monthly payments of $1,000, an interest rate of 9%, and the loan amortized over 30 years?

    a. $124,282
    b. $155,352
    c. $180,000
    d. $200,000

4. If the seller of a property receives a net payment of $300,000 (assuming no other costs of sales) and the real estate agent receives a 6% commission, what was the selling price of the property?

    a. $300,941
    b. $306,949
    c. $318,100
    d. $319,149

5. The mean of a group of values is the same as:

    a. the average.
    b. the middle.
    c. the most common.
    d. the difference between the high and low numbers.

6. The median of a group of values is:

   a. the average.
   b. the middle number.
   c. the most common.
   d. the difference between the high and low numbers.

7. The mode of a group of values is:

   a. the average.
   b. the middle.
   c. the most common.
   d. the difference between high and low numbers.

8. The range of a group of values is:

   a. the average.
   b. the middle number.
   c. the most common.
   d. the difference between the high and low numbers.

9. Four houses have sales prices of $200,000, $260,000, $238,000, and $224,000. What is the mean?

   a. $60,000
   b. $230,000
   c. $230,500
   d. $249,000

10. Four houses have sales prices of $200,000, $260,000, $238,000, and $224,000. What is the median?

    a. $230,000
    b. $230,500
    c. $238,000
    d. $249,000

11. Four houses have sales prices of $200,000, $260,000, $238,000, and $224,000. What is the range?

    a. $22,000
    b. $24,000
    c. $60,000
    d. $200,000

12. Bob owns a property that he rents out for $600 per month. Bob's property is worth $140,000. Joe owns a property that he rents out for $750 per month. What is the value of Joe's property?

    a. $164,000
    b. $168,000
    c. $172,000
    d. $175,000

13. Find the solution to the following problem: $(10 + 7) + 8 \times 3 - 15/3$

    a. 20
    b. 36
    c. 70
    d. 100

14. What is 5 squared and then cubed?

    a. 5 to the 6th power
    b. 5 to the 8th power
    c. 5 to the 5th power
    d. 5

15. Three square yards is equivalent to:

    a. 1 cubic yard.
    b. 3 cubic yards.
    c. 9 square feet.
    d. 27 square feet.

16. A builder has 217,800 square feet of land. He wants to build single-family homes on 1/3 acre lots, but he has to leave 20% of the land vacant for streets. How many homes can he build?

    a. 10
    b. 12
    c. 15
    d. 20

17. A lot measures 50 feet wide by 150 feet deep. It has a 5 foot setback on each side, a 10 foot setback in the back, and a 15 foot setback in the front. What is the usable square footage?

    a. 5,000 square feet
    b. 5,600 square feet
    c. 7,500 square feet
    d. 9,000 square feet

18. If a 30 year $100,000 straight note mortgage has an interest rate of 8%, what will the loan balance be after five years?

    a. $36,190
    b. $83,333
    c. $95,074
    d. $100,000

19. A lender uses a 70% loan-to-value ratio and makes a $196,000 loan for the purchase of a property. What is the property's sales price?

    a. $245,000
    b. $254,800
    c. $266,000
    d. $280,000

20. What is the area of a trapezoid if the lengths of the parallel sides are 8 feet and 20 feet, and the trapezoid is 5 feet high?

    a. 40 square feet
    b. 50 square feet
    c. 70 square feet
    d. 100 square feet

21. What is the area of a right triangle if its hypotenuse is 5 feet and one leg is 4 feet?

    a. 6 square feet
    b. 10 square feet
    c. 20 square feet
    d. Not enough information is given to solve the problem

22. A buyer paid $4,500 in fees for a loan that is 80% loan-to-value and for which the lender charged 2 points. What is the original sales price?

   a. $112,500
   b. $200,000
   c. $225,000
   d. $281,250

23. A lender charges 2.5 points for a loan that is 75% of the $450,000 sales price. How much are the loan fees?

   a. $6,303.50
   b. $7,500.50
   c. $8,437.50
   d. $9,773.50

24. If a lot contains 1,500 square yards and has a width of 50 feet, the depth is:

   a. 30 feet.
   b. 30 yards.
   c. 90 feet.
   d. 270 feet.

25. An appraiser asks a title company to confirm a sale. The title company confirms the sale as a full value transaction using documentary transfer stamps. The stamps were issued at a rate of $.55 per $500 in value, and they total $308.55. The loan-to-value ratio is 80%, and the buyer didn't assume any pre-existing loans. What was the sales price?

   a. $280,000
   b. $350,000
   c. $561,000
   d. $701,250

26. Interest rates are sometimes discussed in terms of *"basis points."* How much does one basis point equal?

   a. 1%
   b. 1/100th of 1%
   c. 1/10th of 1%
   d. The amount the borrower pays per $100,000 of borrowed money

27. The *median* is the:

    a. range of the data.
    b. average.
    c. mid point.
    d. most frequently occuring statistic.

28. When appraising a property, numbers should be rounded to:

    a. whole numbers.
    b. one decimal places.
    c. two decimal places.
    d. the number of places the appraiser feels is appropriate.

29. When speaking of statistics, a *population* is:

    a. the number of people who live in a specific city.
    b. the number of people who live in a region.
    c. a complete data set.
    d. a portion of a data set.

30. Use the following sales prices of 11 houses to answer the question:

    | $ 67,300 | $ 73,000 | $102,000 |
    | $102,000 | $102,000 | $104,000 |
    | $104,000 | $110,000 | $112,500 |
    | $116,000 | $220,600 | |

    The mean of all the sales is:

    a. $104,000.
    b. $110,309.
    c. $111,855.
    d. $113,005.

31. Use the following sales prices of 11 houses to answer the question.

    | $ 67,300 | $ 73,000 | $102,000 |
    | $102,000 | $102,000 | $104,000 |
    | $104,000 | $110,000 | $112,500 |
    | $116,000 | $220,600 | |

    The median of these 11 sales is:

    a. $104,000.
    b. $109,855.
    c. $110,000.
    d. $112,000.

32. Use the following sales prices of 11 houses to answer the question.

    $67,300 $73,000 $102,000
    $102,000 $102,000 $104,000
    $104,000 $110,000 $112,500
    $116,000 $220,600

    The mode of all the sales is:

    a. $102,000.
    b. $104,000.
    c. $110,000.
    d. $112,000.

33. Regression analysis is used for estimating:

    a. the reproduction cost of a property.
    b. the reconstruction cost of a property.
    c. the most probable sales price of a property.
    d. the future value of a property.

34. Use your financial calculator or a compound interest table to answer the following question. Joe deposits $50,000 into an account that pays 8% per year, compounded annually. At the end of the fifth year, what is the total value of the account?

    a. $70,000.00
    b. $73,466.40
    c. $74,233.60
    d. $173,330.05

35. Use your financial calculator or a compound interest table to answer the following question: What is the reversionary value of a property that has an income stream of $25,000 if the period is 30 years at 8%?

    a. $2,284.20
    b. $2,382.80
    c. $2,484.43
    d. $2,498.38

36. All of the following are elements of comparison used with the sales comparison approach **except**:

    a. special financing.
    b. location.
    c. conditions of sale.
    d. listing price.

37. Sarah purchased a piece of property described as the W ½ of the SW ¼ of the NE ¼ of Section 34. If she paid $128,500 for the property, what was the price per front foot (measured on the W property line)?

    a. $74.60
    b. $97.35
    c. $103.00
    d. $321.25

38. Four comparable properties have adjusted values of $140,000, $145,000, $150,000, and $150,000. Using the sales comparison approach, you determine that the subject property's indicated value should equal the mode of the comparables' values. The indicated value of the subject property is:

    a. $140,000.
    b. $142,500.
    c. $146,240.
    d. $150,000.

39. A developer purchased a parcel of land that she plans to subdivide. She determines that 10% of the parcel is unusable, and another 5% will be set aside for streets and common areas. She divides the remainder of the parcel into lots to be sold off. If she sells 23 acres, how many acres did she originally purchase?

    a. 17.5 acres
    b. 20 acres
    c. 27 acres
    d. 30 acres

40. Trisha deposits $6,707 annually and accumulates $117,700 over 10 years. What was her interest rate?

    a. 10.6%
    b. 12.0%
    c. 12.4%
    d. 13.0%

41. A parcel in a lakefront community with no lake view sells for $100,000, while a parcel in the same community with a lake view sells for 25% more. If you appraised a square lot in this community that measures 10,000 square feet and has a view of the lake, what would be the price of the lot on a front foot basis?

    a. $125
    b. $1,200
    c. $1,250
    d. $1,500

42. Which term describes the disparity between a population of numbers?

    a. Mode
    b. Range
    c. Median
    d. Mean

43. Which of the following is **not** a measure of central tendency?

    a. mode
    b. range
    c. median
    d. mean

44. A parcel of land measures 200 feet directly south, 100 feet southeast, 300 feet directly north, and 80 feet directly west to the original starting point. What is its area?

    a. 0.62 acres
    b. 0.46 acres
    c. 1600 square feet
    d. 2500 square feet

45. Find the mode of the following: $255,000, $265,000, $272,000, $273,000, $275,000, $275,000, $281,000?

    a. $268,000
    b. $271,000
    c. $273,000
    d. $275,000

46. An absorption analysis indicates that the residents of a community are capable of purchasing 10 properties per year that cost $150,000 or more. There are currently 40 homes in the area that are available and valued at $250,000. How many years will it take for all these homes to be purchased?

    a. 1 year
    b. 2 years
    c. 4 years
    d. 10 years

47. A below-grade site needs $1,000 of repairs to bring it up to grade, as well as a sidewalk that will cost $900. Three properties that had similar repairs sold 5 months ago for $18,000 each. If the annual inflation rate is 6%, what is the subject property's value?

   a. $16,500
   b. $16,550
   c. $18,500
   d. $19,950

48. 300 condos are expected to sell over the next six years. If 40% sell the first year, and 20% sell in years two and three, how many must sell each year in years four through six?

   a. 15 condos
   b. 35 condos
   c. 40 condos
   d. 50 condos

49. Use the following information to answer the question.

   Property A sold six months ago for $80,000, which is 10% above market value.
   Property B sold 3 months ago for $83,000. The buyer paid cash and absorbed a $5,000 tax lien.
   Property C sold 1 year ago for $72,000, which is 10% under market value due to foreclosure on the property.
   Residential property is currently increasing 8% per year.

   The current market value for Property B is:

   a. $74,736.
   b. $75,636.
   c. $76,410.
   d. $79,560.

50. Use the following information to answer the question:

   Property A sold six months ago for $80,000, which is 10% above market value.
   Property B sold 3 months ago for $83,000. The buyer paid cash and absorbed a $5,000 tax lien.
   Property C sold 1 year ago for $72,000, which is 10% under market value due to foreclosure on the property.
   Residential property is currently increasing 8% per year.

   What is the current market value for Property A?

   a. $74,736
   b. $75,636
   c. $76,410
   d. $79,560

51. A property is currently valued at $53,280 and sold 2 years ago for $36,000. What is the monthly rate of appreciation?

    a. 2%
    b. 3%
    c. 4%
    d. 10%

52. A group of properties recently sold for $145,000, $150,000, $155,000, $150,000, and $159,000. The _____ is $150,000.

    a. mode
    b. mean
    c. range
    d. median

53. A property recently sold for $1,000,000. A tax assessor determines that 90% of the sales price is appropriate for the market value. He assesses the property at 60% of the market value and taxes it at a rate of $6 per $100. What is the tax bill?

    a. $32,400
    b. $62,600
    c. $63,667
    d. $93,000

54. A property is worth $87,500. A buyer puts down 20% in cash and has to pay $3,150 in loan service fees. How many points was she charged?

    a. 2.5 points
    b. 3.5 points
    c. 4 points
    d. 4.5 points

55. In statistical analysis, the _____ measures the dispersion of numbers in a data set.

    a. mean
    b. mode
    c. standard deviation
    d. range

56. An appraiser selects a comparable property that sold one year ago for $125,000. Today, this comparable is worth 10% more than the subject property. Property values in the market area have appreciated 5% annually. What is the value of the subject property?

    a. $119,318
    b. $121,330
    c. $129,350
    d. $135,375

57. Another word for *average* is:

    a. mean.
    b. median.
    c. mode.
    d. margin.

58. Use the following information to answer the question:

    An apartment complex is the subject of an appraisal assignment. Recent sales of similar apartment buildings reveal the following:

    Sale 1: 20 units, gross annual income of $72,000, gross building area of 19,000 square feet, sales price of $352,800.

    Sale 2: 38 units, gross annual income of $125,400, gross building area of 38,000 square feet, sales price of $627,000.

    Sale 3: 45 units, gross annual income of $170,000, gross building area of 46,125 square feet, sales price of $884,520.

    Sale 4: 28 units, gross annual income of $97,440, gross building area of 25,200 square feet, sales price of $516,432.

    What is the range of the gross income multipliers?

    a. 0.3
    b. 0.4
    c. 0.9
    d. 4.3

59. A children's boutique located in a neighborhood shopping center leases for $500 per month, plus 2% of the gross sales over $50,000. What were the gross sales for the year if the total rent paid for the year is $8,000?

    a. $100,000
    b. $150,000
    c. $175,000
    d. $200,000

60. An office space measures 45 feet by 20 feet and rents for $1,200 per month. What is the annual rent per square foot?

    a. $11.33
    b. $12.00
    c. $16.00
    d. $18.60

61. A specific market area has an estimated demand for 500 new homes per year. A developer expects his new subdivision to capture 10% of the market once completed. What is the new subdivision's expected absorption rate?

    a. 50%
    b. 5%
    c. 50 homes per year
    d. 5 homes per year

62. What are the three reporting options permitted by USPAP?

    a. Narrative, form, and limited use
    b. Real property, review, and consulting
    c. Self-contained, summary, and restricted use
    d. Binding, non-binding, and specific

Answers

1. (b) Since the loan is actually an annuity to the lender, use the monthly table (at the end of the book) for 9% for 30 years, column 5. $900 x 124.281866 = $144,282.

2. (b) The loan amount would be $210,000, which is 75% of the sales price. Multiplying $210,000 by the factor from the 8% monthly table (at the end of the book) for 30 years from column 6 (0.007338) would result in the loan payment of $1,540.98.

3. (b) Using the 9% monthly table for a 30 year loan from column 5 (at the end of the book), since this is an annuity to the lender, the factor is 124.281866. Multiplying the factor by the payment amount of $1,000 equals $124,281.86. This, however, is the loan amount, which is only 80% of the purchase price, so 124,281.86 divided by 0.8 equals $155,352.

4. (d) Since $300,000 equals 94% of the selling price, the selling price equals $300,000 divided by 0.94, which equals $319,149.

5. (a) The mean is the same as the average. The units are added and divided by the number of units.

6. (b) The median is the middle number in a series of numbers.

7. (c) The mode in a series of number is the one that occurs most frequently.

8. (d) The range in a series of numbers is the difference between the high and low numbers.

9. (c) The mean is the average.

10. (d) Since there is an even number on the list, the median is the average of the middle two numbers.

11. (c) The range is the difference between the high and low values

12. (d) Apply the ratio of rents as follows: $750 / $600 = 1.25 x $140,000 (the value of the property) = $175,000.

13. (b) The order of operation is parenthesis, exponent, multiplication, division, addition, and subtraction, therefore 17 + 24 – 5 = 36.

14. (a) When you raise a number to a power and then raise that answer to a power, the powers are simply multiplied together to get the new exponent.

15. (d) There are 9 square feet in 1 square yard, therefore 3 x 9 = 27 square feet.

16. (b) 217,800 x 0.8 = 174,240
    174,240 square feet/43,560 square feet per acre = 4 acres of buildable area
    4 (acres) x 3 (number of 1/3 acre lots per acre) = 12

17. (a) 50 feet – (2 x 5) = 40
    150 – (10 + 15) = 125
    40 x 125 = 5,000

18. (d) A straight note calls for the periodic payment of interest only. At any time in the mortgage, the balance is the original loan amount.

19. (d) Loan amount / LTV = Sales price
    $196,000 / 0.70 = $280,000

20. (c) The area of a trapezoid is the sum of the parallel sides, halved and multiplied by the height. [(8 + 20) / 2] x 5 = 70

21. (a) The area of a triangle is half of the product of the sides. One side is 4 feet. The other side is 3 since it is the square root of the difference between the hypotenuse squared (25) and one leg squared (16), or 9. 3 x 4 = 12 / 2 = 6.

22. (d) Fees divided by points equals the loan amount. The loan amount divided by 0.8 equals the sales price.

23. (c) Fees are based on the loan amount. Sales price x 0.75 x 0.025 = $8,437.50.

24. (d) 1,500 square yards is 13,500 square feet; therefore, the depth of 270 feet is calculated by dividing 13,500 by 50.

25. (a) The stamps are calculated as $0.55 per $500 of new money. 561 x 0.55 = $280,000. It represents the entire transaction amount and not just the loan amount-- there were no loans assumed.

26. (b) 1 point = 1%; however, there are 100 basis points in 1%; therefore, one basis point is 1/100th of 1%.

27. (c) The median is the middle variate in a group of numbers. If the number of variates is odd, the median is the single variate in the middle. If the number of variates is even, the median is the average of the two variates closest to the middle.

28. (d) The amount of rounding depends on the range of value. For example, when an appraiser is appraising a house in the $100,000 range, he or she will probably round to the nearest $1,000, but when appraising a home in the $1 million range, he or she will probably round to the nearest $5,000, or even $10,000.

29. (c) A population is a complete data set or all the data in a certain group.

30. (b) The mean is also the average. It is calculated by dividing the sum of all the variates in a population by the total number of variates.

31. (a) The median is the middle variate in a population. If the total number of variates is odd, the median is the middle variate. If the total number of variates is even, the median is the average of the two middle variates.

32. (a) The mode is the most frequently occurring variate in a population.

33. (c) Regression analysis is used to estimate the most probable sales price of a property.

34. (b) Column 1 of the 8% Annual Compound Interest Table (at the end of the book) shows that at the end of the fifth year, the account would have accrued 1.469328 x 50,000 = 73,466.40.

35. (c) Column 4 of the 8% Annual Compound Interest Table (at the end of the book) shows that in 30 years, the reversionary value would be $2,484.43.

36. (d) The elements of comparison are divided into four categories: time, location, physical characteristics, and conditions of sale. Special conditions and special financing are also elements of comparison.

37. (c) First determine the size of the parcel Sarah purchased. If each section is 1 mile by 1 mile (1 square mile), each perimeter line is a mile in length. The western property line of Sarah's property, described as the W ½ of the SW ¼ of the NE ¼ of Section 34, is ¼ mile in length. To calculate the length in feet, divide the length of a linear mile by four: 5280 ft ÷ 4 = 1320 ft. To determine how much she paid per front foot, simply divide the price by 1,320ft: $12,8500 ÷ 1,320ft = 97.348 or $97.35.

38. (d) The mode is the variate (number) in a population (group of numbers) that occurs most frequently. In this population, $150,000 is the mode.

39. (c) To solve this problem, work backwards. She sold 23 acres. To determine how many acres she had before she set aside the unusable portion and the percentage for streets and common areas, divide 23 acres by 85% (100% – 15%). This equals 27.06, rounded to 27 acres.

40. (b) You will need to use either a financial calculator or a compound interest table (at the end of the book) to solve this problem. To use the annual compound interest tables, look up the factor in Column 2: Future Value Annuity of $1 Per Year; Row: 10 years. Usually, you multiply that factor by the amount you are investing annually ($6,707) to determine how much you will have accumulated by the end of 10 years. However, in this case we already know the result is $117,700, but we need to know the interest rate that gets us there. To do this, work backwards. Divide $117,700 by $6,707. This equals 17.548829. Look in the compound interest tables for the factor that is closest to 17.548829. The 12% compound interest table contains the factor closest to 17.548829.

41. (c) A square lot implies 100 x 100 square feet dimensions (100 x 100 = 10,000 square feet). Therefore, the lot has 100 front feet. Premium parcels sell for $125,000 ($100,000 x 1.25 = $125,000). So $125,000 ÷ 100 = $1,250.

42. (b) Range is a measure of the difference between the highest and lowest numbers in a data set.

43. (b) Range is the difference between the highest and lowest numbers in a data set. All the others are measures of central tendency.

44. (b) Draw the parcel. Pick a starting point and draw a line down to represent the 200 feet directly south, then 100 feet southeast, then 300 feet directly north, and finally 80 feet to the original starting point. The resulting shape is a parallelogram. The formula to find a parallelogram's area is (B1 + B2 ÷ 2) × H. Rotate the drawing 90 degrees so the long, 300 feet side is on the bottom. B1 is 200 feet, and B2 is the 300 feet side. H = height, or the 80 feet side. So (200 feet + 300 feet ÷ 2) × 80 feet equals 20,000 square feet 20,000 square feet is not an answer option, so we have to convert the square footage to acreage. There are 43,560 square feet in one acre, so divide 20,000 square feet by 43,560 square feet to get 0.459 acre, rounded to 0.46.

45. (d) The mode is the number or variate that appears most frequently in a population. $275,000 occurs twice in the data set.

46. (c) Simply divide the number of available homes by the rate at which the residents can purchase them. 40 ÷ 10 = 4.

47. (b) To find the inflation rate, divide 6% by 12 (months in a year) and multiply the result by 5 (months since the comps were sold). 0.06 ÷ 12) × 5 = 0.025. Multiply the comparable price of $18,000 by 0.025 to get $450. This is the inflation rate for the comparables' sales price. Add the inflation rate to the comparables' sales price: 450 + 18,000 = $18,450. Finally, to determine the property's value, subtract the costs incurred to bring the subject up to grade: $18,450 − $1,900 = $16,550.

Appraisal Statistical Concepts - Answers

48. (c) First, find how many condos are remaining after the first three years: 300 x 0.6 = 180. 300 – 180 = 120. Then divide the number of remaining condos by the number of years left: 120/3 = 40 per year.

49. (d) Subtract the tax lien from the price of the property to get the market value 3 months ago. $83,000 – $5,000 = $78,000. Add 2% to the old market value to get the current market value (8% per year divided by 1/4 year). $78,000 × 1.02 = $79,560.

50. (b) The market value for Property A 6 months ago, plus 10%, equals $80,000. So X × 1.10 = $80,000 or X = $80,000 ÷ 1.10 = 72,727, the market value of Property A 6 months ago. Add 4% for 6 months of appreciation. (8% per year divided in half). $72,727 × 1.04 = $75,636, the current market value for Property A.

51. (a) The difference between the two values is $53,280 – $36,000 = $17,280. Divide the difference by the original sales price to determine the amount of change: $17,280 ÷ $36,000 = 0.48 or 48%. Divide 48% by 24 (the number of months in two years) to get the monthly rate of increase: 2%.

52. (a) The mode is the most frequent value in a set of numbers. $150,000 occurs twice in the set of property sales prices.

53. (a) First you must find the property's market value: $1,000,000 × 0.90 = $900,000. Next, find the property's assessed value: $900,000 × 0.60 = $540,000. Then find the millage (or tax) rate: $6.00 ÷ $100.00 = $0.06. Finally, find the tax bill: $540,000 × 0.06 = $32,400.

54. (d) First, find the loan value: $87,500 × 0.80 = $70,000. Then find the point base: $3,150 ÷ $70,000 = 4.5.

55. (c) The standard deviation measures the differences between individual variates, or numbers, and the entire population. To find the standard deviation, determine the mean of all the variates in the population. Then find the deviation of each individual variate from the mean. Square the deviation of each variate. Add all the squared deviations and find the square root of that sum. Finally, divide that number by the number of variates in the population.

56. (a) First, find the appreciated value of the comparable. $125,000 x 1.05 = $131,250. Next, find the value of the subject property by dividing the value of the comparable by the amount it exceeds the subject property. $131,250 ÷ 1.10 = $119,318, the value of the subject property.

57. (a) Mean is another word for average.

58. (b) The gross income multiplier = sales price ÷ gross annual income. The GIM's for the recent sales are: 4.90, 5.00, 5.20, and 5.30. The range is 5.30 – 4.90, or 0.40.

59. (b) $500 x 12 months = $6,000 minimum rent. $8,000 − $6,000 = $2,000 rent due from gross sales. $2,000 ÷ 0.02 = $100,000 gross sales over $50,000. $100,000 + $50,000 = $150,000 total gross sales for the year.

60. (c) 45 x 20 = 900 total square feet. $1,200 x 12 months = $14,400 annual rent. $14,400 ÷ 900 = $16 per square foot.

61. (c) To calculate the absorption rate, simply multiply the total demand by the expected percentage of market capture. 500 x 0.10 = 50 homes per year.

62. (c) The three reporting options allowed by USPAP are the self-contained, summary, and restricted use.

Sales Comparison Approach

1. Assume a buyer makes a 20% down payment on a $300,000 sales price. The lender immediately sells the loan in the secondary market to an investor at a 10% discount. What is the adjusted sales price of this property?

    a. $270,000
    b. $276,000
    c. $290,000
    d. $300,000

2. When is the sales comparison approach used in appraisal?

    a. Single family homes only
    b. Single family homes in an active market only
    c. Both a and b
    d. Most types of properties

3. A comparable has a feature that the subject property does not. What should the appraiser do?

    a. Make a negative adjustment only if the market recognizes the value of the feature.
    b. Make a negative adjustment regardless of the value of the feature.
    c. Make an adjustment only if the feature isn't present in any other comparable.
    d. Make an adjustment to the comparable only if the sales price of the comparable is different from the sales price of the subject property.

4. Which of the following property characteristics is important when selecting a comparable to use?

    a. Similar views
    b. Recent sale
    c. Located closest to the subject property
    d. All of the above are important

5. Which of the following is **true** regarding comparables?

    a. They should be located near the subject property
    b. They should be the most similar to the subject property
    c. They may only need a time adjustment
    d. They should have sales prices within 10% of the sales price of the subject property

6. Which is **true** regarding the best comparables?

   a. They don't require more than a 10% single line adjustment.
   b. They don't require more than a 15% net adjustment.
   c. They don't require more than a 25% gross adjustment.
   d. If there is sufficient support, a good comparable may require greater adjustments.

7. Suppose a comparable property is 12% inferior to the subject property and sold 2 weeks ago for $260,000. What is the adjusted price of this comparable?

   a. $228,800
   b. $260,000
   c. $291,200
   d. $325,000

8. A comparable sold 1 year ago for $300,000. Since then, values have declined 8%. The comparable had creative financing that is recognized in the market and in favor of the buyer by 5%.

   Time Adjustment: -8%
   Financing Adjustment: -5%

   What is the adjusted sales price of this comparable?

   a. $262,200
   b. $289,800
   c. $307,800
   d. $340,200

9. A comparable has a pool, valued at $25,000, and the subject property does not. The comparable property sold 6 months ago for $250,000. In the past year, the market has appreciated 10%. What is the adjusted sales price of this comparable?

   a. $212,500
   b. $250,000
   c. $236,250
   d. $237,500

10. Comparable A sold 2 weeks ago, comparable B is a model match, and comparable C is across the street from the subject property. Which is the best comparable?

    a. 1
    b. 2
    c. 3
    d. Not enough information

11. Which of the following adjustments should be made first?

    a. Location
    b. Conditions of sale
    c. Financing
    d. Physical characteristics

12. Which of the following adjustments should be made last?

    a. Financing
    b. Physical characteristics
    c. Market conditions
    d. Location

13. The sales comparison approach would be least effective if applied to which of the following?

    a. A four unit dwelling
    b. A police station
    c. An inactive market
    d. A seller's market

14. When appraising a single-family residence, the appraiser should consider all sales of the subject property that occurred in the previous:

    a. 6 months.
    b. 1 year.
    c. 3 years.
    d. 5 years.

15. An appraiser should use which of the following as a data source for comparables?

    a. Title company
    b. Escrow documents
    c. Assessor's records
    d. All of the above

16. Assume the following comparables have these adjusted prices:

    Comp 1: $225,000
    Comp 2: $240,000
    Comp 3: $230,000
    Comp 4 (a current listing): $260,000

    What is the value of the subject property?

    a. $230,000
    b. $231,667
    c. $240,000
    d. Less than $260,000

17. A comparable sold for all cash in a neighborhood where sales typically have 80% loan-to-value financing. What percent of the net amount (sale price less closing costs) did the seller receive?

    a. 20%
    b. 80%
    c. 100%
    d. None of the above

18. Two properties sell simultaneously. They both sell for the same price and both sellers pay normal closing costs. However, one sale is an all cash transaction and the other uses an 80% loan with a 20% down payment. Which of the following is **true**?

    a. The sellers net the same amount
    b. The buyers' costs are the same
    c. The sellers' discount points are the same
    d. The sellers net different amounts

19. A comparable sold 1 year ago for $300,000. Since then, values have declined 8%. The comparable had creative financing that is recognized in the market and in favor of the buyer by 5%.

    Time Adjustment: −8%
    Financing Adjustment: −5%

    What is the adjusted sales price of this comparable?

    a. $262,200
    b. $289,800
    c. $307,800
    d. $340,200

20. One step in the sales comparison approach requires the appraiser to adjust for differences between properties such as square footage, age, and quality of construction. What is the economic principle on which these adjustments are based?

    a. Anticipation
    b. Contribution
    c. Substitution
    d. Surplus productivity

21. You are appraising a property in order to establish its listing price and have found an identical comparable to use in your appraisal. The comparable sold six months ago for $100,000. You must make an adjustment for the difference in time between the two sales. You find a paired sale of two other houses, one of which sold one year ago for $80,000 and the other sold yesterday for $88,000.

    a. $88,000
    b. $100,000
    c. $105,000
    d. $110,000

22. The sales comparison approach is best used with:

    a. single-family residential only.
    b. single-family and multi-family residential only.
    c. vacant land only.
    d. any type of property except special purpose property.

23. Which of the following is not an appropriate pairing when using the paired sales techniques?

    a. Very similar properties in very dissimilar locations
    b. Very similar properties with very dissimilar times of sale
    c. Very similar properties with very dissimilar physical features
    d. Very dissimilar properties in very similar locations

24. Which of the following is true regarding the paired sales technique?

    a. The paired sales technique is best used with dissimilar properties to provide a diverse example of property values.
    b. Adjustments should be made by dollar amounts or percentages, depending on how the adjustment is derived from the market.
    c. The paired sales technique is best used when there is a limited quantity of data available.
    d. Adjustments are necessary only if the properties being analyzed are located in dissimilar areas.

25. Which of the following conditions limits the sales comparison approach?

    a. The quantity and quality of comparable data
    b. An excessive number of comparables
    c. An overly active market
    d. Knowledgeable buyers and sellers

26. An appraiser is using the sales comparison approach and must eliminate sales that do not meet the minimum criteria for being a legitimate comparable. What is usually the most important consideration during this process?

    a. Location
    b. Time of sale
    c. Age of property
    d. Conditions of sale

27. When using the sales comparison approach, the proper sequence for making adjustments is:

    a. Property rights, conditions of sale, market conditions, financing, location, and physical characteristics.
    b. Financing, conditions of sale, market conditions, property rights, location, and physical characteristics.
    c. Property rights, financing terms, conditions of sale, market conditions, location, and physical characteristics.
    d. Physical characteristics, location, property rights, financing, conditions of sale, market conditions.

28. The sales comparison approach to value is based on which economic principle?

    a. Supply and demand
    b. Contribution
    c. Balance
    d. Substitution

29. Which approach estimates value by analyzing sales prices of similar properties that have recently sold?

    a. Income approach
    b. Sales comparison approach
    c. Cost approach
    d. Sales value approach

30. All of the following are elements of comparison used with the sales comparison approach **except**:

    a. special financing.
    b. location.
    c. conditions of sale.
    d. listing price.

31. The sales comparison approach uses the economic principle of _____ when estimating value.

    a. change
    b. substitution
    c. supply and demand
    d. conformity

32. Which process is used to reconcile the adjusted values of comparables?

    a. Average the adjusted results from the appropriate comparables.
    b. Review the comparables and use a median of the adjusted values.
    c. Review the comparables and use the top four values to compare to the subject property.
    d. Review each sale and judge its comparability to the subject property.

33. What does an appraiser need in order to obtain an accurate view of the marketplace and its activity?

    a. To locate a sufficient number of sales to determine a market pattern
    b. To know the standard deviation
    c. To know the sales history of the neighborhood in order to determine a market pattern
    d. To determine the sales average of surrounding properties

34. What are adjustments based on?

    a. Similarities between the subject and comparable properties
    b. Differences between the subject and comparable properties
    c. Median construction costs
    d. Differences in sales prices over a 4 month period

35. An appraiser must verify _____ before a sale may be used as a comparable property.

    a. whether any special concessions were granted by either party
    b. the date the comparable property was originally constructed
    c. the number of times the comparable has sold in the last three years
    d. whether the comparable had been previously appraised

36. A good source of data verification is the:

    a. seller, buyer, or broker.
    b. neighbors.
    c. tax assessor.
    d. previous owners.

37. The primary source of information for adjustments is:

    a. standard deviation tables.
    b. market data.
    c. compound interest tables.
    d. other appraisers.

38. The _____ method determines the value of an adjustment by using data from two sales where only one difference is present.

    a. matched pairs
    b. percentage adjustments
    c. regression analysis
    d. reconciliation

39. An appraiser is trying to estimate the value of a property. What process does he use to select which data and approach to use?

    a. Adjustment
    b. Reconciliation
    c. Comparison
    d. Substitution

40. All of the following sales would make good comparables **except** a sale:

    a. with typical mortgage financing.
    b. to a relative at below market price.
    c. by a willing seller to a willing buyer, free from compulsion.
    d. with reasonable market exposure.

41. When market data is _____, it usually provides the best indication of market value.

    a. carefully collected and analyzed
    b. estimated
    c. averaged
    d. provided by trusted sources

42. Which of the following situations would result in the best comparable?

    a. A parent who sold the family home to one of her children
    b. A corporation that transferred an employee and bought their home
    c. A seller who has relocated to a more expensive home
    d. An owner who sold his home to avoid foreclosure

43. Which of the following is normally **true** of houses that are listed substantially above market price?

    a. They will sell before other competing properties.
    b. They will eventually sell given enough time on the open market.
    c. They will not be subject to the principle of substitution.
    d. They will not sell despite adequate market exposure and time.

44. The first step in the sales comparison approach is to:

    a. select comparable sales.
    b. state the problem.
    c. collect data.
    d. analyze each comparable.

45. Which of the following is important when selecting comparables?

    a. How recently the property sold and its similarity to the subject property
    b. The number of previous sales and previous owners
    c. The financing terms and market exposure
    d. none of the above

46. When an appraiser is reviewing data, he does not need to verify:

    a. the reported price and terms.
    b. the old mortgage information.
    c. the rate of depreciation.
    d. the physical measurements.

47. While researching comparables, an appraiser finds a sale that resulted when the buyer exercised an option. The sales price of this sale:

   a. may not be typical of the current market.
   b. would increase the subject property's indicated value.
   c. would have no affect on the appraisal.
   d. may not be the correct sales price.

48. Dollar or percentage adjustments should reflect:

   a. previous sales.
   b. similarities.
   c. differences.
   d. market trends.

49. Regression analysis may solve which of the following problems for an appraiser?

   a. Doubling up on adjustments
   b. Missing information or data
   c. Excessive adjustments
   d. Inaccurate adjustments

50. Which of the following adjustments can **not** be made using percentage adjustments?

   a. Time
   b. Location
   c. Special conditions
   d. Ownership

51. Which of the following often requires more than one adjustment?

   a. Financing terms
   b. Special conditions
   c. Physical characteristics
   d. Location

52. Cumulative percentage adjustments are calculated by:

   a. averaging the percentage adjustments and multiplying by the unadjusted price.
   b. adding the percentage adjustments and multiplying by the unadjusted price.
   c. adding the percentage adjustments to the unadjusted price.
   d. subtracting the percentage adjustments from the unadjusted price.

53. Which adjustment takes into account the differences in ownership between the subject property and the comparable?

    a. location
    b. financing terms
    c. property rights conveyed
    d. physical characteristics

54. Which of the following is considered the key to the sales comparison approach?

    a. Market abstraction of the adjustments
    b. Accurate physical measurements
    c. Accurate adjustments
    d. Selection of appropriate comparables

55. What should an appraiser do to obtain necessary information about comparables?

    a. Make accurate physical measurements.
    b. Inspect the comparables and verify the data.
    c. Rely on the recorded facts of the sale and analyze the data.
    d. Inspect the comparables and interview the lender.

56. Which adjustment converts the transaction price of a comparable into a cash equivalent?

    a. Property rights conveyed
    b. Location
    c. Condition of sale
    d. Financing terms

57. An appraiser is using the sales comparison approach and is searching for comparables. Which of the following is least important?

    a. Square footage
    b. Lot size
    c. Room count
    d. Sales price

58. A subject property has a pool and a comparable does not. On what does an appraiser base his adjustments for the pool?

    a. The appraiser's opinion
    b. The lender's rate
    c. The market's reaction
    d. The builder's cost

59. Use the following information to answer the question:

   Comparable 1 1 acre   2 car garage $51,000
   Comparable 2 0.5 acre   1 car garage $46,000
   Comparable 3 0.5 acre   2 car garage $49,000
   Subject   1 acre   1 car garage $

   What is the value of the subject property?

   a. $45,000
   b. $47,000
   c. $48,000
   d. $50,000

60. Use the following information to answer the question:

   Comparable 1 1 acre   2 car garage $51,000
   Comparable 2 0.5 acre   1 car garage $46,000
   Comparable 3 0.5 acre   2 car garage $49,000
   Subject   1 acre   1 car garage $

   If an appraiser performed a matched pairs analysis, what would she adjust for?

   a. + $2,000 for garage, − $3,000 for lot size
   b. − $2,000 for garage, + $3,000 for lot size
   c. + $2,000 for lot size, − $3,000 for garage
   d. − $2,000 for garage, + $3,000 for lot size

61. When making adjustments as part of the sales comparison approach, which adjustment should be made first?

   a. Financing terms
   b. Condition of sale
   c. Market conditions
   d. Locations and physical characteristics

62. An appraiser can determine how much an adjustment for time should be worth by:

   a. calculating the property's age.
   b. studying the sale and resale prices of the property.
   c. studying an amortization table.
   d. studying the property's price relative to comparable properties.

63. An appraiser considers all of the following when determining property comparability **except**:

    a. zoning classification.
    b. site.
    c. form of ownership.
    d. view.

64. You are appraising a property in the Sweet Meadow neighborhood. In this neighborhood, swimming pools are considered to add value to a property. You have found comparables in the same neighborhood that are larger than the subject property, but they do not have swimming pools. What should you do?

    a. Subtract from the subject property for the difference in size and the value of the pool.
    b. Add to the subject property for the difference in size and subtract the value of the pool.
    c. Subtract from the comparable for the difference in size and add for the value of the pool.
    d. Subtract from the comparable for the value of the pool and add for the difference in size.

65. You determine that the subject property's neighborhood has appreciated 5% per year for the last five years. A comparable in the neighborhood sold 4 years ago for $100,000. What is the subject property's current adjusted value?

    a. $121,550
    b. $122,500
    c. $150,000
    d. $175,520

66. Which of the following statements is **correct** regarding the sales comparison approach?

    a. When selecting comparable sales, the appraiser does not consider the age of the property.
    b. When using the sales comparison approach, the appraiser adjusts the comparable properties to the subject property.
    c. An appraiser should never use comparable sales that are more than six months old.
    d. The sales prices of comparables are always conclusive evidence of market value in the area.

67. Which of the following conditions is a limitation when using the sales comparison approach?

    a. The approach's reliance on historical data
    b. Comparables that are too similar
    c. An active market
    d. An appraiser using the approach to value residential properties

68. In which type of market is the sales comparison approach most reliable?

    a. Seller's market
    b. Buyer's market
    c. Active market
    d. Inactive market

69. An appraiser using the sales comparison approach must adjust for differences between the subject property and the comparables. The dollar value of a positive feature present in the subject property but not present in a comparable is _____, while the dollar value of a positive feature present in a comparable but not present in the subject property is _____.

    a. subtracted, added
    b. added, subtracted
    c. subtracted, subtracted
    d. added, added

70. You select a comparable sale that recently sold for $50 per square foot. You study the market and determine you need to make the following adjustments to the price of the comparable:

    Time adjustment   +8%
    Physical adjustment −5%
    Age adjustment   −6%

    What is the value of the comparable sale per square foot?

    a. $48.06
    b. $48.60
    c. $50.60
    d. $52.50

71. The sales comparison approach is most reliable when a(n) _____ market exists.

    a. active
    b. stable
    c. efficient
    d. seller's

72. What does the term *plottage* mean?

    a. The incremental value created by combining two or more sites to produce greater utility
    b. The value created by subdividing land, surveying it, and mapping it on a plat map
    c. The value of land according to the assessor's office plat maps
    d. The partial value of a piece of land that has been subdivided

73. A prudent purchaser would pay no more for a property than the cost to acquire one with equal utility refers to the principle of:

    a. adjustment.
    b. substitution.
    c. comparison.
    d. contribution.

74. The primary strength of the Sales Comparison Approach is that:

    a. it is the most mathematically accurate.
    b. it is always the easiest approach to use.
    c. it is a direct reflection of buyers and sellers in the marketplace.
    d. it considers the cost to reproduce improvements.

75. Which of the following is the correct order of sequence for adjustments in the sales comparison approach?

    a. Time, property rights, conditions of sale, financing, physical characteristics
    b. Conditions of sale, time, property rights, financing, other adjustments
    c. Time, property rights, conditions of sale, financing, location
    d. Property rights, financing, conditions of sale, time, location

76. A property for which there is no identifiable market is called a(n):

    a. unique property.
    b. limited market property.
    c. special purpose property.
    d. exclusive use property.

77. A property for which there is a market, although the market is not readily identifiable is called a(n):

    a. unique property.
    b. limited market property.
    c. special purpose property.
    d. exclusive use property.

78. The primary limitation to the Sales Comparison Approach is that:

    a. comparable data may not be readily available.
    b. it is the least reliable.
    c. it is the most dificult approach to use.
    d. it always sets the upper limit of value.

Answers

1. (b) The original loan amount was $240,000 (80% of $300,000). The $240,000 is then discounted by 10%, or $24,000. Therefore, the adjusted sales price is the discounted loan amount of $216,000 + the down payment of $60,000 (20% of $300,000).

2. (d) The sales comparison approach can and must be used or at least considered in most types of properties. There are some property types, such as public or civic buildings, public lands, etc., that never sell, hence there are no sales to compare.

3. (a) Not only must a feature exist, but there also has to be value for that feature before an adjustment is made.

4. (d) All of the above characteristics are important to consider when selecting comparables.

5. (b) Regardless of the other factors, the comps should be the most similar.

6. (d) Although FNMA guidelines have restrictions based on a-c, that doesn't necessarily make it the best comparable. For example, maybe a view in the neighborhood is worth 30% of the value and no other adjustment is made, yet there is significant data to support the adjustment. Although it exceeds all of the parameters of FNMA guidelines, it may still be a good and reliable comparable.

7. (c) $260,000 x (1 + 0.12) = 291,200.

8. (a) Since the comp is superior in both regards, adjust it negatively for the financing and time differences. $300,000 x (1 – 0.05) x (1 – 0.08). Cash equivalency is always adjusted first, then time.

9. (d) You must adjust for the pool. $250,000 x 1.05 (6 months appreciation) – $25,000 = 237,500.

10. (d) Although all may be good comparables, factors may exist with regard to each of the comparables, such as conditions of sale, which may discount a property as a comparable.

11. (c) Adjustments should be made in the following order: financing, conditions of sale, market conditions, location, and physical characteristics.

12. (b) Adjustments should be made in the following order: financing, conditions of sale, market conditions, location, and physical characteristics.

13. (c) The sales comparison approach produces the least reliable results when the market is inactive.

14. (c) An appraiser should consider all sales that occurred in the previous three years.

15. (d) A, B, and C are all commonly used by appraisers as data sources.

16. (d) Listings are typically the upper limit of value, so the value of the subject property is probably less than $260,000.

17. (c) The seller pockets the same amount regardless of the loan, or loan-to-value ratio.

18. (a) All else being equal, cash or cash equivalent (80% loan with 20 % down payment) the sellers net the same.

19. (a) Since the comp is superior in both regards, adjust it negatively for the financing and time differences. $300,000 x (1 − 0.05) x (1 − 0.08). Cash equivalency is always adjusted first, then time.

20. (b) The principle of contribution states that any improvement to a property is worth only what it adds to the property's market value, regardless of the improvement's construction cost.

21. (c) Based on the paired sales, property is appreciating 10% in one year. Since the difference in time between the subject property and the comparable is only six months, the sales price should be adjusted half of 10% or 5%. 5% of 100,000 is 5,000. Add this to the sales price of the comparable.

22. (d) The primary limitation of the sales comparison approach relates to the availability of comparable data. When there is no identifiable market for a property, such as in the case of special purpose properties, the sales comparison approach cannot be used.

23. (d) When using the paired sales technique, the appraiser must use similar properties. Even though the properties may be in similar locations, using dissimilar properties is inappropriate and will not yield accurate results.

24. (b) The type of adjustment necessary in the paired sales analysis depends on how the information is derived from the market. Several adjustments are usually necessary in order to isolate the affect of one variable. The analysis is more reliable if a large amount of data is available. If only a limited amount of data exists, other methods should be used to determine the effectiveness of this approach.

Sales Comparison Approach - Answers

25. (a) The primary limitation of the sales comparison approach is the availability of comparable data. In markets where sales activity is slow, there may not be enough sales and listings against which to compare the subject property.

26. (d) The most important consideration when choosing which comparables to use in the sales comparison approach is the circumstances surrounding the sale of the comparable. The appraiser must consider the terms of the sale, the price, and whether it was at arm's length.

27. (c) Adjustments should be made in this order: property rights conveyed, financing, conditions of sale, market conditions (time), location, and physical characteristics.

28. (d) The principle of substitution is used in every appraisal to some extent; however, it is primarily used with the sales comparison approach.

29. (b) The sales comparison approach values real property based on what similar properties in the same area have recently sold for.

30. (d) The elements of comparison are divided into four categories: time, location, physical characteristics, and conditions of sale. Special conditions and special financing are also elements of comparison.

31. (b) The sales comparison approach uses the economic principle of substitution when estimating value in reference to comparable properties.

32. (d) The process to reconcile the adjusted values of comparables is to review each sale and judge its comparability to the property being appraised.

33. (a) The value of a property is generally accurate when the sales comparison approach is based on a sufficient number of sales similar to the subject property with appropriate adjustments.

34. (b) When the appraiser is using the sales comparison approach, he or she must adjust the sales or listing price of each comparable for differences between it and the subject.

35. (a) The criteria used to verify a comparable property before its use includes whether any special concessions were granted by either party.

36. (a) The appraiser should personally inspect every comparable used in the appraisal report and confirm the data with the buyer, seller, or broker.

37. (b) Adjustments are derived from market data.

38. (a) The matched pairs method of determining adjustment value uses two sales from the market that have one defining difference between them. The difference in their sales price is then attributed to that difference.

39. (b) Once the appraiser has collected all the data and obtained value estimates using the appropriate approaches, the appraiser must reconcile the estimates from each approach to produce a final estimate.

40. (b) A sale to a relative at below market price is not an "arm's length" transaction, one of the criteria for good comparables.

41. (a) Market data usually provides the best indication of market value for a property when it is carefully collected, analyzed, verified, and reconciled.

42. (c) Every comparable property must be sold in an arm's length transaction in which neither buyer nor seller is acting under duress, the property is offered on the open market for a reasonable amount of time, and both buyer and seller have a reasonable knowledge of the property.

43. (d) Houses that are listed substantially above market value usually do not sell, regardless of how long they are offered for sale.

44. (a) The first step in the sales comparison approach is to study the market and select the sales and listings of properties that are most comparable to the subject property. Stating the problem is the first step in the appraisal process.

45. (a) The more recently the comparable sold and the more similar it is to the subject property, the better it will be as an indicator of value.

46. (b) The appraiser must verify facts concerning the comparables, such as depreciation, measurements, and reported price and terms.

47. (a) Reported sales prices may differ from the actual market value of a property due to several reasons, including a buyer who exercises an option.

48. (c) Adjustments may be made to reflect the dollar or percentage value of the noted differences.

49. (a) Doubling up on adjustments exists when more than one set of matched pairs is used and some comparison elements may interact. Regression analysis may help measure the interaction of data.

Sales Comparison Approach - Answers

50. (d) Percentages are often used to express the differences between a subject property and a comparable sale. This is especially true for time, special conditions, and location adjustments. Residential appraisals use sales price as the unit of comparison, and the adjustments are made in dollars, not percentages.

51. (c) There is often more than one physical characteristic that requires adjustment.

52. (b) Cumulative percentage adjustments are calculated by adding the percentages together and multiplying the sum by the unadjusted price.

53. (c) The adjustment for the property rights conveyed takes into account the differences in legal estate between the subject property and the comparable.

54. (d) Appropriate comparables are essential to the sales comparison approach. The best comparables require no or very minimal adjustment.

55. (b) In order to obtain all of the information needed to use a comparable sale, the appraiser should inspect each comparable property and verify the nature of the sale with the buyer, seller, or broker.

56. (d) The financing terms adjustment converts the transaction price of the comparable into its cash equivalent or modifies it to match the financing terms of the subject property.

57. (d) The goal of any approach to value is to seek the value indication. Using sales price as a search parameter is like seeking a predetermined result.

58. (c) An adjustment for differences between the subject property and a comparable is based on a typical buyer's reaction to the difference.

59. (c) A matched pair analysis between Comp 2 and Comp 3 shows a $3,000 adjustment for the garage space; which is then applied to Comp 1 to result in an adjusted value for the Subject Property of $48,000. An analysis of Comp 1 and Comp 3 shows a $2,000 adjustment for the difference in site area. When applied to Comp 2 this also indicates an adjusted value for the Subject Property of $48,000.

60. (c) Find the two comparables that are exactly the same, except for the adjustment you are trying to determine. The difference in price between the two comps will equal the value of the adjustment. For example, Comp 1 and 3 are identical except for the lot size. Comp 3 is ½ acre smaller and $2,000 less expensive. Therefore, ½ acre is equal to $2,000.

61. (a) Financing terms is the best answer of those provided. However, property rights have priority over financing.

62. (b) By studying sale and resale prices, an appraiser can extract the differences in value. For example, a house that sold in April 2003 at $300,000 then sells for $330,000 in April 2004 demonstrates a 10% annual increase during that period, or 5% over the preceding 6 months or 2.5% over the preceding 3 months, etc.

63. (c) View, type of zoning, site size and shape are points of comparison. Type of ownership can be important in determining the definition of the problem and the type of value for the subject property, but not for comparing other properties to the subject.

64. (c) You always adjust the value of the comparable. Subtract from the comparable for the difference in size and add the value of the missing pool.

65. (a) Compound the interest, or appreciation rate, as 1.054 and multiply the result by the comparable's sales price. $1.05^4 = 1.2155 \times 100,000 = 121,550$.

66. (b) Comparable properties are always adjusted to the subject property, never the subject property to the comparables.

67. (a) You may have to adjust historical data of comparable sales to reflect the current market. All of the other choices are advantages to the sales comparison approach.

68. (c) The sales comparison approach is most reliable when the market is active, with many buyers and sellers, and many recent sales for comparison.

69. (b) If the subject property has a positive feature that is not present in the comparable, the dollar value of the feature is added to the comparable. If the comparable has a positive feature that the subject property does not, the dollar value of the feature is subtracted from the comparable.

70. (a) First, calculate the adjustment for time. $50 x 1.08 = $54.00. Next, calculate the adjustment for the physical and age differences. The two negative adjustments add up to 11%. Subtract this from 1.00 (100%) to get 0.89. $54 x 0.89 = $48.06, the value of the comparable per square foot.

71. (a) The sales comparison approach is most reliable when an active market exists. The more activity in the market, the more reliable the collected data will be.

72. (a) Plottage refers to the incremental value created by combining two or more sites to produce greater utility. The joining of the sites does not necessarily produce incremental value, it must also create greater utility.

73. (b) By definition.

74. (c) The sales comparison approach is easily understood and directly reflects the actions of buyers and sellers in the marketplace.

75. (d) These five of the seven steps are in the correct order.

76. (c) By definition.

77. (b) By definition.

78. (a) The sales comparison approach relies on comparable data. Lack of data would limit the reliability of the sales comparison approach.

Site Value

1. Which technique for determining improvement value requires an appraiser to deduct the net income applicable to the land, and then capitalize the remainder and attribute the result to the improvements?

    a. Abstraction
    b. Allocation
    c. Developmental
    d. Building residual

2. The term *plottage* refers to:

    a. creating a metes and bounds description of a plot of land.
    b. combining two or more adjacent land units that results in greater value.
    c. the abstracted value of a plot of land.
    d. subdividing a plot of land into two or more adjacent lots, which increases the total value.

3. Site value for an existing home is usually computed using:

    a. the cost approach.
    b. comparison only.
    c. comparison or abstraction.
    d. the income it generates.

4. A property's total value is estimated to be $150,000. The appraiser concludes that 76% of the total value is attributable to a single-family residence built on the land. What is the estimated value of the land?

    a. $12,000
    b. $36,000
    c. $114,000
    d. $160,000

5. Which of the following defines *plottage* value?

    a. The incremental value created by combining two or more sites to create greater utility
    b. The value of the land on which the improvement is built
    c. The value of a parcel of land according to tax rolls
    d. The total value of a parcel of land that has been subdivided to create greater utility

6. The term *economic obsolescence* means the same as:

    a. physical deterioration.
    b. functional obsolescence.
    c. external depreciation.
    d. functional utility.

7. An appraiser considers all of the following when analyzing the physical characteristics of a lot **except**:

    a. whether it is an inside lot or a corner lot.
    b. whether it is a rectangular lot or an odd-shaped lot.
    c. the presence of storm sewers.
    d. the extent of landscaping.

8. The area at the rear of a site is considered _____ if that area does not serve the existing improvements.

    a. excess land
    b. raw, usable land
    c. a superadequacy
    d. functional obsolescence

9. When making a series of adjustments in sequence, the appraiser adjusts for which of the following first?

    a. Special conditions
    b. Special financing
    c. Location
    d. Physical characteristics

10. Dollar adjustments may be based on all of the following **except**:

    a. total price of the property.
    b. front foot price.
    c. net sales price.
    d. square foot price.

11. An appraiser who is determining property value may not base it on the principle of:

    a. supply and demand.
    b. surplus productivity.
    c. increasing and decreasing returns.
    d. balance.

12. Which of the following is **not** an acceptable alternate means of valuing a residential property?

    a. Income approach
    b. Land residual technique
    c. Capitalizing ground rent
    d. Extraction method

13. Which of the following statements is **true**?

    a. Factors that affect value differ according to land use
    b. Factors that affect value are not affected by land use
    c. Value is not influenced by location
    d. Value is not affected by frontage

14. An appraiser may use _____ to estimate the value of a finished lot.

    a. the developer's estimates of sales price
    b. appropriate comparables from existing subdivisions
    c. sales prices from unadjusted raw land
    d. current interest rates

15. The _____ method of site valuation assumes the site to be at its highest and best use.

    a. extraction
    b. allocation
    c. land residual technique
    d. sales comparison

16. All of the following are units of comparison used to estimate the value of a site **except**:

    a. front foot.
    b. square foot.
    c. cubic foot.
    d. square yard.

17. An appraiser may estimate the market value of a residential property using all of the following methods **except** the:

    a. sales comparison approach.
    b. allocation procedure.
    c. extraction method.
    d. cost approach.

18. Which of the following is true if a comparable is in the same neighborhood as the subject property?

    a. Often, no neighborhood adjustment is needed
    b. It is always a better comparable sale than a site in another neighborhood
    c. A neighborhood adjustment is never necessary
    d. Comparables in the same neighborhood should be avoided

19. Three parcels each have an estimated value of $10,000. If the parcels were combined, an appraiser has estimated their assembled value would be $40,000. The parcels' increase in value when joined is an example of:

    a. accumulation.
    b. agglomeration.
    c. superadequacy.
    d. plottage.

20. What does the term *plottage* mean?

    a. The incremental value created by combining two or more sites to produce greater utility
    b. The value created by subdividing land, surveying it, and mapping it on a plat map
    c. The value of land according to the assessor's office plat maps
    d. The partial value of a piece of land that has been subdivided

21. When appraising land value, which is the most reliable method?

    a. Land residual technique
    b. Sales comparison
    c. Allocation
    d. Subdivision development

22. What are the two components that comprise the total value of an improved property?

    a. The value of the improvements and the contribution of the site
    b. The contribution of improvements and the value of the site
    c. The demolition of the improvements and the redevelopment of the site
    d. The highest and best use of the improvements and the anticipation of the site

23. When an oversupply of land is coupled with stable demand, typically prices:

    a. will decline.
    b. will increase.
    c. will remain static.
    d. are not affected.

24. Which of the following is not one of the six recognized methods for land and site valuation?

    a. Allocation
    b. Building residual
    c. Extraction
    d. Sales comparison

25. When valuing a site, which appraisal method deducts the value of site improvements from the overall sales price of a property?

    a. Allocation
    b. Extraction
    c. Ground rent capitalization
    d. Sales comparison

26. What is a factor that expresses a relationship between value and a particular property feature?

    a. Element of comparison
    b. Unit of measure
    c. Unit of comparison
    d. Essential element

27. Which method is a technique used to estimate land value in which the appraiser views the land parcel as if subdivided into smaller lots?

    a. Allocation
    b. Extraction
    c. Ground rent capitalization
    d. Subdivision method

28. Matched pair analysis is typically used in which appraisal method?

    a. Allocation
    b. Extraction
    c. Sales comparison
    d. Subdivision method

29. Which method of site valuation would be used to appraise a surface parking lot in a downtown area leased to a parking lot operator?

    a. Allocation
    b. Land residual
    c. Sales comparison
    d. Ground rent capitalization

30. Which method of site valuation is rarely used?

    a. Allocation
    b. Land residual
    c. Sales comparison
    d. Ground rent capitalization

31. Which method of site valuation is most commonly used?

    a. Allocation
    b. Land residual
    c. Sales comparison
    d. Ground rent capitalization

32. Which of the following improvements is considered an onsite improvement?

    a. Utility hookups
    b. Curbs
    c. Storm sewer drains
    d. Sidewalks

33. Improvements that are outside the confines of the site are called:

    a. onsite improvements.
    b. over improvements.
    c. offsite improvements.
    d. owner improvements.

34. Which economic principle states that land must always be estimated as if vacant and available for development to its most economic and profitable use, even if already improved?

    a. Substitution
    b. Highest and best use
    c. Supply and demand
    d. Anticipation

35. Which of the following is **not** a physical characteristic that my influence the value of a parcel of land?

    a. Size
    b. Drainage
    c. Shape
    d. Zoning

Answers

1. (d) When using the building residual technique, the appraiser first deducts the NOI that the land must earn to justify its value. The resulting balance must be earned by the building. This building income is then capitalized at the interest rate plus the rate of recapture to arrive at the building's value.

2. (b) Two or more contiguous properties are worth more when combined under one ownership than if they remain separate parcels of land.

3. (c) Comparison is preferred, but no comparable sales may be available. Abstraction is commonly used to determine site value in subdivided lots.

4. (b) 76% of $150,000 = $114,000, which is the value of the single-family residence. $150,000 − $114,000 = $36,000, which is the value of the land.

5. (a) Plottage value is the increase in value that results when two or more adjacent sites are combined to create greater utility.

6. (c) Economic obsolescence and external depreciation are the same thing.

7. (d) When analyzing the physical characteristics of a lot, the items an appraiser considers include whether it is an inside lot or a corner lot, rectangular lot or an odd-shaped lot, the if there is storm water disposal, and whether it is a flat lot or a sloping lot or one that drops off significantly. However, landscaping is not considered.

8. (a) The market considers a lot with an area that does not serve the improvements as excess land.

9. (b) Adjustments are made in the following order: special financing, special conditions, market conditions, location, and physical characteristics.

10. (c) If dollar adjustments are used, they may be based on either the total price of the whole property, or on the other units of comparison, such as price per square foot, price per front foot, price per acre, or per dwelling unit permitted by zoning on the site. Net sales price is the result of all the adjustments, not an adjustment by itself.

11. (a) An appraiser may base the value of a site on the principles of balance, contribution, surplus productivity, and increasing and decreasing returns.

12. (a) The value of residential property may be estimated using the sales comparison approach, the allocation procedure, extraction method, capitalization of ground rent, or land residual technique. The income approach does not apply.

13. (a) Value factors differ according to the type of land use. Value factors in a residential neighborhood may include proximity to a good school or daycare facilities. Value factors in commercial area may include traffic flow and frontage.

14. (b) An appraiser can determine the estimated value of a finished lot by analyzing appropriate comparables from existing, competitive subdivisions that have recently been developed.

15. (c) In the land residual technique, the site is assumed to be improved to its highest and best use.

16. (c) When using dollar adjustments, the appraiser may base them on either the total price of the whole property or on the other units of comparison, such as price per square foot, price per front foot, price per acre or per dwelling unit permitted by zoning.

17. (d) The five basic procedures for estimating market value of residential property are the sales comparison approach, the allocation procedure, the extraction method, the capitalization of ground rents, and the land residual technique.

18. (a) If a comparable site is in the same neighborhood as the appraised site, it is likely that no neighborhood adjustment would be necessary.

19. (d) When a group of adjacent properties are combined into one property through a process called assemblage, the increase in unit value is called plottage.

20. (a) Plottage refers to the incremental value created by combining two or more sites to produce greater utility. The joining of the sites does not necessarily produce incremental value, it must also create greater utility.

21. (b) Sales comparison is the most common approach and is the most reliable when there is enough data. Allocation method is used when where is an inadequate number of comparable sales available to use the sales comparison method. The subdivision method is a technique used to estimate land value in which the appraiser views the land parcel as if subdivided into smaller lots. The land residual technique is rarely used.

22. (b) By definition.

23. (a) More supply than demand indicates a decrease in prices.

24. (b) Land residual, not building residual, is one of the methods of site valuation.

25. (a) By definition.

Site Value - Answers

26. (c) By definition.

27. (d) By definition.

28. (c) By definition.

29. (a) By definition.

30. (b) By definition.

31. (c) When adequate comparable data is available, this method is the one most frequently used.

32. (a) Onsite improvements include those within the confines of the site.

33. (c) By definition.

34. (b) By definition.

35. (d) Zoning determines what is legally permissible and is not a physical characteristic.

Cost Approach

1. If a property has an economic life of 50 years, its actual age is 35, and its effective age is 20, what is the total loss in value, using straight-line depreciation?

    a. 20%
    b. 35%
    c. 40%
    d. 50%

2. The condition of the subject property affects which of the following?

    a. Actual age
    b. Effective age
    c. The cost approach
    d. Both b and c

3. An appraiser is estimating the replacement cost of a property using the quantity survey method. He needs to determine the cost of completing a patio. How many cubic yards of concrete would be necessary to complete a 162 square foot patio that is 4 inches thick? (Round to the nearest whole number)

    a. 1 square yard
    b. 2 square yards
    c. 9 square yards
    d. 118 square yards

4. The cost to produce a structure of the same size, quality of construction, and utility is called:

    a. reproduction cost.
    b. replication cost.
    c. replacement cost.
    d. approximation cost.

5. Economic obsolescence is usually:

    a. curable.
    b. too expensive to correct.
    c. incurable physical deterioration.
    d. impossible for the owner to correct.

6. An outdated architectural style is an example of what type of depreciation?

    a. External obsolescence
    b. Functional obsolescence
    c. Economic obsolescence
    d. Physical deterioration

7. All of the following are examples of functional obsolescence **except**:

    a. a one-car garage.
    b. a house with an unworkable floor plan.
    c. a stairway suffering from wear and tear.
    d. no air conditioning in a desert location.

8. All of the following are examples of external obsolescence **except**:

    a. an oversupply of similar properties.
    b. adverse zoning regulations.
    c. environmental restrictions.
    d. a one-bathroom house.

9. Effective age is influenced by which of the following?

    a. Original cost of construction
    b. Physical age according to tax assessor's records
    c. Quality of construction and maintenance
    d. All of the above

10. An appraiser calculates effective age:

    a. using a complex mathematical formula.
    b. as an estimate based on the market area.
    c. using a published field service manual for the area.
    d. only after consulting with another appraiser.

11. If a building does not contribute any value to a site, the appraiser must:

    a. add salvage value.
    b. compute the original cost of the building.
    c. deduct demolition costs.
    d. add the cost new of similar construction to the value opinion.

12. Economic life is:

    a. the length of time the property has appreciated in value.
    b. the past use of the property.
    c. the value of the property less its economic obsolescene.
    d. the length of time the improvments will contribute to the value.

13. Which is usually shorter in duration, physical life or economic life?

    a. Physical life
    b. Economic life
    c. They are usually the same
    d. The two cannot be compared

14. The period of time between the total economic life and the effective age of an improvement is called:

    a. estimated depreciation.
    b. sum of the years.
    c. remaining economic life.
    d. obsolescence.

15. Appraisers use _____ to determine the age of improvements.

    a. tax assessor's records
    b. the age-life method
    c. the owner's assertion
    d. the legal description of the property

16. In the straight-line method of estimating depreciation, the appraiser:

    a. calculates the economic obsolescence.
    b. disregards the economic life of the property.
    c. compares the structure's effective age with its total economic life.
    d. provides for the recapture of depreciation by allowing for accruals.

17. All of the following are usually curable forms of depreciation **except**:

    a. physical deterioration.
    b. wear and tear.
    c. functional obsolescence.
    d. external obsolescence.

18. An appraiser's definition of depreciation is:

    a. a loss in value from any cause.
    b. a way of reducing the cost basis of a property.
    c. a way of minimizing the tax consequence.
    d. a reduction in a property's aesthetic appeal.

19. The replacement cost new of an office building is estimated at $1,500,000. The depreciation from wear and tear on the existing structure is $100,000. Due to lack of fiber optics in the building and inadequate parking on-site, functional obsolescence is estimated at $250,000. Its location in a declining part of the city (economic obsolescence) is estimated at $200,000. What is the total depreciation of this office building?

    a. $450,000
    b. $550,000
    c. $950,000
    d. There is not enough information to answer

20. The definition of *depreciation* is:

    a. the difference between functional and external obsolescence.
    b. the difference between appraised value and replacement cost.
    c. the difference between economic life and physical life.
    d. the difference between effective age and chronological age.

21. Which of the following is **not** a step in the cost approach to value?

    a. Estimating site value
    b. Determining accrued depreciation
    c. Adding site improvement values
    d. Estimating appreciation

22. A house is located in an upscale neighborhood, but it backs to a busy street and traffic noise is a problem. This property suffers from:

    a. economic obsolescence.
    b. functional obsolescence.
    c. physical depreciation.
    d. superadequacy.

23. *Superadequacy* is:

    a. excess land.
    b. plottage.
    c. unearned increment.
    d. over improvement.

24. A property suffering from superadequacy experiences:

    a. economic obsolescence.
    b. functional obsolescence.
    c. plottage.
    d. progression.

25. A residential property has a one-car garage in a market area where two-car garages are the norm. The property suffers from:

    a. regression.
    b. aggregation.
    c. economic obsolescence.
    d. functional obsolescence.

26. A house is located near a dairy farm and is affected by a strong odor and the presence of flies. The property suffers a loss in value due to:

    a. functional obsolescence.
    b. economic obsolescence.
    c. physical depreciation.
    d. regression.

27. The cost approach is least reliable when appraising:

    a. new construction.
    b. an old structure with severe functional obsolescence.
    c. a single-family residence.
    d. a library.

28. The cost approach is the most reliable approach to value that can be used when appraising:

    a. a single-family residence.
    b. office buildings.
    c. large income properties.
    d. special purpose properties like city halls, public schools, and public libraries.

29. When developing an estimate of cost, an appraiser should treat a developer's profits as:

    a. irrelevant to the cost approach.
    b. entrepreneurial reward.
    c. built in to the cost per square foot.
    d. optional in most markets.

30. A developer's profits are:

    a. excessive in most markets.
    b. minimal.
    c. the difference between sales price and all direct and indirect costs.
    d. the difference between asking price and cost.

31. In a cost handbook, how are the developer's marketing materials classified?

    a. Basic costs
    b. Indirect costs
    c. Profit
    d. Excess costs

32. Which method would an appraiser most likely use to appraise a city hall?

    a. Capitalization
    b. Sales comparison
    c. Income
    d. Cost

33. Which of the following is a cause of economic obsolescence?

    a. An unworkable floor plan
    b. Excessive wear and tear
    c. Proximity to the city dump
    d. Advanced age

34. The cost approach is most reliable when used on:

    a. new or newer structures.
    b. older, seasoned properties.
    c. income properties.
    d. vacant land.

35. Which of the following sources may provide an appraiser with reliable cost data?

    a. The multiple listing service
    b. A cost service handbook
    c. A dictionary of appraisal terms
    d. The consumer price index

36. The economic life of an improvement has expired when:

    a. the improvements no longer contribute to the property value.
    b. the improvements no longer earn sufficient income to justify their continued operation.
    c. the property value as improved is no longer greater than the value as vacant.
    d. all of the above

37. Structural over improvements are generally:

    a. curable.
    b. incurable.
    c. economically and physically possible to correct.
    d. correctable if permits can be obtained.

38. Why is it not always possible to determine the reproduction cost of an older home?

    a. The building costs from many years ago may not be available.
    b. The precise details of workmanship and materials may not be available.
    c. Current materials are not comparable to materials used in the past.
    d. The labor costs from many years ago may not be available.

39. Reproduction cost is:

    a. the original cost to construct an exact duplicate of the improvements.
    b. the original cost to construct a structure of the same utility.
    c. the current cost to construct a structure of the same utility.
    d. the current cost to construct an exact duplicate of the improvements.

40. Replacement cost is:

    a. the original cost to construct an exact duplicate of the improvements.
    b. the original cost to construct a structure of the same utility.
    c. the current cost to construct a structure of the same utility.
    d. the current cost to construct an exact duplicate of the improvements.

41. The most accurate method of estimating building cost, and the one most commonly used by contractors is:

    a. square foot.
    b. quantity survey.
    c. unit-in-place.
    d. cubic foot.

42. The index method of estimating current building cost is based on:

    a. comparing the changes in building cost over time.
    b. multiplying the construction cost of each component part by the number of units used in the construction.
    c. itemizing the cost to install all the component parts of a new structure.
    d. devising a square foot figure to account for all construction costs.

43. Which method of estimating building cost do appraisers typically use?

    a. The index method
    b. The square foot method
    c. The quantity survey method
    d. The unit-in-place method

44. A single–family residence cost $75,000 to construct in 1985. At that time, the cost index indicated that the numerical factor reflecting the cost to construct that house was 204. The same cost index today indicates the appropriate numerical factor reflecting the cost to construct that house is 408. According to the index method, what is the replacement cost of that single–family residence today?

    a. $105,000
    b. $125,000
    c. $150,000
    d. $200,000

45. The improvements on a site are 25 years old, but an appraiser has determined their effective age is 15 years. The economic life of the property is 55 years. Using the straight-line method, what is the percentage of accrued depreciation?

    a. 15%
    b. 21%
    c. 25%
    d. 32%

46. Total economic life is calculated by:

    a. adding actual age to remaining economic life.
    b. adding effective age to remaining economic life.
    c. subtracting effective age from remaining economic life.
    d. adding recaptured depreciation to remaining economic life.

47. What is the formula for calculating accrued depreciation using the straight line method?

    a. Divide actual age in years by remaining economic life.
    b. Divide actual age in years by total economic life.
    c. Divide effective age in years by total economic life.
    d. Divide effective age in years by remaining economic life.

48. In the cost approach to value, depreciation applies to:

    a. the improvements only.
    b. the improvements and the land.
    c. the land only.
    d. the materials only.

49. The cost approach provides an opinion of value based on which of the following concepts?

    a. Costs are basically the same over long periods of time.
    b. Building costs are consistent even in different geographical areas.
    c. A person would not normally pay more for a property than it would cost to purchase land and build a similar structure.
    d. The opinion of value offered by the cost approach is valid only if the site value is determined by comparison.

50. The cost approach is the most accurate approach when:

    a. the house is older with significant functional obsolescence.
    b. the house suffers from significant depreciation.
    c. the house has unique amenities and comparable sales are few.
    d. the property is an office building.

51. Which term refers to the expense of constructing a building in a manner that replicates a previous structure's design, layout, materials, and quality of workmanship?

    a. Remodeling cost
    b. Replacement cost
    c. Reproduction cost
    d. Replication cost

52. A building is 10 years old, which is also its effective age. It has a total economic life of 50 years. Using straight-line depreciation, what is its percentage of accrued depreciation?

    a. 15%
    b. 20%
    c. 40%
    d. 50%

53. *Accumulated depreciation* means the:

    a. amount of accrued capital recapture written off on the annual accounting statements.
    b. total loss in value that has accrued since the property was purchased by the current owner.
    c. loss in value that has accrued since the property was built.
    d. difference between a structure's reproduction or replacement cost and its market value as of the date of the appraisal.

54. A building that sold for $100,000 has an annual straight-line depreciation expense of $2,500. What will be the accumulated deprecation in three years?

    a. $2,500
    b. $7,000
    c. $7,500
    d. $25,000

55. Which of the following is a step in the cost approach?

    a. Estimate the net operating income of the property.
    b. Determine the value of the land using its assessed value and tax rate.
    c. Estimate the accrued depreciation.
    d. Verify the acquisition price of the construction material used when the structure was built.

56. Which method of measuring accrued depreciation analyzes each cause of depreciation separately and then adds the separate estimates together to calculate the total?

    a. Breakdown method
    b. Age-life method
    c. Modified economic age-life method
    d. Straight-line method

57. Which of the following is the best example of economic obsolescence?

    a. A house that has only a small wood stove for heating
    b. The largest employer in an area moves relocates to another state and lays off all its employees
    c. A house that has a leaky roof and a cracked foundation
    d. A house with five bedrooms and only one bathroom

58. Which of the following is not an acceptable method of estimating building costs?

    a. unit-in-place method
    b. quantity survey method
    c. breakdown method
    d. comparative unit method

59. Accrued depreciation is estimated using the age-life method by calculating the ratio of a property's effective age to its _____, and applying the ratio to the property's reproduction cost new.

    a. physical age
    b. depreciated age
    c. chronological age
    d. total economic life

60. An appraiser may use which of the following methods to estimate accrued depreciation?

    a. Economic age-life, modified economic age-life, sales comparison, breakdown method, or capitalized value method.
    b. Economic age-life, comparative unit, sales comparison, breakdown method, or effective value method.
    c. Economic age-life, modified economic age-life, quantity survey, replacement method, or breakdown method.
    d. Economic age-life, modified economic age-life, sales comparison, comparative unit, or reconstruction method.

61. The cost approach may be unreliable if:

    a. the property suffers from functional obsolescence.
    b. the property suffers from external obsolescence.
    c. the property has accrued extensive depreciation.
    d. a substantial number of comparables are available.

62. All of the following items must be considered and incorporated into the cost approach to value **except**:

    a. replacement cost.
    b. functional obsolescence.
    c. vacancy allowance.
    d. physical wear and tear.

63. An appraiser who is using the cost approach values a site as if it is:

    a. occupied and being used under its existing use
    b. improved under the current zoning ordinances
    c. improved and available for income-generating purposes
    d. vacant and available to be used under its highest and best use

64. An appraiser is evaluating a single-family residence and observes a foundation that is cracked, has only one bathroom for 4 bedrooms, and has an oversupply of single-family residences for sale in the local market due to a recent local recession. What has the appraiser observed?

    a. Physical deterioration, functional obsolescence, and economic obsolescence
    b. Functional obsolescence, physical deterioration, and economic obsolescence
    c. Economic obsolescence, physical deterioration, and locational obsolescence
    d. Economic obsolescence, functional obsolescence, and locational obsolescence

65. An asset's loss in value due to wear and obsolescence is referred to as:

    a. incurable external obsolescence.
    b. curable functional obsolescence.
    c. curable economic obsolescence.
    d. depreciation.

66. If an improvement is _____, the cost approach is more reliable.

    a. older with many improvements and remodels
    b. new but suffering from economic obsolescence
    c. the highest and best use and suffers no functional obsolescence
    d. new, has no accrued depreciation, and is the highest and best use

67. The cost approach:

    a. determines future rights.
    b. converts cost-to-construct figures to market value figures.
    c. determines the difference between the cost to construct and sales price.
    d. converts reproduction costs to sales prices.

68. Depreciation is the difference between:

    a. the cost of the improvement on the date of the appraisal and the value of the improvement.
    b. the size of the improvement and the cost of the improvement.
    c. the cost to construct and the cost to reproduce the improvement.
    d. the value of the raw land and the cost of improvements.

69. Which of the following is **not** considered a direct cost?

    a. labor.
    b. contractor profit.
    c. taxes.
    d. materials.

70. The _____ appraisers use to estimate reproduction or replacement cost is also used by contractors, builders, and cost estimators.

    a. quantity survey method
    b. unit-in-place method
    c. square foot method
    d. cubic foot method

71. In general, superadequacies are:

    a. found in newer homes rather than older ones.
    b. curable.
    c. incurable.
    d. found only in homes valued in excess of $100,000.

72. Depreciation is measured by all of the following **except** the:

    a. unit-in-place method.
    b. age-life method.
    c. abstraction method.
    d. breakdown method.

73. When an appraiser uses the _____, she multiplies the construction cost per square foot by the number of square feet in the subject property.

    a. square foot method
    b. unit-in-place method
    c. quantity survey method
    d. breakdown method

74. The unit-in-place method:

    a. estimates the cost of labor and materials for each component of a building.
    b. estimates the cost of the current improvement as is.
    c. compares the construction cost with another building that has recently sold.
    d. includes units of land as part of the cost of construction.

75. Curable physical deterioration is used in which method of estimating accrued depreciation?

    a. Breakdown
    b. Age-life
    c. Abstraction
    d. Unit-in-place

76. The _____ of a building is the longest portion or most advanced point in its life cycle.

    a. chronological age
    b. effective age
    c. economic life
    d. physical life

77. An appraiser who uses the quantity survey method must:

    a. prepare a detailed inventory of all materials and equipment used to construct the building.
    b. separate total depreciation into physical deterioration, functional obsolescence, and external obsolescence.
    c. use sales data to determine an estimate of property value.
    d. prepare a detailed inventory of the property owner's personal property and assets.

78. An appraiser uses the abstraction method to determine the average annual amount of depreciation, which is indicated by the comparable properties sold. To find this information, the appraiser:

    a. multiplies the total depreciation by economic life.
    b. divides the average annual amount of depreciation by physical life.
    c. divides the total depreciation by effective age.
    d. multiplies the chronological age by total depreciation.

79. The unit-in-place method is used to:

    a. estimate building replacement cost.
    b. estimate building reproduction cost.
    c. estimate land value.
    d. determine a property's highest and best use.

80. When using the cost approach to appraise a 4 unit building, an appraiser considers all of the following **except**:

    a. permit fees per square foot.
    b. market lease rate.
    c. architect's fees.
    d. depreciation theory.

81. A property owner remodels his kitchen at a cost of $30,000. The remodel adds $15,000 of value to the property. This is an example of:

    a. economic obsolescence.
    b. functional obsolescence, curable.
    c. functional obsolescence, incurable.
    d. physical deterioration.

82. An appraiser is determining if a property suffers from functional obsolescence. She should:

    a. determine the age-life ratio of the improvements.
    b. consider the remaining life of the short lived improvements.
    c. use the comparative unit method.
    d. compare the utility and function of the subject property with that of other properties in the neighborhood.

83. The cost approach determines the cost new of improvements as of the:

    a. date of construction.
    b. original purchase date.
    c. effective date of the appraisal.
    d. renovation date.

84. An office building sells for $100,000. Its annual straight-line depreciation is $2,500. What will the accumulated depreciation be in three years?

    a. $3,500
    b. $5,250
    c. $7,500
    d. $12,250

85. A home loses value after an industrial plant is built nearby. Which form of depreciation is it suffering from?

    a. Curable functional obsolescence
    b. Economic obsolescence
    c. Physical depreciation
    d. Incurable functional obsolescence

86. A home that lacks central air conditioning would suffer from functional obsolescence when:

    a. comparable properties lack air conditioning as well.
    b. the home has no comparables.
    c. comparable properties have central air-conditioning.
    d. the home is less than ten years old.

87. When an improvement _____, the cost approach is more reliable.

    a. is the highest and best use, and is less than 15 years old
    b. has accrued significant depreciation
    c. suffers no functional obsolescence
    d. is new, has no accrued depreciation, and is the highest and best use

88. Land site value is evaluated using the cost approach:

    a. at its present use if currently improved.
    b. at its highest and best use as if vacant.
    c. according to current zoning regulations.
    d. at its present use, as long as the value is greater than the cost to demolish it.

89. What is the term for a building's age based on its physical condition and utility?

    a. Economic age
    b. Economic life
    c. Effective age
    d. Actual age

90. Which of the following could cause economic obsolescence in a residential property?

    a. Lack of periodic maintenance and repairs on the house
    b. Construction of an industrial plant on the adjacent lot
    c. A change in area zoning, prohibiting commercial land use
    d. Lack of central heat and air conditioning in the house

91. What is term for the difference between the present value of an improvement and its reproduction cost new?

    a. Accumulated deterioration
    b. Accrued depreciation
    c. Physical deterioration
    d. Value of the improvement

92. Curable, physical deterioration is measured by the:

    a. cost to restore the item to new or reasonably new condition.
    b. cost of the item as if new, less accrued depreciation.
    c. cost of replicating the item.
    d. cost of the item as if new, less functional obsolescence.

93. The cost approach is based on which valuation principle?

    a. Conformity
    b. Contribution
    c. Highest and best use
    d. Substitution

94. When _____, the cost approach to value will usually be more accurate.

    a. the land is raw and undeveloped
    b. the building is new and is being used under its highest and best use
    c. the building is old and suffers from significant depreciation
    d. the land is slated for development, but is not yet improved

95. Which of the following must be true in order for functional obsolescence to be curable?

    a. The cost of reproducing the obsolete item must be less than the value of the item.
    b. The property without the obsolete item must be more valuable than with the item.
    c. The cost of replacing the obsolete item must be the same as or less than the anticipated increase in value.
    d. The cost of replacing the obsolete item must be the same as or more than the anticipated increase in value.

Answers

1. (c) Depreciation is effective age divided by economic life. Therefore, simply divide 20 by 50 = 40%.

2. (d) When the property's condition affects the effective age, it also impacts the cost approach because it impacts depreciation.

3. (b) You need to determine the volume to solve this problem. The formula to find volume is V = Length x Width x Height. We can simplify the formula to V = Area x Depth. First, convert all the figures into yards. There are 9 square feet in 1 square yard, so to find the Area, divide 162 by 9 to get 18 square yards (Area). There are 36 inches in 1 yard, so to find the Depth, divide 4 by 36 to get 0.111. To find the Volume, multiply the Area by the Depth, or 18 x 0.111 = 1.98, rounded up to 2.

4. (c) Reproduction cost refers to the cost to build an exact replica at current prices. Replacement cost refers to the cost to build an improvement with the same utility.

5. (d) Since economic (external) obsolescence originates outside the property lines, there is little a property owner can do to change these influences.

6. (b) An outdated architectural style is an example of functional obsolescence, originating within the property lines.

7. (c) A stairway suffering from wear and tear is an example of physical deterioration. The other three choices are examples of functional obsolescence.

8. (d) A one-bathroom house is an example of functional obsolescence. The other three choices are examples of external obsolescence.

9. (c) Construction costs and physical age have no impact on effective age. The quality of construction and maintenance determine effective age.

10. (b) Effective age is an estimate based on the local market area. Estimates of effective age are best expressed in increments of five years, since it is not a precise finding, but an estimate.

11. (c) The appraiser cannot ignore anything that impacts value, and since the structure does not contribute anything to value, this too cannot be ignored. Demolition costs must be deducted. In rare instances, salvage value may help offset demolition costs, but C is the answer that will apply in most cases.

12. (d) Economic life deals with the future use of an improvement. An improvement that has used up its economic life is usually ready for demolition.

13. (b) A structure will usually stand beyond its estimated useful life.

14. (c) Economic life is the estimated useful period of the improvements. Effective age is how old the structure appears to be. The difference between the two is the remaining economic life.

15. (a) Tax assessors' records are the best source of information to determine the age of improvements.

16. (c) The straight-line, or age-life method of calculating depreciation is the easiest to understand and use. The formula is effective age/total economic life = accrued depreciation.

17. (d) Since external obsolescence originates outside the property lines, there is usually nothing the property owner can do fix its influence.

18. (a) Depreciation is a loss in value from any cause. Reducing the property's cost basis and minimizing taxes deal with accounting practices for tax purposes. A loss in aesthetic appeal is a description of obsolescence.

19. (b) To calculate the total depreciation, add all the types of depreciation together.

20. (b) The difference between the replacement cost new and the actual appraised value equals the depreciation of an improvement.

21. (d) Estimating appreciation is not a step in the cost approach.

22. (a) Economic obsolescence is a cause of depreciation that originates outside the property lines. A house that is located close to a busy street and is subject to traffic noise suffers from economic obsolescence.

23. (d) Superadequacy is a type of functional obsolescence caused by a structural component that is too large or of a higher quality than what is needed for the highest and best use of a property. The component's cost exceeds its value.

24. (b) Superadequacy exists within the property lines, therefore it is functional obsolescence.

25. (d) A garage that is smaller than the market area's norm is an example of functional obsolescence. Functional obsolescence is a loss in value due to a feature, design, or layout that is undesirable in the market.

26. (b) The property suffers from economic obsolescence due to the odor and flies from the nearby dairy farm. Economic obsolescence is a cause of depreciation that originates outside the property lines.

Cost Approach - Answers

27. (b) An old structure with a lot of functional obsolescence requires the appraiser to estimate of a significant amount of depreciation. This produces a large margin of error and decreased reliability.

28. (d) These kinds of properties don't produce a stream of income to capitalize and there are no, or very few, comparable sales that could be applied. The cost approach is the only approach possible.

29. (b) A developer is entitled to a financial reward for investing in land and building. This should be incorporated into the appraiser's estimate of cost.

30. (c) The difference between the sales price and the total costs is the developer's profit.

31. (b) Marketing materials are indirect costs, not covered in profits or the basic costs of the cost handbook.

32. (d) A city hall produces no stream of income and has no comparable sales. The only method practical is the cost approach.

33. (c) Economic obsolescence, also called external obsolescence, is caused by factors outside the property lines such as proximity to the city dump.

34. (a) Older structures have a lot of depreciation to estimate, making the cost approach less reliable. Income properties are appraised using the income capitalization approach. The cost approach does not apply to vacant land.

35. (b) A cost handbook, such as Marshall & Swift, would provide an appraiser with reliable cost data.

36. (d) All of these answer choices indicate that the improvements no longer contribute to value and it's time to demolish them.

37. (b) Structural overimprovements lose value due to functional obsolescence. It is not cost effective to tear down the structure and replace it or repair the overimprovement. The overimprovement is simply incurable.

38. (b) Reproduction cost refers to an exact duplicate, and because knowledge of the workmanship and duplication of materials may not be possible, the appraiser usually settles for replacement cost, the new cost of a structure of the same size, quality of construction, and utility.

39. (d) Reproduction cost is the current cost to construct an exact duplicate of the improvements

40. (c) Replacement cost is the current cost to construct a structure of the same utility.

41. (b) The quantity survey method is the one most commonly used by contractors, not appraisers. It is most accurate because it accounts for all the component parts of a structure, including costs of labor.

42. (a) To calculate current building cost, the present index is divided by the index at time of construction, which results in a fraction or ratio. The ratio is then multiplied by the original cost. The resulting figure is present building cost.

43. (b) Appraisers typically use the square foot method and is a reasonably accurate method to apply if used correctly in conjunction with an authoritative cost handbook. The quantity survey method and the unit-in-place method require specialized knowledge of the construction industry. The index method may not be reliable enough for good appraisal work.

44. (c) Today's cost index factor (408) is divided by the original cost index factor (204). The resulting ratio is 2.0. Multiply 2.0 by the original cost of construction in 1985 to arrive at the answer.

45. (b) To find the percentage of accrued depreciation, divide the effective age by the total economic life, $15 \div 70 = 21\%$.

46. (b) Total economic life is calculated by adding the effective age to the remaining economic life.

47. (c) Dividing effective age by total economic life will give the accrued depreciation as a percentage.

48. (a) Depreciation applies to improvements only and is the loss in value from the original construction costs.

49. (c) The cost approach deals with replacement and reproduction costs. If it costs someone more to purchase raw land and reconstruct an improvement than purchase an existing one, they will most likely purchase the existing one.

50. (c) There may be few, if any, comparable properties to compare the subject property to, and the house does not produce an income, so the cost approach would be most accurate and appropriate.

51. (c) Reproduction cost is the current construction cost to create an exact duplicate of a structure. Replacement cost is current construction cost to create a structure with the same utility as a previous structure.

52. (b) The straight-line method formula is Effective Age/Total Economic Life = Accrued Depreciation. 10/50 = 0.2 or 20% accrued depreciation.

53. (d) Accumulated (accrued) depreciation is the difference between a structure's.

54. (c) $2,500 x 3 years = $7,500.

55. (c) In the cost approach, the appraiser estimates the value of the improvements in terms of their reproduction or replacement cost as though new, subtracts any loss in value due to depreciation, and then adds the site value.

56. (a) When estimating accrued depreciation with the breakdown method, the appraiser analyzes each cause of depreciation separately and estimates the dollar or percentage amount of depreciation association with each cause.

57. (b) Economic depreciation is caused by factors outside the property itself, including zoning changes, proximity to nuisances, changes in land use, and market conditions.

58. (c) The breakdown method is used to estimate accrued depreciation.

59. (d) Accrued depreciation = effective age/total economic life.

60. (a) When estimating accrued depreciation, an appraiser may use the economic age-life method, the modified economic age-life method, the sales comparison method, the breakdown method, or the capitalized value method.

61. (c) Ideally, for the cost approach to be applicable and reliable, the improvements must be new or nearly new and they must represent the highest and best use of the site.

62. (c) Vacancy allowance must be considered when using the income approach, not the cost approach.

63. (d) The cost approach to value requires the appraiser to estimate the value of the site as if vacant and available for use under the land's highest and best use. The use may or may not be the land's current use.

64. (a) Physical deterioration is loss in value due to neglected repairs or maintenance. Functional obsolescence results from defects in a building or structure that detract from its value such as an unworkable design or layout, or features that are outdated. Economic obsolescence is loss in value due to forces outside the property, such as changes in optimum land use, zoning, or the balance of supply and demand.

65. (d) Depreciation is defined as a loss in utility, and therefore value, from any cause. Depreciation may be physical, functional, or economic.

66. (d) For the cost approach to be applicable and reliable, the improvements must be new or nearly new, and the improvements must represent the highest and best use of the site.

67. (b) The cost approach estimates the value of improvements by converting the cost to construct into market value.

68. (a) Depreciation is defined as the difference between the cost of an improvement on the date of appraisal and the value of the improvement.

69. (c) Direct costs are the costs of labor, materials, and contractors' and subcontractors' overhead and profit. All of the answers are direct costs except taxes.

70. (a) The quantity survey method is generally used by cost estimators, contractors and builders as well as appraisers.

71. (c) Virtually all superadequacies are incurable.

72. (a) The three techniques used to measure depreciation are the age-life method, the breakdown method, and the abstraction or market method.

73. (a) When using the square foot method, the appraiser multiplies the construction cost per square foot by the number of square feet in the subject property.

74. (a) The unit-in-place cost estimate is calculated by breaking up a building into components and estimating the cost of the material and labor required to construct that unit, on the date of appraisal.

75. (a) The breakdown method is accomplished by dividing depreciation into its three separate components: physical deterioration, functional obsolescence, and external obsolescence. Physical deterioration is further broken down into curable and incurable.

76. (d) Effective age, economic life, and chronological age are all shorter periods of time in the life of a building. Physical life is the total life of a building.

77. (a) An appraiser using the quantity survey method must prepare a detailed inventory of all materials and equipment used to construct the building.

78. (c) When using the abstraction method, an appraiser divides the total depreciation by the effective age in order to determine the average amount of depreciation indicated by each of the sold properties.

Cost Approach - Answers

79. (b) The unit-in-place method is used to estimate reproduction cost. The construction cost per unit of each of the structure's component parts is multiplied by the number of units of that component part.

80. (b) The market lease rate is used with the income approach.

81. (c) If an upgrade costs more than the value it adds, it is considered incurable functional obsolescence.

82. (d) Functional obsolescence is a feature or improvement that is undesirable or unnecessary, or one that is desirable in the marketplace, but the property lacks. To determine functional obsolescence, the appraiser should compare the subject property's improvements and features against those of other properties in the surrounding or comparable area.

83. (c) The cost approach analyzes the cost new of improvements as of the effective date of the appraisal.

84. (c) 3 x $2,500 per year = $7,500.

85. (b) Economic obsolescence occurs when factors outside a property cause it to lose utility or value.

86. (c) Functional obsolescence is the loss in value within an improvement due to changes in tastes, preferences, technical innovations, or market standards. If comparable properties have a feature that is lacking in the subject property, such as central air-conditioning, the subject property suffers from functional obsolescence.

87. (d) The cost approach is most reliable when an improvement is new, has no accrued depreciation, and is the land's highest and best use.

88. (b) When an appraiser uses the cost approach, he or she values the land at its highest and best use as if vacant.

89. (c) Effective age is a building's age based on its physical condition and utility. It is greatly affected by maintenance and repairs.

90. (b) Economic obsolescence is a loss in value due to factors or conditions outside a property. This would include construction of an industrial plant on an adjacent lot.

91. (b) Accrued depreciation is the difference between the present value of an improvement and its reproduction cost new.

92. (a) Physical, curable deterioration is measured by the cost to restore the property to new or reasonably new condition.

93. (d) The cost approach is based on the principle of substitution, which states that the value of a parcel of real estate is determined by the cost to acquire an equally desirable substitute.

94. (b) The value estimated using the cost approach is most accurate when an improvement is new and being used under its highest and best use. Older improvements can result in less accurate results, and vacant or unimproved land is not appraised using the cost approach.

95. (c) Curable functional obsolescence is measured by the cost to fix or replace the obsolete item or condition. If the property value increases more than what it costs to cure the obsolescence, then it is considered curable.

Income Approach

1. A property is valued at $900,000 and its net operating income is $99,000. What is its capitalization rate?

    a. 0.11%
    b. 1.1%
    c. 11%
    d. 11.1%

2. An income-producing property has a capitalization rate of 10% and its property taxes increase by $400 per month. Which of the following is **true** of the property's value?

    a. It will increase by $4,000.
    b. It will increase by $48,000.
    c. It will decrease by $48,000.
    d. It will decrease by $4,000.

3. The formula to calculate the operating expense ratio is:

    a. operating expenses divided by scheduled gross income.
    b. operating expenses divided by effective gross income.
    c. operating expenses divided by net operating income.
    d. none of the above

4. A property's net operating income is $80,000 and its capitalization rate is 8%. What is the property value?

    a. $100,000
    b. $640,000
    c. $800,000
    d. $1,000,000

5. An office building is valued at $300,000, and earns an annual net operating income of $52,000. What is the direct capitalization rate?

    a. 3.7%
    b. 15.3%
    c. 17.3%
    d. 23.7%

6. Which of the following is calculated using the band-of-investment technique?

    a. Replacement cost
    b. Overall capitalization rate
    c. Net operating income
    d. Return on investment rate

7. A property is purchased with favorable financing. What would be the reaction of the overall capitalization rate?

    a. Unaffected
    b. Lower
    c. Higher
    d. Cannot be determined

8. The definition of *capitalization* as it is used in appraising is the:

    a. initial funds invested in a project.
    b. process of converting net income into an estimate of value.
    c. value resulting from any one of the three approaches.
    d. process of calculating the amount of capital available for investment.

9. An office building has an effective gross income of $185,000, a vacancy rate of 10%, and an effective gross income multiplier of 5.5. What is the office building's indicated value?

    a. $33,636
    b. $101,750
    c. $1,017,500
    d. $1,175,000

10. An office building is valued at $100,000 and has a net income of $10,000. If the net income remains the same, but the capitalization rate increases by one full percentage point, what would the estimate of value be?

    a. $19,111
    b. $90,909
    c. $91,019
    d. $190,010

11. An apartment complex earns an annual effective gross income of $64,000. It has $30,000 in fixed expenses and $17,000 in variable expenses. What is the apartment complex's operating expense ratio?

    a. 0.13
    b. 0.73
    c. 2.13
    d. 3.76

12. You are reconstructing an apartment complex's income statement. You estimate that gross income is $500,000, vacancy and bad debt allowance are 6%, and operating expenses are $205,000. What is the operating expense ratio? (Round to the nearest whole number)

    a. 43%
    b. 44%
    c. 47%
    d. The operating expense ratio cannot be determined without knowing the property taxes

13. The estimated market value of an apartment building is $5,000,000. Its potential gross income is $1,000,000, its vacancy loss is $50,000, and its operating expenses total $350,000. What is the effective gross income multiplier?

    a. 3.19
    b. 4.20
    c. 5.26
    d. 9.63

14. The gross income of a property is $125,000 and its operating expenses are 32% of the gross income. If the capitalization rate is 14%, what is the value of the property? (Round to the nearest whole number)

    a. $607,143
    b. $677,857
    c. $832,571
    d. $931,025

15. A property with a gross income of $24,000 sells for $210,000. What is the gross income multiplier?

    a. 5.64
    b. 7.33
    c. 8.75
    d. 11.97

16. An office building has a net income of $18,000 and an annual debt service of $14,000. It recently sold for $140,000 What is the overall capitalization rate? (Round to the nearest tenth)

    a. 8.9%
    b. 10.0%
    c. 12.9%
    d. 22.9%

17. A two-story office building rents for $16 per square foot. The first floor measures 80 feet by 100 feet. The second story measures 80 feet by 80 feet. What is the annual rent?

    a. $160,000
    b. $124,200
    c. $230,400
    d. $260,800

18. Vacancy and collection loss allowance is usually estimated as a percentage of what?

    a. Effective gross income
    b. Potential gross income
    c. Rental property value
    d. Highest and best use

19. What is the relationship between the level of risk and the capitalization rate?

    a. The capitalization rate increases when the risk increases.
    b. The capitalization rate decreases when the risk increases.
    c. The capitalization rate increases when the risk decreases.
    d. The capitalization rate remains the same as long as there is positive net income.

20. The income approach to value:

    a. is based on the principle of anticipation.
    b. converts the ability of property to generate income into an indication of value.
    c. requires an estimate of net operating income of property.
    d. all of the above

21. An appraiser uses which of the following calculations to find a gross rent multiplier?

    a. GRM = NOI x sales price
    b. GRM = NOI ÷ sales price
    c. GRM = monthly gross rent x sales price
    d. GRM = sale price ÷ monthly gross rent

22. When using the GRM income approach, an appraiser should look for homes that _____ in order to select comparables.

    a. are owner occupied
    b. were rented at the time of sale
    c. are from different neighborhoods
    d. are currently for sale

23. If _____, then the GRM approach is considered a reliable approach to estimate value.

    a. the data used is verified and is representative of the market
    b. the appraiser is experienced, skilled, and knowledgeable
    c. the data is current and taken from reputable sources
    d. all of the above

24. The **correct** income capitalization formula is:

    a. income ÷ rate = value.
    b. income x rate = value.
    c. income − expenses = value.
    d. income ÷ expenses = value.

25. Given the following market rents and a vacancy rate of 5%, what is the potential gross income of the apartment building?

    5 one-bedroom units @ $800 each
    2 two-bedroom units @ $1,000 each
    4 three-bedroom units @ $1,500 each

    a. $140,000
    b. $142,000
    c. $144,000
    d. $164,000

26. On a reconstructed operating statement, which of the following items is considered a fixed expense?

    a. Property taxes
    b. Payroll taxes
    c. Employee benefits
    d. Employee payroll

27. The income approach would be unreliable if the appraiser uses:

    a. unsupported room adjustments.
    b. unverified age adjustments.
    c. unsupported rent adjustments.
    d. unsupported location adjustments.

28. Expenses that occur infrequently are included in which section of a building's operation expense analysis?

    a. Fixed expenses
    b. Operating expenses
    c. Reserves
    d. Other expenses

29. Which of the following is effected most by the risk that an apartment building's projected income will not be collected?

    a. Return on investment
    b. Property value
    c. Capitalization rate
    d. Interest rate

30. What is the first step when reconstructing an operating statement?

    a. Capitalize the net operating income.
    b. Determine the potential gross income.
    c. Calculate the variable and fixed expenses.
    d. Deduct vacancy allowance.

31. An investor requires a 10% rate of return to invest in a building. The building is expected to have a remaining economic life of 25 years. What is the appropriate building capitalization rate, using the straight-line method?

    a. 11%
    b. 11.4%
    c. 13%
    d. 14%

32. A property's potential gross income, less its vacancy and collection loss equals its:

    a. effective gross income.
    b. net operating income.
    c. operating income.
    d. cash flow.

33. When estimating the net operating income of a property, an appraiser considers all of the following expenses **except**:

    a. property insurance.
    b. mortgage payments.
    c. decorating expenses.
    d. real estate taxes.

34. You are appraising an income-producing property and need to estimate its replacement allowance. You should be careful to avoid duplicating replacement items that you may also have included in:

    a. property management fees.
    b. repair and maintenance.
    c. fixed expenses.
    d. insurance accounts.

35. When an appraiser analyzes the market using the gross rent multiplier technique, she estimates value by:

    a. dividing historic rent by the gross rent multiplier.
    b. subtracting market rent from net income.
    c. multiplying operating expenses by market rent.
    d. multiplying monthly market rent by the gross rent multiplier.

36. An appraiser calculates _____ by subtracting a property's vacancy and collection loss allowance from potential income.

    a. effective gross income
    b. net operating expenses
    c. cash flow
    d. effective net income

37. By using the income approach, an appraiser can estimate value by applying an overall capitalization rate to:

    a. net operating expenses.
    b. net operating income.
    c. effective gross income.
    d. gross income.

38. Which of the following items should be included in a reconstructed statement of net operating income?

    a. Debt service
    b. Management charges
    c. Internal rate of return
    d. Mortgage interest payments

39. To estimate value, an appraiser divides the overall capitalization rate into:

    a. effective gross income.
    b. net operating income.
    c. vacancy rate.
    d. operating expenses.

40. When an appraiser is calculating net operating income, which of the following expenses should not be deducted from gross income?

    a. Vacancy rate
    b. Income tax expense
    c. Total operating expense
    d. Maintenance and repairs

41. You are trying to find an apartment complex's net operating income. All of the following operating expenses might be included in the reconstructed operating statement **except**:

    a. fixed expenses.
    b. variable expenses.
    c. replacement allowance.
    d. mortgage debt service.

42. What is the formula for calculating *effective gross income*?

    a. Total income less operating expenses
    b. Gross potential income less an allowance for vacancy and collection loss
    c. Total income plus appreciation
    d. Total income if all rentable space is leased

43. All of the following operating expenses are usually considered fixed expenses **except**:

    a. debt service.
    b. fire insurance.
    c. property management fees.
    d. replacement reserves.

44. What is the definition of *fixed expenses*?

    a. Expenses that are constant for the term of ownership
    b. Expenses that are determined by the landlord and defined in the lease terms
    c. Expenses that do not vary with the level of occupancy of the property
    d. Expenses that are based on typical market rates

45. Capitalization is the process of:

    a. forecasting the future price of a property.
    b. calculating the investment to return ratio.
    c. deducting expenses to find net income.
    d. converting income into a value indication.

46. An appraiser reconstructs an operating statement when using the income approach to:

    a. study the historical trends of price in the market area.
    b. develop an estimated projection of vacancy rate and maintenance costs of the property.
    c. develop an estimated projection of expected income and expense that reflect the earning capacity of the property.
    d. develop a reliable historical record of income and expenses for the property.

47. The term GIM refers to:

    a. gross income modifier.
    b. gross income multiplier.
    c. general income multiplier.
    d. general investment manager.

48. The management fee in a reconstructed operating statement is usually computed as a:

    a. percentage of net operating income.
    b. percentage of effective gross income.
    c. fixed expense.
    d. percentage of potential gross income.

49. What is the term for the total income from a property before any expenses are deducted?

    a. Net income
    b. Gross income
    c. Operating income
    d. Return on investment

50. What is the difference between potential gross income and effective gross income?

    a. Operating expenses
    b. Vacancy
    c. Collection loss
    d. Vacancy and collection loss

51. Which of the following is **not** used to calculate effective gross income?

    a. Other income (e.g., vending machines)
    b. Vacancy
    c. Operating expenses
    d. Collection loss

52. What is the term for income from a property or business, after deducting operating expenses, but before deducting income taxes and financing expenses?

    a. Net effective income
    b. Cash flow
    c. Effective gross income
    d. Net operating income

53. In order to estimate effective gross income, an appraiser needs to know which of the following?

    a. Net income and operating expenses
    b. Potential gross income and vacancy and collection loss
    c. Potential gross income, vacancy rate, and debt service
    d. Gross income, collection loss, and debt service

54. Which of the following would be included in a reserve for replacements?

    a. Building replacement at the end of its economic life
    b. Roof replacement when it is worn out
    c. Allowance for painting
    d. Refinancing fees

55. How much net operating income is necessary to support a property value of $200,000 at a 12% capitalization rate?

    a. $2,400
    b. $16,667
    c. $24,000
    d. $240,000

56. Use the following income ladder to answer the question.

Gross Income	$100,000
Vacancy	−3,000
Effective Gross Income	$97,000
Operating Expenses	−30,000
Net Operating Income	$67,000
Debt Service −	20,000
Pre Tax Cash Flow	$47,000

    An office building has the preceding income ladder, a 10% cap rate, and the owners paid a down payment of $250,000. The operating expense ratio equals:

    a. 30%.
    b. 30.93%.
    c. 44.78%.
    d. 52.63%.

57. Which is an appropriate method of estimating replacement reserves?

    a. Straight line
    b. Sinking fund
    c. Future value of an annuity
    d. Both a and b

58. Which of the following is **not** included in operating expenses?

    a. Loan payments
    b. Property taxes
    c. Utilities
    d. Replacement reserves

59. A rental property has an annual gross income of $100,000, a vacancy allowance of $5,000, operating expenses of $30,000, and an annual total loan payment of $10,000 ($8,000 is interest). What is its net operating income?

    a. $57,000
    b. $65,000
    c. $70,000
    d. $95,000

60. Which of the following is considered when calculating the vacancy allowance?

    a. Rent concessions
    b. Vacancy
    c. Collection losses
    d. All of the above

61. Which of the following is **true** of a fixed expense?

    a. It varies with vacancy.
    b. It varies with gross income.
    c. It varies with effective gross income.
    d. It is not affected by income or other expense factors.

62. Which of the following is considered an operating expense?

    a. Weekly pool maintenance
    b. Income taxes
    c. Loan interest payments
    d. Rent concessions

63. Why are income and expenses annualized for non-residential properties when using the income approach?

    a. The cap rate is an annual figure.
    b. They allow a more accurate estimate of a stabilized income stream to be calculated.
    c. Long term leases are for a period not less than 1 year.
    d. Property taxes are always based on an annual figure.

64. Which of the following is one of the six functions of a dollar?

    a. Simple interest
    b. Calculating loan payments
    c. Adjusting for discounts of sales prices
    d. Residual calculations

65. What is the best explanation for why an appraiser conducts a rent survey?

    a. To establish a comparable's contract rent
    b. To establish a comparable's economic rent
    c. To establish the subject property's contract rent
    d. To establish the subject property's economic rent

Answers

1. (c) The cap rate is equal to the net operating income divided by the value, and that equals 0.11, which is the same as 11%.

2. (c) The $400 monthly tax increase must be annualized (multiplied by 12) and then capitalized. Since property taxes increase, the net operating income would decrease, and result in a loss of value by $4,800 divided by 0.10, which equals $48,000.

3. (b) The operating expense ratio is calculated by dividing the operating expenses by the effective gross income.

4. (d) Value equals net operating income divided by the capitalization rate. $80,000/0.08 = 1,000,000

5. (c) Net operating income/value = capitalization rate. $52,000/$300,000 = 0.173 or 17.3%.

6. (b) The band-of-investment technique is commonly used to calculate overall capitalization rate, or overall rate.

7. (b) Favorable financing indicates a safer investment with lower risk, which results in a lower capitalization rate.

8. (b) Capitalization refers to the process of converting net income into an estimate of value.

9. (c) The formula for the income capitalization approach is: gross income x gross income multiplier = market value.

10. (b) Net income/value = capitalization rate. $10,000/$100,000 = 0.10 or 10%. If the capitalization rate increases by 1%, then $10,000/0.11 = $90,909.

11. (b) The formula to calculate the operating expense ratio is: operating expenses/effective gross income = operating expense ratio

12. (b) The formula to find the operating expense ratio is operating expenses/effective gross income = operating expense ratio. First you must calculate effective gross income. Gross income – vacancy and collection losses = effective gross income. 6% of $500,000 is 30,000. $500,000 – $30,000 = $470,000 effective gross income. $205,000/$470,000 = 0.436 rounded up to 0.44 or 44%

13. (c) The formula to find the effective gross income multiplier is: sales price/effective gross income = effective gross income multiplier. First you must find the effective gross income. $1,000,000 − $50,000 = 950,000 effective gross income. $5,000,000/$950,000 = 5.26

14. (a) The formula to find value is: net operating income/capitalization rate = value. First you must find the net operating income. $125,000 x 0.32 = 40,000. 125,000 − 40,000 = 85,000 (net operating income). 85,000/0.14 = 607,142.85 rounded up to $607,143.

15. (c) The formula to find the gross income multiplier is: sales price/gross income = gross income multiplier. $210,000/$24,000 = 8.75.

16. (c) The formula to find the capitalization rate is: net operating income/value = capitalization rate. 18,000/140,000 = 0.1285 or 12.85 rounded to 12.9%.

17. (c) [(80 x 100) + (80 x 80)] x 16 = 230,400

18. (b) Vacancy and collection loss is typically based on potential gross income. Deducting vacancy and collection loss from potential gross income results in effective gross income.

19. (a) A high level of risk equals a high capitalization rate. A high level of risk implies a high possibility of loss on the investment, a high-risk property will have a lower selling price or value.

20. (d) The income approach to value is based on the principle of anticipation, and converts the ability of the property to generate income into an indication of value. It also requires the appraiser to estimate a property's net operating income in order to estimate its value.

21. (d) To find the gross rent multiplier, an appraiser divides the sales price by the monthly gross rent.

22. (b) The GRM is selected by finding properties similar to the subject property in the same or nearby neighborhoods that were rented at the time they were sold.

23. (d) All of the choices contribute to a reliable estimate.

24. (a) The formula used with the income capitalization approach is income divided by rate.

25. (c) Potential gross income is the sum of all the income from a property. 5 units at $800 each = $4,000, 2 units at $1,000 each = $2,000, and 4 units at $1,500 each = $6,000. These totals added together and multiplied by 12 months equals $144,000. The vacancy rate is factored in only when calculating effective gross income.

26. (a) Fixed expenses are the property taxes and casualty insurance. The rest are variable expenses that may vary depending on occupancy.

27. (c) The income approach may be unreliable if the appraiser uses unsupported market rent adjustments.

28. (c) Expenses that occur infrequently and are not operating expenses are included in the reserve section.

29. (d) The greater the risk, the higher the amount of interest necessary to entice investors.

30. (b) The steps taken to reconstruct an operating statement are: determine potential gross income, deduct for vacancy and collection losses, determine effective gross income, subtract operating expenses and replacement reserves, determine total operating expenses, and determine net operating income.

31. (d) First you need to find the recapture rate using the formula: 100%/years of useful life = annual recapture rate. 100/25 = 4% recapture rate. Add this to the required return on investment of 10% to equal 14%.

32. (a) Effective gross income is calculated by subtracting the vacancy and collection loss from a property's potential gross income.

33. (b) Mortgage payments are not a factor in determining net operating income.

34. (b) Replacement allowances may often be mistakenly placed in with the repair and maintenance category. An appraiser must analyze all expenses carefully to avoid duplicating certain items or not counting them at all.

35. (d) When using a gross rent multiplier technique, an appraiser estimates value by multiplying the monthly market rent by the gross rent multiplier. The resulting number is an estimate of what the value would be, based on the gross rents and sales prices of other properties.

36. (a) Effective gross income is potential gross income less vacancy and collection loss allowance.

37. (a) The overall capitalization rate can be applied only to the net operating income. The formula used in the income approach is value = income ÷ overall capitalization rate.

38. (b) Management expenses should be included in the net operating income statement. The other expenses are not operating expenses.

39. (b) The overall capitalization rate is always applied to the net operating income.

40. (b) Income taxes should not be deducted from gross income because they are not operating expenses. They are used only to calculate after-tax cash flow.

41. (d) Mortgage debt service is not a deduction when calculating net operating income.

42. (b) Effective gross income is calculated by subtracting vacancy and collection loss from gross potential income.

43. (c) Property management's fee is usually based on a percentage of the actual income collected, so it is not a fixed expense.

44. (c) A fixed expense is one that does not vary with the level of occupancy of the property.

45. (d) Income is converted into a value indication by direct capitalization or yield capitalization. Direct capitalization only considers the first year's income or an average of incomes. Yield capitalization discounts the future benefits of the property to find a present value estimate.

46. (c) The income approach is based on the present value of future cash flows, so a reasonable estimate of actual cash flow is necessary to calculate value.

47. (b) GIM stands for gross income multiplier. The GIM equals the value of the property divided by the gross annual income.

48. (b) Management fees are usually calculated as a percentage of effective gross income.

49. (b) Gross income is a property's total income before expenses are deducted.

50. (d) Potential gross income less vacancy and collection loss equals effective gross income.

51. (c) Effective gross income is calculated before deducting operating expenses. Effective gross income less operating expenses equals net operating income.

52. (d) Net operating income = gross income − operating expenses.

53. (b) In order for an appraiser to estimate effective gross income, she must know the potential gross income, vacancy and collection loss. Effective gross income = potential gross income − vacancy and collection loss.

54. (b) Reserves apply to long-term items that will need to be replaced before the end of the economic life of the property.

55. (d) Net operating income = value x rate
    Net operating income = $200,000 x 0.12 = $24,000

56. (b) The operating expense ratio is the operating expenses divided by the effective gross income. $30,000/$97,000 = 0.3092 or 30.92%.

57. (d) Both methods are appropriate to estimate replacement reserves. When using a straight-line method, you find the necessary annual payment by dividing the cost of the item to be replaced by the number of years of economic life. In a sinking fund, you make periodic payments that are compounded annually to arrive at the amount necessary to replace the item.

58. (a) Loan payments are not included in operating expenses. They are factored in after calculating net operating income.

59. (b) Net operating income = effective gross income − operating expenses. Effective gross income is the annual gross income less the vacancy allowance, or $95,000. Loan payments are not included in operating expenses, so that figure is irrelevant to our calculations. $95,000 − $30,000 = $65,000.

60. (d) The vacancy allowance includes rent concessions, actual vacancies, and other money that is not collected from such items as vending machines and laundries.

61. (d) Fixed expenses do not vary according to the vacancy rate or other factors.

62. (a) An operating expense is directly related to the operation of the property such as maintenance. Income taxes, rent concessions, and debt service are not operating expenses.

63. (b) Residential properties are appraised using monthly income and expenses. Non-residential properties are appraised using annualized expenses. This is done to calculate a more accurate estimate of a stabilized income stream, regardless of seasonal variations in occupancy and one-time expenses such as major repairs or tax bills. These expenses could affect a single month's income.

64. (b) Calculating loan payments is a future value annuity of $1 per period. The other five functions of $1 include the future value of $1, the sinking fund factor, the present value of $1, the present value annuity of $1 per period, and the installment to amortize $1.

65. (d) A survey helps to determine the stability of the income stream and its affect on the property's value. Economic or market rent is what the subject property should earn given the local marketplace, and is the best measure of potential rent. If the contract rate is higher, the overage is more risky and requires additional consideration in the yield capitalization. If it's lower, it is an adverse encumbrance that limits the income potential and the resulting value to an investor.

Valuation of Partial Interests

1. What is the greatest possible interest one can have in real property?

    a. A fee simple
    b. A fee defeasible
    c. A life estate
    d. A reversionary estate

2. What is a primary difference between a cooperative building and a condominium?

    a. A cooperative building is financed by a single mortgage and a condominium building is financed by a series of individual mortgages.
    b. A cooperative building is financed by a series of individual mortgages and a condominium building is financed by a single mortgage.
    c. Condominium owners are not responsible for common area maintenance costs.
    d. A cooperative is subject to property taxation and a condominium is not.

3. What form of ownership allows title to real estate to be held in unequal shares?

    a. Tenants in common
    b. Ownership in severalty
    c. Joint tenancy with right of survivorship
    d. Community property

4. A _____ may be subject to double taxation when earnings from a property are distributed.

    a. general partnership
    b. limited partnership
    c. corporation
    d. community property

5. In a real estate investment, the _____ is responsible for the management decisions of a property.

    a. limited partner
    b. general partner
    c. shareholders
    d. general counsel

6. Which type of entity is created to hold title to property in cooperative interest ownership?

    a. Corporation
    b. Partnership
    c. Condominium association
    d. Board of trustees

7. A brother and sister inherit title to a property in unequal shares. They hold title to the property:

    a. as tenants in common.
    b. as joint tenants.
    c. in severalty.
    d. as community property.

8. Which of the following is not the responsibility of a condominium's Homeowners' Association?

    a. Providing a lifeguard at the pool
    b. Landscaping and maintenance
    c. Establishing a private school for residents' children
    d. Providing grounds security

9. All of the following may limit the public rights of a property owner **except**:

    a. ad valorem taxation.
    b. escheat.
    c. easements.
    d. eminent domain.

10. Your supervisor signs your appraisal on the line reserved for the reviewer. Who is responsible for the contents of this report?

    a. You
    b. Your supervisor
    c. Both of you
    d. The client

11. A property owner offers a tenant one month free rent if she signs a one-year lease for $900 per month. What is the effective monthly rent?

    a. $825
    b. $850
    c. $900
    d. $975

12. A clothing store tenant agrees to pay $20,000 rent per year if sales are under $300,000 and 5% of sales in excess of that amount. If the tenant pays $35,000 in rent, what were the sales for that year?

    a. $300,000
    b. $500,000
    c. $600,000
    d. $900,000

Answers

1. (a) A fee simple estate is the greatest possible interest one can have in real property. It is unqualified, indefinite in duration, freely transferable, and inheritable.

2. (a) A cooperative building is financed by a single mortgage. A condominium building is financed by a series of individual mortgages.

3. (a) Individuals may own unequal shares of a property if they own it as tenants in common.

4. (c) Income received by the stockholders of a corporation is often subject to double taxation.

5. (b) General partners usually develop the partnership, retain special benefits (including the right of management decisions), and are solely responsible for all liabilities.

6. (a) Cooperative ownership is a form of ownership in which a corporation is created to hold title to the entire property.

7. (a) A tenancy in common is often created when a property owner dies without a will and leaves several descendants who inherit unequal shares.

8. (c) A Homeowners' Association is responsible for the governance of the condominium and maintenance of the common areas. Establishing private schools is not one of its responsibilities.

9. (c) All of the answers are limitations on the public rights of property owners, except for easements, which do not limit public rights.

10. (c) An appraiser who signs any portion of a report is also required to sign the certification, and in doing so is completely responsible for the appraisal and its contents.

11. (a) You need to multiply the rent per month by the actual number of months she will be paying rent (11), and divide that result by the number of months in one year (12). (900 x 11) /12 = 825 effective rent.

12. (c) If the tenant paid $35,000 in rent, that means that $15,000 rent was paid to account for exceeding the $300,000 limit. To determine the total sales, divide the overage by the percentage of sales. $15,000/0.05 = $300,000. Add the base rent to the amount of additional sales to get the total sales for the year. $300,0000 + $300,000 = $600,000.

Appraisal Standards and Ethics

1. What is the Appraisal Foundation?

    a. A government agency
    b. A for-profit organization of professional appraisers
    c. The independent board that develops USPAP
    d. A private non-profit organization

2. The Appraisal Subcommittee's activities are funded by:

    a. the U.S. Government.
    b. The Appraisal Foundation.
    c. a collection of registry fees from state licensed and certified appraisers.
    d. fines paid by appraisers who violate USPAP.

3. State appraisal boards are monitored by the Appraisal Subcommittee to determine:

    a. the percentage of appraisers who join appraisal organizations.
    b. whether their licensing procedures are consistent with Title XI of FIRREA.
    c. whether their policies are consistent with Fair Housing Laws.
    d. the number of lenders using licensed or certified appraisers.

4. Which economic crisis precipitated appraisal licensing?

    a. The Great Depression of the 1930's
    b. The recession of the 1970's
    c. The savings and loan crisis of the late 1980's
    d. The recession and decline in property values of the early 1990's

5. USPAP achieves legal authority through:

    a. the standards and contracts of private enterprises.
    b. Title XI of FIRREA.
    c. adoption, citation, or implementation by government agencies.
    d. both a and c

6. Which of the following is **not** a characteristic of a profession?

    a. Primarily physical labor and skill
    b. Primarily mental labor and skill
    c. Standards of practice
    d. Education and special knowledge

7. Valuation services:

    a. fall under the definition of appraisal practice.
    b. must be performed by appraisers.
    c. include appraisal practice.
    d. must comply with USPAP.

8. What is the primary purpose of USPAP?

    a. Promote and maintain the public trust.
    b. Create absolute standards and rules that appraisers must follow in all appraisal assignments.
    c. Provide minimum standards that appraisers must follow in performing valuation services.
    d. Improve the quality of valuation services.

9. When an appraiser fails to comply with USPAP in an assignment, what is the most serious potential consequence?

    a. The appraiser may lose his or her license.
    b. The public may lose trust and confidence in the appraisal profession.
    c. The appraiser may be restricted to non-federally related appraisal assignments.
    d. The appraiser may end up in an expensive lawsuit.

10. Which of the following is not an important element in the scope of work decision?

    a. Intended users
    b. Effective date of value
    c. Sales history
    d. Purpose of assignment

11. A Comment is a/an _____ part of USPAP.

    a. required
    b. integral
    c. binding
    d. optional

12. USPAP contains _____ RULES.

    a. three
    b. five
    c. six
    d. seven

13. The ETHICS RULE consists of _____ sections.

    a. three
    b. four
    c. five
    d. seven

14. USPAP is designed to serve all of the following **except**:

    a. all providers of valuation services.
    b. users of appraisal services.
    c. all providers of appraisal services.
    d. licensed appraisers.

15. An appraiser must retain a workfile for:

    a. written appraisal reports only.
    b. appraisals for federally-related transactions.
    c. appraisal reports that follow binding requirements.
    d. any assignment that is covered by Standards Rules.

16. An appraiser who has never appraised a commercial property is asked to appraise a small commercial property. She wants to keep the assignment. She should:

    a. accept the assignment and disclose her lack of experience in the final report.
    b. accept the assignment and perform the appraisal to the best of her ability.
    c. disclose the lack of experience to the client; describe the lack of experience and the steps taken to competently complete the assignment in the report.
    d. accept the assignment and invoke the DEPARTURE RULE, which releases her from any requirement to disclose her incompetence.

17. The DEPARTURE RULE may be applied to:

    a. hypothetical conditions.
    b. Advisory Opinions.
    c. a specific requirement.
    d. a binding requirement.

18. According to the Conduct section of the ETHICS RULE, an appraiser must perform assignments with all of the following **except**:

    a. impartiality.
    b. objectivity.
    c. independence.
    d. timeliness.

19. According to the JURISDICTIONAL EXCEPTION RULE, it is not a violation of USPAP if an appraiser:

    a. complies with the recommendations of an attorney.
    b. disregards a requirement of USPAP that conflicts with a law of a jurisdiction, as long as there is proper disclosure in the report.
    c. disregards a requirement of USPAP that conflicts with a law of a jurisdiction.
    d. invokes the DEPARTURE RULE.

20. A specific requirement applies when:

    a. it addresses analysis that is typical practice in such an assignment.
    b. it addresses analysis that is not typical practice in a given assignment.
    c. it addresses analysis that would not provide meaningful results in an assignment.
    d. it addresses conditions not present in a given assignment.

21. An appraiser does not use one of the usual approaches to value. In the Summary Appraisal Report, this exclusion must be:

    a. stated and explained.
    b. stated in the certification.
    c. included if requested by the client.
    d. referred to as irrelevant.

22. When an appraiser uses a hypothetical condition:

    a. he has an overactive imagination.
    b. the hypothetical condition must be disclosed according to the JURISDICTIONAL EXCEPTION RULE.
    c. the hypothetical condition must be approved by the client's attorney.
    d. the hypothetical condition must be clearly disclosed in the report.

23. An opinion of the highest and best use of a property is a/an:

    a. binding requirement in every appraisal.
    b. specific requirement that may be necessary in some appraisals.
    c. part of the scope of work.
    d. optional step in the appraisal process.

24. While appraising a residence, an appraiser found that the subject property had sold two years before the date of the appraisal. According to USPAP, the appraiser must:

    a. analyze the sale because it occurred within three years of the date of the opinion of value.
    b. disregard the sale because it would not influence current market value.
    c. take no action because the sale occurred more than one year before the date of value.
    d. use the prior sale of the subject property as a comparable.

25. A scope of work is acceptable when it is:

    a. consistent with expectations of participants in the market.
    b. consistent with what the appraiser's peers' actions would be.
    c. both a and b
    d. neither a nor b

26. Which of the following statements about an extraordinary assumption is **false**?

    a. It relates directly to a specific assignment.
    b. If it is found to be false, it could alter the appraiser's conclusions.
    c. It is contrary to what exists, but is assumed for the purpose of analysis.
    d. It presumes uncertain information to be certain.

27. When developing an opinion of highest and best use, land is appraised:

    a. as if it is improved.
    b. according to its current use.
    c. as though it is vacant and available for development to its highest and best use.
    d. based on market area trends.

28. A hypothetical condition may be used when:

    a. it is necessary for reasonable analysis.
    b. it results in a credible analysis.
    c. the appraiser complies with disclosure requirements.
    d. all of the above

29. Which type of appraisal report is intended for client use only?

    a. Restricted use
    b. Summary
    c. Self-contained
    d. Narrative

30. An appraiser who signs a certification is responsible for:

    a. the certification, assignment results, and contents of the report.
    b. the contents of the report only.
    c. the opinion of value only.
    d. the certification only.

31. When performing an appraisal review, an appraiser may evaluate all of the following **except**:

    a. the quality of another appraiser's work.
    b. the analysis in an appraisal consulting report.
    c. the relevance of another appraiser's work.
    d. the competency of another appraiser.

32. Which of the following is not a proper procedure for an appraiser performing a review appraisal?

    a. Research their own comparable sales data
    b. Use the same effective date as the work under review
    c. Use a different effective date than the work under review
    d. Apply data that became available after the effective date of the original appraisal to form an opinion of the quality of the appraiser's work

33. In a review appraisal assignment:

    a. the appraiser does not need to identify any extraordinary assumptions used in the assignment.
    b. the effective date of the reviewer's opinion must be the same as the effective date of the original appraisal.
    c. the appraiser may be asked to form an opinion of value of the subject property and of the quality of the original appraiser's work.
    d. the appraiser does not need to comply with USPAP.

34. It is not necessary for an appraiser performing a review appraisal to:

    a. replicate the steps completed by the original appraiser.
    b. make conclusions that are in line with the intended use of the review.
    c. disclose the ownership interest appraised in the work under review.
    d. perform the review in the context of market conditions as of the effective date of the original opinion of value.

35. Which RULE is violated by a misleading or fraudulent appraisal review report?

    a. SUPPLEMENTAL STANDARDS RULE
    b. JURISDICTIONAL EXCEPTION RULE
    c. COMPETENCY RULE
    d. ETHICS RULE

36. According to STANDARD 3, an appraiser performing an appraisal review must do all of the following **except**:

    a. develop a scope of work decision.
    b. include all known pertinent information.
    c. state the nature, extent, and detail of the review process undertaken.
    d. develop his or her own opinion of value.

37. Is an appraiser performing a review appraisal required to explain why he or she disagrees with the original appraiser?

    a. Yes
    b. Only if the original appraiser failed to invoke the DEPARTURE RULE
    c. No, because the reviewer is expected to find flaws in the original appraisal
    d. There is no such requirement

38. The general requirements for developing a real property appraisal review are:

    a. very different from STANDARD 1.
    b. identical to STANDARD 1.
    c. very similar to STANDARD 1.
    d. there is no comparison.

39. An appraisal review assignment may be performed from all the following **except**:

    a. the office.
    b. the field with an interior inspection of the property.
    c. the field without an interior inspection of the subject property.
    d. examination of sales documents only.

40. Which of the following is not performed by an appraiser who is performing a review appraisal?

    a. Signing the certification
    b. Signing in the right corner of the original appraisal report
    c. Preparing a separate report
    d. Identifying the appraiser who completed the work under review

41. Which of the following is not part of a real property consulting service?

    a. Signing the certification
    b. Scope of work decision
    c. Advocacy
    d. Integrity

42. What is the difference between the certification requirements for written appraisal reports and written appraisal consulting reports?

    a. There is no difference
    b. The location of the signatures
    c. Signing the written appraisal consulting report makes the appraiser responsible for only the final value conclusion
    d. The signed certification of a written appraisal consulting report is not an integral part of the appraisal report

43. The DEPARTURE RULE:

    a. may be applied to Standards Rule 4-1.
    b. may be applied to STANDARD 4 only if its specific requirements are not applicable or necessary to produce credible results in the assignment.
    c. does not apply to any part of STANDARD 4.
    d. applies to all requirements of STANDARD 4.

44. STANDARD 4 is similar to _____ in purpose and principle.

    a. STANDARD 1
    b. STANDARD 2
    c. STANDARD 3
    d. STANDARD 6

45. STANDARD 5 is similar to _____ in purpose and principle.

    a. STANDARD 1
    b. STANDARD 2
    c. STANDARD 3
    d. STANDARD 6

46. When developing a real property appraisal consulting assignment:

    a. the consulting appraiser may or may not include an opinion of value.
    b. the consulting appraiser must include their own opinion of value in the report.
    c. the consulting appraiser must not include their own opinion of value in the report.
    d. the opinion of value may or may not be that of the consulting appraiser.

47. All of the following are binding requirements of STANDARD 5 **except**:

    a. Standards Rule 5-1.
    b. Standards Rule 5-2.
    c. Standards Rule 5-3.
    d. Standards Rule 5-4.

48. According to Standards Rule 5-3:

    a. the consulting appraiser is not responsible for the information provided by individuals who did not sign the certification.
    b. a description of the assistance provided by any individuals must be included in the certification.
    c. names of individuals who provided significant assistance in the appraisal consulting assignment but did not sign the certification must be stated in the certification.
    d. names of individuals who provided significant assistance in the appraisal consulting assignment but did not sign the certification need not be stated in the certification.

49. In an appraisal consulting assignment, a hypothetical condition:

    a. must lead to credible results.
    b. must not be disclosed.
    c. must not be used.
    d. may be used only if required for legal purposes.

50. Which of the following is **false**?

    a. A real property appraisal consulting assignment requires research and analysis.
    b. Misrepresenting the purpose of an appraisal consulting assignment is a violation of the ETHICS RULE.
    c. The purpose of a real property appraisal consulting assignment can be limited to an opinion of value.
    d. The appraiser performing an appraisal consulting assignment must comply with the ETHICS and COMPETENCY RULES.

51. Find the solution to the following problem: $(10 + 7) + 8 \times 3 - 15/3$

    a. 20
    b. 36
    c. 70
    d. 100

52. An appraiser who conducts a review appraisal and signs an appraisal report prepared by another:

    a. is not responsible for the contents of the report.
    b. must have written at least 35% of the report.
    c. must have physically inspected the property.
    d. is fully responsible for the contents of the report.

53. When an appraiser reviews an appraisal report, he or she must observe all of the following specific guidelines **except**:

    a. identify the subject of the appraisal review assignment.
    b. identify the appraiser(s) who completed the work under review.
    c. form an opinion as to the competency of the appraiser whose report is being reviewed.
    d. develop an opinion as to the completeness of the material under review, given the scope of work.

54. Which provision or standard of USPAP requires an appraiser who has reviewed an appraisal to form an opinion regarding the adequacy and appropriateness of the report he or she reviewed and to clearly disclose the nature of the review process he or she used?

    a. Standard 6
    b. Standard 3
    c. COMPETENCY RULE
    d. Standard 5

55. Which of the following is not a description of an appraisal?

    a. supported opinion
    b. objective opinion
    c. unbiased opinion
    d. statement of fact

56. An appraiser may offer a client all of the following **except**:

    a. experience.
    b. advocacy.
    c. objectivity.
    d. integrity.

57. What should the Certificate of Appraisal state?

    a. The appraiser has never previously appraised the subject property.
    b. The appraiser has no present or prospective interest in the subject property.
    c. The appraiser has never owned the subject property.
    d. The appraiser has never had a contemplated interest in the subject property.

58. An appraiser is hired by a seller to appraise his property. During the course of the appraisal, the appraiser reviews the property's confidential income statement. A potential buyer later asks the appraiser if she can see the appraisal data. What should the appraiser do?

    a. Give the data to the potential buyer as requested.
    b. Give the data to the buyer only if the seller specifically authorizes its release to the buyer.
    c. Direct the buyer to the county assessor's records, where she can obtain the information after it is recorded.
    d. Refuse to give the buyer the information under any circumstances.

59. A/An _____ is the study of the cost-benefit relationship of an economic endeavor involving real estate.

    a. cost analysis
    b. feasibility analysis
    c. limited appraisal
    d. investment analysis

60. A written appraisal report must do all of the following **except**:

    a. contain sufficient information to enable the user to understand it.
    b. present the appraisal in a manner that is not misleading.
    c. disclose any extraordinary limiting conditions.
    d. disclose the client's desired result.

61. Which of the following is **not** a requirement of a written appraisal report?

    a. It must contain a copy of the deed
    b. It must define the value to be estimated
    c. It must state the purpose of the appraisal
    d. It must identify the real estate being appraised

62. An advertisement for an appraisal company in the local yellow pages claims, "highest and best values always found." Which of the following statements about this ad is true?

    a. It is misleading and therefore violates the ETHICS RULE.
    b. It is an exaggeration, but still ethical because it is advertising.
    c. It is ethical only in limited appraisals.
    d. It is ethical if used only for ad valorem taxation appraisals.

63. What is the difference between a binding requirement and a specific requirement in USPAP?

    a. Departure from binding requirements is not permitted, while departure from specific requirements is permitted under certain limited conditions.
    b. Specific requirements are absolute, while binding requirements are conditional.
    c. Specific requirements can only be used in certain types of appraisals, while binding requirements are applicable to every assignment.
    d. There is no difference, the terms are synonymous.

64. The primary function of USPAP is to:

    a. protect professional appraisers and the appraisal profession from frivolous lawsuits.
    b. promote and maintain a high level of public trust in professional appraisal practice.
    c. educate appraisers about the appraisal profession.
    d. provide appraisers with a quick reference for appraisal questions.

65. Is it ethical if an appraiser pays a fee to be included on a lender's "approved appraiser" list?

    a. Yes, provided the lender discloses payment of the fee to his or her borrowers.
    b. Yes, provided the appraiser discloses the fee in the appraisal report.
    c. No, such a situation causes a conflict of interest and compromises the validity of the appraisal report. It is a violation of the ETHICS RULE.
    d. It depends on the nature of the appraisal, and the intended use and users.

66. It is ethical if an appraiser offers a client a reduced fee on an appraisal because the client's real estate transaction is not completed?

    a. Yes, provided the appraiser discloses in the appraisal report that a discount was given.
    b. Yes, provided the appraiser notifies the lender that the client is receiving a reduced fee.
    c. No, this practice is a violation of the ETHICS RULE.
    d. It depends on the nature of the appraisal, and the intended use and users.

67. A client's business partner requests information relating to an appraisal report you prepared for your client. Can you disclose the results of the appraisal the client's business partner?

    a. No, the appraiser may disclose the results of an appraisal only to the intended user(s) listed in the report.
    b. No, disclosure of the results to anyone besides the intended user is a violation of the ETHICS RULE.
    c. Yes, provided you receive authorization from the client before sharing any confidential information.
    d. Both a and b

68. An appraiser must retain a workfile for at least:

    a. 5 years after preparation or at least 2 years after final disposition of judicial proceedings in which testimony was given, whichever period expires last.
    b. 3 years after preparation or at least 1 year after final disposition of judicial proceedings in which testimony was given, whichever period expires last.
    c. 3 years after preparation or at least 5 years after final disposition of judicial proceedings in which testimony was given, whichever period expires last.
    d. 5 years, regardless of the result of the report or any testimony for a judicial proceeding.

69. You performed an appraisal two years ago that was never used in loan underwriting or in any other manner by the client. She now requests that you destroy the workfile and any records of the appraisal. Is this ethical?

    a. Yes, since the client requested the appraisal and paid for the appraisal, the client now owns the report and can request its destruction.
    b. Yes, since it has been two years since the appraisal was performed, the report and files may be destroyed.
    c. No, USPAP does not permit appraisers to destroy written records prior to five years after preparation for any reason.
    d. It depends on whether loan underwriting was stated as an intended use in the appraisal report.

70. Does USPAP require every appraisal report to include a complete legal description of the subject property?

    a. Yes, Standards Rule 2-1 requires a complete and accurate legal description
    b. No, USPAP Rule 2-2 requires sufficient information to identify the real estate
    c. Yes, if the report does not include a complete legal description of the subject property, the report is considered an incomplete appraisal
    d. It depends on the intended use of the appraisal report

71. The URAR form is what kind of appraisal report?

    a. Summary Appraisal Report
    b. Self-contained Appraisal Report
    c. Restricted Use Report
    d. Oral Report

72. You don't charge a fee for your appraisal services, therefore you:

    a. do not have to follow USPAP.
    b. cannot perform appraisals.
    c. must still follow USPAP.
    d. are not considered an appraiser.

73. All of the following must be retained in an appraiser's workfile **except**:

    a. the client's name and the identity of any other intended user(s).
    b. a complete legal description of the subject property.
    c. a summary of any oral reports or testimony, or a transcript of testimony.
    d. true copies of any written reports.

74. The three conditions that must be met before invoking the DEPARTURE RULE and performing a Limited Appraisal are: 1) determine that the appraisal process to be performed is not so limited that the results of the assignment are no longer credible, 2) advise the client that the assignment calls for a Limited Appraisal and that any departure(s) will be clearly identified in the appraisal report, and 3):

    a. confirm the intended use and users of the appraisal report with the client.
    b. reassure the client that you are competent to perform a Limited Appraisal.
    c. be aware of, understand, and correctly employ the recognized methods and techniques that are necessary to produce a credible appraisal.
    d. be certain the client agrees that performing a Limited Appraisal would be appropriate for the assignment.

75. An appraiser may invoke the JURISDICTIONAL EXCEPTION RULE when:

    a. When there is a conflict between the requirements of USPAP and the applicable law or public policy requirements of a jurisdiction
    b. When there is a conflict between the appraiser's knowledge and the scope of work required by the appraisal assignment
    c. When there is a conflict between the client's desired estimate of value and the appraiser's professional opinion of value
    d. When there is a conflict between the appraiser's competency in a given area and the public policy requirements of a jurisdiction

76. A hypothetical condition is a(an):

    a. conditional Standards Rule that only applies to appraisals performed on specific types of properties.
    b. n appraisal that is not actually performed but is hypothesized for the purpose of valuation.
    c. assumption about the subject property that is presumed to be correct, which if found false, could alter the appraiser's opinion of value.
    d. condition of the subject property that is contrary to what exists, but is assumed for the purpose of analysis.

77. An extraordinary assumption is a(n):

    a. assumption that is presumed to be fact about the competency of the appraiser, which if found to be false, could call into question the validity of the appraisal.
    b. assumption about the value of a subject property, used by an appraiser when the research performed on the property does not yield sufficient information to estimate its value.
    c. assumption that is presumed to be fact about the physical, economic, or legal condition of the subject property, which if found to be false, could alter the appraiser's estimate of value.
    d. assumption about the correct approach to value that should be used to valuate a specific subject property, used by an appraiser that is unfamiliar with the area.

78. The Appraisal Foundation is a:

    a. government regulatory agency.
    b. private regulatory agency.
    c. government sponsored enterprise.
    d. banking regulatory agency.

79. If an appraiser does not develop one of the three approaches to value while performing an appraisal because that approach is not applicable to the appraisal problem, the appraisal is considered:

    a. incomplete.
    b. null and void.
    c. complete.
    d. unreliable.

80. Which Rule does an appraiser invoke when performing a limited appraisal?

    a. COMPETENCY RULE
    b. Standards Rule 1-3
    c. DEPARTURE RULE
    d. Standards Rule 4-2

81. The _____ is/are responsible for deciding if any supplemental standards apply to an appraisal assignment.

    a. client only
    b. property owner
    c. lender
    d. appraiser and client

82. Which Standards apply to developing an appraisal?

    a. Standards 1, 3, 4, and 8
    b. Standards 1, 5, 8, and 10
    c. Standards 1, 6, 7, and 9
    d. Standards 1, 6, 7, and 10

83. One example of a situation in which a hypothetical condition may be used is when:

    a. appraising proposed construction as of a current date.
    b. an appraisal is not actually performed, but is hypothesized.
    c. an appraiser does not inspect the interior and assumes the interior condition of a property is good.
    d. the client requests a minimum value opinion for tax purposes.

84. Which Standards apply to reporting an appraisal?

    a. Standards 2, 4, 7, and 10
    b. Standards 2, 6, 8, and 10
    c. Standards 3, 5, 8, and 10
    d. Standards 4, 5, 8, and 9

85. You are asked to review an appraisal report and limit your review to only the income approach to value. You:

    a. must not comply with this request, as it violates the ETHICS RULE.
    b. can comply with this request, only if you invoke the DEPARTURE RULE.
    c. can comply with this request, because of Standards Rule 3-1(b).
    d. cannot comply with this request, as it violates the COMPETENCY RULE.

86. Which section of USPAP states that an appraiser complies with the Standards either by choice or by requirements placed upon them or the service they provide?

    a. DEFINITIONS
    b. ETHICS RULE
    c. COMPETENCY RULE
    d. PREAMBLE

87. Which of the following Rules prohibits an appraiser from communicating results in a misleading or fraudulent manner?

    a. ETHICS RULE
    b. Standards Rule 3-1
    c. JURISDICTIONAL EXCEPTION
    d. Standards Rule 1-1

88. You are asked to perform a "condition and marketability report." You are not asked to give a value conclusion as part of the assignment. You:

    a. cannot take this assignment as it violates the ETHICS RULE.
    b. do not have to follow USPAP since there is no conclusion of value requested.
    c. must follow USPAP since this is a valuation service, even though no conclusion of value was requested.
    d. may take this assignment, but may not receive a fee since it is not a complete appraisal as no value conclusion will be given.

89. You work for an appraisal company and occasionally hire independent contractors to perform appraisals. You generally keep the workfiles for all appraisals at your office however, Kathy, one of the independent contractors, has requested that she keep all the files pertaining to her work in her possession. According to USPAP, which appraiser should keep access to the workfiles?

    a. You, since you were hired by the client and in turn hired Kathy to perform the appraisals
    b. Kathy, the independent contractor who performed the appraisals
    c. Both of you, since you both are connected to the appraisals
    d. The client, who hired you and whose property was appraised

90. Which Standards Rule requires an appraiser to develop a value opinion for personal property, trade fixtures, or intangible items during the course of a real property appraisal?

    a. Standards Rule 1-4
    b. Standards Rule 8-5
    c. Standards Rule 2-2
    d. Standards Rule 3-2

91. You are asked to appraise a property that has sold 3 times in the last year. According to USPAP, you must analyze:

    a. the most recent sale.
    b. the average of all the sales.
    c. all of the sales.
    d. the two most recent sales.

92. Which section of USPAP describes the overall structure of USPAP?

    a. Advisory Opinions
    b. DEPARTURE RULE
    c. DEFINITIONS
    d. PREAMBLE

93. Which section of USPAP contains terms and their meanings that are specific to appraisals?

    a. DEFINITIONS
    b. ETHICS RULE
    c. COMPETENCY RULE
    d. Advisory Opinions

94. Which organization has final authority over USPAP and any changes to USPAP?

    a. The Appraisal Subcommittee
    b. The Appraisal Qualifications Board
    c. FNMA
    d. The Appraisal Standards Board

95. Which organization sets the minimum standards for state licensed and certified appraisers?

    a. The Appraisal Subcommittee
    b. The Appraisal Qualifications Board
    c. The Appraisal Foundation
    d. The Association of Appraisal Regulatory Organizations

96. Which federal organization oversees the activities of The Appraisal Foundation?

    a. Appraisal Subcommittee
    b. Appraisal Qualifications Board
    c. Appraisal Standards Board
    d. The House Committee on Appraisal Activities

97. The purpose of USPAP is to:

    a. establish requirements for professional appraisal practice.
    b. develop and promulgate new appraisal techniques.
    c. adhere to local laws.
    d. uniformly develop and enforce state appraisal laws.

98. The intent, and primary reason for the creation of USPAP is to:

    a. promote the appraisal profession.
    b. develop new appraisal techniques.
    c. promote and maintain the public trust.
    d. uniformly enforce state laws.

99. The Standards are intended for:

    a. users of appraisal services only.
    b. state licensed and certified appraisers.
    c. appraiser trainees.
    d. appraisers and users of appraisal services.

100. Appraisers must develop and communicate their results to intended users:

    a. via the appropriate peer review committee.
    b. only if presenting a predetermined value.
    c. in a manner that is meaningful and not misleading.
    d. in order to be paid.

101. The ETHICS RULE requires an appraiser to perform assignments with:

    a. cultural understanding of divergent groups.
    b. polite behavior throughout the appraisal assignment.
    c. integrity, impartiality, objectivity, and independent judgment.
    d. consistent application of state laws.

102. The COMPETENCY RULE requires an appraiser to be competent:

    a. prior to accepting an assignment.
    b. at the beginning of the assignment.
    c. during the assignment.
    d. by the completion of the assignment.

103. What are the two types of requirements found in USPAP?

    a. Development and reporting
    b. Verbal and written
    c. Binding and non-binding
    d. Binding and specific

104. Departure is never permitted from:

    a. binding requirements.
    b. non-binding requirements.
    c. specific requirements.
    d. general requirements.

105. Departure from _____ is permitted under certain limited conditions.

    a. specific requirements
    b. binding requirements
    c. constitutional
    d. foundational

106. The requirements in USPAP deal with the procedures appraisers should follow when developing and reporting an appraisal, appraisal review, and an appraisal consulting assignment. These requirements complement:

    a. FNMA guidelines.
    b. Appraisal Qualifications Board requirements.
    c. the appraisal process.
    d. minimum state requirements.

107. Which Standards deal with the development and reporting of a real property appraisal?

    a. Standards 1 and 2
    b. Standards 4 and 5
    c. Standards 7 and 8
    d. Standards 9 and 10

108. Most of the Standards are paired together. One of the pair deals with development, and the other deals with reporting. Which two Standards are not paired?

    a. Standard 3 Review and Standard 4 Consulting
    b. Standard 5 Consulting and Standard 6 Mass Appraisal
    c. Standard 8 Personal Property and Standard 9 Business Appraisal
    d. Standard 3 Review and Standard 6 Mass Appraisal

109. Each Standard contains _____, which clarify, interpret, explain, or elaborate on USPAP and have the full weight of a Standards Rule.

   a. supplemental standards
   b. Statements
   c. Advisory Opinions
   d. definitions

110. Which of the following are an integral part of USPAP and are extensions of the Rules and Standards Rules?

   a. Comments
   b. Statements
   c. Advisory Opinions
   d. Definitions

111. If a section of USPAP is contrary to a local law, an appraiser in that area must use which of the following to complete an appraisal assignment?

   a. DEPARTURE RULE
   b. JURISDICTIONAL EXCEPTION RULE
   c. COMPETENCY RULE
   d. Hypothetical condition

112. The COMPETENCY RULE states that if an appraiser has insufficient knowledge and/or experience to complete an assignment, the appraiser must:

   a. refuse to perform the assignment.
   b. accept the assignment and note his incompetence by invoking the DEPARTURE RULE.
   c. accept the assignment only if he feels that he has a reasonable chance of finding help to complete the appraisal with a credible result.
   d. disclose his incompetence to the client before accepting the assignment, determine the necessary steps to complete the assignment, and describe these steps to the client.

113. The purpose of the SUPPLEMENTAL STANDARDS RULE is to:

   a. provide a reasonable means to augment USPAP with requirements that add to the requirements set forth in USPAP.
   b. provide a reasonable means to depart from portions of USPAP that conflict with laws or public policies of a jurisdiction.
   c. provide a reasonable means to substitute appraisal policies dictated by government sponsored enterprises for USPAP requirements as applicable.
   d. all of the above

114. Which of the following best describes a limited appraisal?

    a. The act or process of developing an opinion of value without invoking the DEPARTURE RULE
    b. The act or process of developing an opinion of value while invoking the DEPARTURE RULE
    c. The act or process of developing an opinion of value while invoking the JURISDICTIONAL EXCEPTION RULE
    d. The act or process of developing an opinion of value while invoking a hypothetical condition

115. Which of the following best describes a complete appraisal?

    a. The act or process of developing an opinion of value without invoking the JURISDICTIONAL EXCEPTION RULE
    b. The act or process of developing an opinion of value without invoking the DEPARTURE RULE
    c. The act or process of developing an opinion of value while invoking the DEPARTURE RULE
    d. The act or process of developing an opinion of value without using a hypothetical condition

116. You recently appraised a single-family residence for the owner, who is selling the property. A potential buyer has just contacted you to obtain a copy of the appraisal. What should you do?

    a. Comply with the buyer's request because all the information you used to do the appraisal is public record, so there is nothing confidential in the report
    b. Give him a copy as the information in the appraisal report will enable the buyer to make an informed decision and help ensure an arm's-length transaction
    c. Do not give the buyer a copy until you have obtained permission from the lender and if the lender agrees, you can send a copy to the potential buyer
    d. Do not give the buyer a copy. The seller is your client, so he is the only one who can authorize you to disclose the information

117. A property owner asks you to appraise her property and states that you will be compensated if you arrive at a value of $100,000. You should:

    a. refuse to do the appraisal and tell her it is unethical to accept compensation based on a predetermined value.
    b. report her to the lender for attempting to falsify a loan.
    c. perform the assignment with the hopes of finding the property's value at $100,000.
    d. perform the assignment according to the owner's request.

118. Your supervisor signs your appraisal on the line reserved for the reviewer. Who is responsible for the contents of this report?

    a. You
    b. Your supervisor
    c. Both of you
    d. The client

119. You appraise a large rural property and arrive at an opinion of value that is $100,000 less than the property is actually worth because you are not knowledgeable of water rights. Which rule of USPAP did you violate?

    a. Competency Rule
    b. Jurisdictional Exception Rule
    c. Ethics Rule
    d. Supplemental Standard Rule

120. An appraiser who performs an appraisal review must keep the report for at least _____ year(s).

    a. 1
    b. 3
    c. 4
    d. 5

121. A buyer who is applying for a mortgage asks an appraiser to appraise his property. The appraiser should not concern himself with the:

    a. client's opinions.
    b. tax rate of the subject property.
    c. amount of financing necessary.
    d. evidence that supports constructions costs.

122. An appraiser's assignment fee is determined by:

    a. the ultimate value of the property being appraised.
    b. the scope of work and complexity of the assignment.
    c. the level of expertise held by the appraiser and the amount of time she spens on the assignment.
    d. the lender.

123. According to USPAP, who usually sets the supplemental appraisal standards for commercial banks that are insured by the federal government?

   a. The Federal Reserve Districts
   b. The Appraisal Standards Board
   c. The appraiser
   d. The FDIC

124. If a specific requirement is not applicable to an appraisal assignment, it is irrelevant and:

   a. no departure is needed.
   b. departure is permitted.
   c. departure is sometimes necessary.
   d. none of the above

125. If a specific requirement is applicable and necessary to produce a credible opinion of value, then:

   a. departure is not permitted.
   b. no departure is needed.
   c. you may depart from all specific requirements.
   d. both b and c

126. If a specific requirement is applicable, but **not** necessary to produce credible results:

   a. departure is permitted.
   b. departure is not permitted.
   c. departure is not necessary.
   d. none of the above

127. In which step of the appraisal process does an appraiser decide which valuation approach to use and whether to invoke the DEPARTURE RULE?

   a. Define the problem
   b. Collect, verify, and analyze all relevant information
   c. Scope of work
   d. Reconciliation

128. In which of the following circumstances may an appraiser's role be misunderstood?

   a. An appraiser, who is also a real estate broker, acting as a broker
   b. An appraiser when appraising a property
   c. A broker listing a property
   d. When using the DEPARTURE RULE

129. When an appraiser is developing and communicating an appraisal report, bias is:

   a. permitted.
   b. tolerated.
   c. discouraged.
   d. forbidden.

130. Which of the following is a violation of the ETHICS RULE?

   a. Reporting a predetermined value
   b. A commission that is based on a percentage of the appraised value
   c. A commission that is contingent on the occurrence of a subsequent event, such as receiving financing
   d. All of the above

131. Which of the following is a violation of the ETHICS RULE?

   a. Reporting a predetermined value
   b. A commission that is based on a percentage of the appraised value
   c. A commission that is contingent on the occurrence of a subsequent event, such as receiving financing
   d. All of the above

132. Which of the following is not permitted under USPAP?

   a. Advocacy and contingent fees
   b. Impartial analysis
   c. Independent results
   d. Objective decisions

133. Advocacy is permitted in which of the following circumstances?

   a. Appraisal practice
   b. Appraisal review
   c. Appraisal consulting
   d. Non-appraisal practice

134. An appraiser sometimes pays a referral fee or commission in order to obtain appraisal assignments. This practice is:

   a. sometimes necessary in declining marketplaces.
   b. allowed if it is disclosed.
   c. prohibited by Advisory Opinion 24.
   d. never permitted.

135. If an appraisal report has an effective date of 10/16/1995, and testimony concerning this report was given on 7/30/1997, the appraiser must keep her work file until:

    a. 10/16/1999.
    b. 10/16/2002.
    c. 10/16/2000.
    d. 7/30/1999.

136. Every appraisal report must contain two dates, which are the:

    a. inspection date and report date.
    b. completion date and effective date of valuation.
    c. effective date of valuation and report date.
    d. effective date of valuation and filing date.

137. Which Standard in USPAP deals with the development and reporting of an opinion about the quality of another appraiser's work?

    a. Standard 3 – appraisal review
    b. Standard 4 – appraisal consulting
    c. Standard 9 – business appraisal
    d. Standard 11 – appraisal advising

138. The purpose of an _____ assignment is to develop an analysis, recommendation, or opinion where an opinion of value is a component of the analysis leading to the assignment results.

    a. appraisal practice
    b. appraisal review
    c. appraisal consulting
    d. appraisal advocacy

139. An appraiser is best described as:

    a. one who performs appraisals competently and fairly.
    b. either state licensed or certified.
    c. one who is expected to perform valuation services in a timely manner and at a reasonable price.
    d. one who is expected to perform valuation services competently and in a manner that is independent, impartial, and objective.

140. Appraisal practice is best described as:

   a. performed only by an appraiser.
   b. valuation services performed by an individual acting as an appraiser, but not limited to appraisal, appraisal review, or appraisal consulting.
   c. valuation services performed by an individual acting as an appraiser.
   d. valuation services performed only by an appraiser and limited to appraisal review or appraisal consulting.

141. Services pertaining to all aspects of value are:

   a. valuation services.
   b. performed by appraisers and others.
   c. both a and b
   d. none of the above

142. An appraiser's compensation must not be influenced by:

   a. the amount of effort required to complete the assignment.
   b. the value estimated in the appraisal.
   c. the expenses paid by the appraiser to complete the assignment.
   d. the time required to complete the appraisal.

143. An appraiser must consider and analyze any prior sales of the subject property that occurred within what period of time?

   a. Three years for all property types
   b. Two years for one-to-four family residential property and five years for all other property types
   c. One year for one-to-four-family residential property and three years for all other property types
   d. One year for one-to-four family residential property and two years for all other property types

144. Which of the following is true of an appraiser who signs a real estate appraisal report prepared by another, even as a reviewer?

   a. The appraiser is not responsible for the appraisal or the contents of the report.
   b. The appraiser must have contributed at least 65% to the report.
   c. The appraiser must have physically inspected the property and performed the reconciliation.
   d. The appraiser must accept full responsibility for the appraisal and the contents of the report.

145. An appraiser estimates the market value of an industrial park for use in a property tax appeal. The appraisal report is completed on May 22, 1996. On August 13, 1997, the appraiser testifies in court on behalf of the owner of the industrial park. The state Supreme Court rules in favor of the owner with the final disposition on September 29, 1997. At a minimum, how long must the appraiser keep her records?

    a. May 22, 1999
    b. May 22, 2001
    c. August 13, 2002
    d. September 29, 2002

146. In which section of analysis would you find the statement: "My compensation is not contingent upon the reporting of a predetermined value."

    a. Cover letter
    b. Letter of transmittal
    c. Certification statement
    d. Assumptions and limiting conditions

147. Standard 2 of USPAP requires the appraiser to include all of the following statements in the certification statement **except**:

    a. "My actual compensation for this assignment is $___."
    b. "My compensation is not contingent upon the reporting of a predetermined value."
    c. "I have (or have not) made a personal inspection of the property."
    d. "I have no (or the specified) present or prospective interest in the property."

148. An appraisal's effective date:

    a. establishes the context of the value estimate.
    b. is always the same date as the appraisal report.
    c. must not be later than the date of the appraisal report.
    d. must not be prior to the date of the appraisal report.

149. All of the following statements must be included in an appraisal's certification **except**:

    a. the appraiser's compensation is not contingent upon the development or reporting of a predetermined value.
    b. the effective date of the appraisal and the date of the report are the same.
    c. no one provided significant professional assistance to the person signing this report.
    d. the appraiser has or has not made a personal inspection of the property that is the subject of this report.

150. What is the term for a preference or inclination used in the development or communication of an appraisal assignment that precludes an appraiser's impartiality?

   a. Favoritism
   b. Bias
   c. Consulting
   d. Advocacy

151. What is the term for representing the cause or interest of another, even if that cause or interest does not necessarily coincide with one's own beliefs, opinions, conclusions, or recommendations?

   a. Activism
   b. Bias
   c. Advocacy
   d. Sponsorship

152. An appraiser's peers are:

   a. all other appraisers.
   b. appraisers who work in the same office together.
   c. other appraisers in the same general geographic area.
   d. other appraisers who have expertise and competency in the same or a similar type of assignment.

153. USPAP defines a report as:

   a. any communication, written or oral, of an appraisal, appraisal review, or consulting service that is transmitted to the client upon completion of an assignment.
   b. regular communication, usually due at the end of the month.
   c. any communication, written or oral, with the client.
   d. oral communication with the client.

154. All appraisal reports must be signed by which one of the following methods?

   a. Hand written signature only
   b. Either hand written or electronic signature that the appraiser has sole personalized control over
   c. Either hand written or electronic signature
   d. Electronic signature only

155. When may an appraiser use the racial make-up of an area to define a neighborhood?

   a. When the racial boundaries are clearly marked
   b. Never
   c. When it is predominantly a white neighborhood
   d. When the appraiser imposes the jurisdictional exception rule

156. A seller asks a licensed real estate broker for his opinion of value. The broker tells the seller that he should list his home for $295,000. Which of the following is **true**?

   a. The broker may give his opinion of value at any time.
   b. The broker may only render an opinion of value if he includes a disclaimer that he is invoking the departure provision of USPAP.
   c. The broker may be guilty of a criminal action.
   d. The broker may only perform such a task if he is also a licensed appraiser.

157. The Confidentiality Section of the ETHICS RULE states that the results of an appraisal may be disclosed only to:

   a. the client and those authorized by the client.
   b. state enforcement agencies.
   c. duly authorized peer review committees.
   d. all of the above

158. Which of the following terms is defined as an assumption directly related to a specific assignment, which if found to be false, could alter the appraiser's opinions or conclusions?

   a. Standard assumption
   b. Binding assumption
   c. Extraordinary assumption
   d. Hypothetical condition

159. When can an appraiser use the tax assessor's number as a legal description?

   a. Never
   b. If no other legal description is available
   c. If the appraiser is appraising a new home and the only description is metes and bounds
   d. If the property is located in an unincorporated area

160. You are asked to perform an appraisal in a neighborhood that you are familiar with. The lender informs you that he needs a value of $250,000 to make the deal. You know that the values are probably higher than that, due to your experience with the neighborhood. What should you do?

    a. Accept the assignment because you know the desired value is more than substantiated.
    b. Accept the assignment, but inform the lender that they cannot ask for a value.
    c. Refuse the assignment.
    d. Ask another appraiser to appraise it, but don't tell him of the lender's request.

161. Which of the following terms is defined as that which is contrary to what exists, but is supposed for the purpose of analysis?

    a. Extraordinary assumption
    b. Condition subsequent
    c. Hypothetical condition
    d. Binding requirement

162. An appraiser may perform a retrospective appraisal for a property as it was in 1995 if:

    a. the appraiser has experience appraising property during that period of time.
    b. the appraiser has data to support an appraisal from that period of time.
    c. appraisers are not permitted to appraise property more than 5 years in the past.
    d. the appraiser was licensed at that time to appraise that type of property.

163. Which standard of USPAP deals with real property appraisal reporting?

    a. STANDARD 1
    b. STANDARD 2
    c. STANDARD 3
    d. none of the above

164. Which standard of USPAP deals with real property appraisal reporting?

    a. STANDARD 1
    b. STANDARD 2
    c. STANDARD 3
    d. STANDARD 7

165. A local builder hires you to provide a market value appraisal in order to secure construction loan financing. He provides you with the necessary plans and specifications for the proposed construction. The site is currently zoned R-1 single-family residential, but the developer is planning to build a duplex. He has already filed to change the zoning to R-2 with the city zoning department and is quite confident that his application will be approved. The change will permit up to two residential units to be built on one lot. You treat the zoning as R-2 for the purpose of your analysis. In order to conform to USPAP, you must use a(n):

   a. extraordinary assumption.
   b. specific requirement.
   c. hypothetical condition.
   d. zoning variance.

166. A feasibility analysis is:

   a. a study of the cost-benefit relationship of an economic endeavor.
   b. a detailed study of the asset depreciation of a development.
   c. an analysis of a site's zoning and topography.
   d. none of the above

167. A market analysis is:

   a. a study of the national real estate market.
   b. a study of market conditions for a specific type of property.
   c. a study of the local real estate market's historical behavior.
   d. a study to determine the future trends of a specific real estate market.

168. A cash flow analysis is:

   a. a study of the historical trends of an investment's cash flow.
   b. a study of an investment's assets and depreciation.
   c. a study of the anticipated movement of cash into or out of an investment.
   d. a study of the economic stability of an investment.

169. If the client is the only intended user, an appraiser may report her conclusions and opinions using a:

   a. Restricted Use Appraisal Report.
   b. Summary Appraisal Report.
   c. Self-contained Appraisal Report.
   d. Narrative Appraisal Report.

170. Which of the following terms is defined as the amount and type of information researched and the analysis applied in an assignment?

    a. Specific requirement
    b. Scope of work
    c. Assignment conditions
    d. Feasibility analysis

171. Which of the following terms is defined as any party identified by the appraiser based on communication with the client at the time of the assignment?

    a. An intended user
    b. An associate of the client
    c. A member of a peer review committee
    d. An attorney representing the client

172. You are a practicing appraiser in Irvine, CA, and have been hired to appraise a farmhouse on 5 acres in Chowchilla, CA. You have never been to Chowchilla, but you research the average price for agricultural land and residential properties in Chowchilla on the Internet before you arrive in town. You tell the client before you start work that you are not familiar with the area, but she still wants you to do the work. Have you violated the COMPETENCY RULE?

    a. No, you disclosed your lack of knowledge before you started the work
    b. Yes, research on recent sales prices is not adequate to know a market
    c. Yes, you must disclose any lack of knowledge or experience before accepting the assignment
    d. Both b and c

173. A developer offers 50 single-family homes for sale at $350,000 with special financing. However, he is also offering the same homes for $340,000 if the buyers secure their own financing. What should an appraiser do with this information?

    a. It depends on whether the client is concerned about financing.
    b. Nothing because the buyer makes the financing decision, not the appraiser.
    c. Discuss the special financing in the report and give his or her opinion about the value it adds or detracts.
    d. Complete the appraisal "as is".

174. The main difference between _____ is the content and level of detail presented.

   a. binding requirements, specific requirements, and non-binding requirements
   b. self-contained appraisal reports, summary appraisals reports, and restricted use appraisal reports
   c. extraordinary assumptions, hypothetical conditions, and jurisdictional exceptions
   d. none of the above

175. All appraisal reports must contain a:

   a. signed certification.
   b. specific requirement.
   c. general disclaimer.
   d. hypothetical condition.

176. Which of the following is a requirement from which an appraiser may **not** depart?

   a. Specific requirement
   b. Non-binding requirement
   c. Binding requirement
   d. Mandatory requirement

177. Which of the following is a requirement from which an appraiser may depart if the requirement is applicable to the assignment, but not necessary?

   a. Specific requirement
   b. Non-binding requirement
   c. Binding requirement
   d. Optional requirement

178. Valuation services include:

   a. appraisal, review, real estate, and personal property consulting.
   b. mass appraisals for ad valorem taxation and other purposes.
   c. valuation of antiques, boats, cars, real estate, and intangibles such as franchises, trademarks, and licenses.
   d. all of the above

179. Which of the following instances would permit an individual to act in the capacity of an advocate?

   a. Determining the scope of work
   b. Performing as a real estate broker
   c. Collecting information to be used in an appraisal
   d. Forming an opinion as to the quality of another appraiser's work

180. When an appraiser decides to use a hypothetical condition or an extraordinary assumption, he makes this decision as part of the:

   a. scope of work.
   b. development.
   c. data collection.
   d. reconciliation.

181. Which of the following is always presumed to be prior to the appraisal's effective date and is always the opinion of the appraiser, **not** the client?

   a. Exposure time
   b. Market time
   c. Sales time
   d. All of the above

182. What does a hypothetical condition have in common with an extraordinary assumption?

   a. An appraiser must analyze its affect on value.
   b. An appraiser must disclose its use in the appraisal report.
   c. An appraiser decides whether to use it during the scope of work section of the assignment.
   d. All of the above.

183. If an appraiser has an interest in a property, may he perform and report an appraisal and not violate USPAP?

   a. No, this is a violation of the conduct and management sections of the ETHICS RULE.
   b. Yes, partial interest rights are not covered under USPAP.
   c. Yes, but only for a retrospective appraisal, not a current appraisal.
   d. Yes, as long as the appraiser discloses the interest in the certification.

184. What is the term for the set of requirements issued by governmental agencies, government sponsored enterprises, or other entities that establish public policy and add to USPAP?

   a. Extraordinary Requirements
   b. Advisory Opinions
   c. Specific Requirements
   d. Supplemental Standards

185. What is the term for the set of requirements issued by governmental agencies, government sponsored enterprises, or other entities that establish public policy and add to USPAP?

   a. Extraordinary Requirements
   b. Advisory Opinions
   c. Specific Requirements
   d. Supplemental Standards

186. You are hired to appraise a home that fronts a two-lane residential street. It is public knowledge that the City Council has voted to widen the street to four lanes next year. However, you are not familiar with the City's proposal and so did not consider the effects of the street widening in the appraisal. Have you violated the COMPETENCY RULE?

   a. No, it was a two-lane street on the effective date of valuation and should be appraised as a two-lane street.
   b. Yes, this is public information so the street should be treated as if it were already a four-lane street.
   c. Yes, the appraiser did not consider the relevant characteristic. The market will react today to this change in the future and the appraiser should consider this reaction and note its affect on value.
   d. No, the appraiser must wait to see if the proposed street widening produces a positive or negative reaction.

187. An appraiser must include which of the following in every certification?

   a. Number of years of appraisal experience
   b. Disclosure of any personal interest the appraiser has in the property being appraised
   c. Disclosure of any hypothetical conditions, extraordinary assumptions, or limiting conditions used in the appraisal assignment
   d. Length of time spent on the appraisal assignment

188. You complete an appraisal, and 6 months later, the client requests an update of the opinion of value. What is the client asking you to perform?

   a. A recertification of value
   b. A recertified appraisal
   c. A new appraisal assignment
   d. An appraisal review

189. How does USPAP identify information that the client labels confidential and that the appraiser cannot get from any other source?

    a. Relevant information
    b. Pertinent information
    c. Confidential information
    d. Private information

190. According to the ETHICS RULE, an appraiser may accept a referral fee, management fee, commission, or anything of value in connection with obtaining an assignment as long as the appraiser:

    a. arrives at the desired opinion of value.
    b. adheres to all other requirements of the ETHICS RULE.
    c. does not tell anyone about the fee.
    d. discloses the fee in the appraisal report.

191. If an appraiser is completing a rental survey as well as an appraisal on the same property, what type of valuation service is the appraiser performing?

    a. Appraisal advocacy
    b. Appraisal consulting
    c. Appraisal valuation
    d. Appraisal surveying

192. You were hired to appraise all of the personal property in an estate. You reported the condition of every item of personal property, which required you to authenticate many rare and valuable antique ivory and jade carvings from the Manchu Dynasty. You had never authenticated property before, but you made educated guesses and felt confident that you performed competently. Since you felt so confident, you didn't mention your inexperience to the client. Did you violate the COMPETENCY RULE?

    a. No, you violated the ETHICS RULE, not the COMPETENCY RULE.
    b. No, the property owners are responsible for providing authentication since they most likely purchased the items and have a better understanding of their age and condition.
    c. Yes, you did not have the knowledge or experience, you did nothing to become knowledgeable or experienced, and you did not disclose your incompetence and inexperience to the client.
    d. None of the above.

Answers

1. (d) The Appraisal Foundation is a non-profit, private organization that was established for scientific and educational purposes.

2. (c) The Appraisal Subcommittee is funded by the registration fees paid by certified or licensed appraisers.

3. (b) The Appraisal Subcommittee was established to monitor the state regulatory agencies to determine whether their policies are consistent with Title XI of FIRREA.

4. (c) The Savings and Loan Crisis of the 1980's led to the licensing of appraisers and motivated the federal government to pass FIRREA.

5. (d) USPAP achieves legal authority through its adoption, citation, or implementation by government agencies or by the standards or contract requirements of private enterprise.

6. (a) A profession is defined as a vocation that calls for predominantly intellectual labor and skill, education, and special knowledge that imply professional attainments, standards of practice, and that the observation of these standards be monitored.

7. (c) Valuation services are defined as "services pertaining to aspects of property value." These services include services performed by appraisers as well as others.

8. (a) The primary objective of USPAP is to promote and maintain a high level of public trust in professional appraisal practice.

9. (b) The primary goal of USPAP is to promote public trust. If an appraiser does not comply with USPAP, that trust is broken.

10. (c) Elements in the scope of work decision include intended use, intended users, the purpose of the assignment and the type of value, the effective date(s), relevant property characteristics, and assignment conditions. Sales history of the subject property is not one of these elements.

11. (b) Comments are an integral part of USPAP. Comments interpret and establish the context and conditions for the application of DEFINITIONS, Rules, and Standards Rules. They have the same weight as these components.

12. (b) USPAP contains five RULES: the ETHICS RULE, the COMPETENCY RULE, the DEPARTURE RULE, the JURISDICTIONAL EXCEPTION RULE, and the SUPPLEMENTAL STANDARDS RULE.

13. (b) The ETHICS RULE contains four sections: Conduct, Management, Confidentiality, and Record Keeping.

14. (a) USPAP is designed to serve appraisers and users of appraisal services.

15. (d) An appraiser must retain a work file for each appraisal, appraisal review, or appraisal consulting assignment.

16. (c) The COMPTENCY RULE requires an appraiser who lacks sufficient knowledge or experience to competently complete an assignment to disclose the lack of knowledge and/or experience to the client before accepting the assignment. The appraiser must also take the steps necessary or appropriate to complete the assignment competently, and describe in the appraisal report the lack of knowledge and/or experience and the steps taken to complete the assignment competently.

17. (c) If a specific requirement is applicable, but not necessary, departure is permitted.

18. (d) An appraiser must perform assignments ethically and competently, with impartiality, objectivity, independence, and without accommodation of personal interest.

19. (b) It is not a violation of USPAP for an appraiser to disregard the part or parts of USPAP that are contrary to the law or public policy of a jurisdiction, as long as the appraiser discloses the exception.

20. (a) A specific requirement is applicable when it addresses factors or conditions that are present in a given assignment, or it addresses analysis that is typical practice in such an assignment.

21. (a) In a Summary Appraisal Report, an appraiser must state and explain the reason for excluding any of the usual appraisal approaches and any permitted departures from the specific requirements of Standard 1.

22. (d) An appraiser must state all assumptions, hypothetical conditions, and limiting conditions that affect their analysis, opinions, and conclusions.

23. (b) When an appraiser is developing an opinion of market value, he or she must develop an opinion of the highest and best use of the subject property.

24. (a) An appraiser must analyze all sales of the subject property that occurred within the three years prior to the effective date of the appraisal.

25. (c) A scope of work decision is acceptable when it is consistent with the expectations of participants in the market for the same or similar appraisal services, and it is consistent with what the appraiser's peers' actions would be if they were performing the assignment.

26. (c) An extraordinary assumption presumes something as fact about the physical, legal, or economic characteristics of the subject property or about external conditions such as market conditions or trends, or about the integrity of the data used in analysis. If the presumption is found to be false, it could alter the appraiser's opinions or conclusions.

27. (c) When developing an opinion of highest and best use, the appraiser must appraise the land as though vacant and available for development to its highest and best use.

28. (d) A hypothetical condition may be used in an assignment when it is clearly required for legal purposes, reasonable analysis, or comparison; when its use results in a credible analysis; and when the appraiser complies with the disclosure requirements stated in USPAP.

29. (a) An appraiser may use a Restricted Use Appraisal Report if the intended users do not include parties other than the client.

30. (a) An appraiser who signs an appraisal report's certification accepts full responsibility for all elements of the certification, the assignment results, and the contents of the appraisal report.

31. (d) An appraisal review is the development of an opinion about the quality of another appraiser's work, including the appraisal report, appraisal review report, or an appraisal consulting report. The reviewer considers the completeness, adequacy, relevance, appropriateness, and reasonableness of the work under review.

32. (d) An appraisal review must be conducted in the context of market conditions as of the effective date of the appraisal being reviewed. The reviewer must not use any information or data that could not have been available to the original appraiser.

33. (c) An appraisal review is the development of an opinion about the quality of another appraiser's work. The review assignment may also require the reviewer to develop his or her own opinion of value. See Standards Rule 3-1 (c), Comment, lines 1196-1211, and Standards Rule 3-2 (d) including the Comment.

34. (a) The review appraiser is not required to replicate the steps taken by the original appraiser. The reviewer may use an extraordinary assumption about those items in the original appraisal that the reviewer concludes are credible and in compliance with the applicable Standard(s).

35. (d) The ETHICS RULE prohibits an appraiser from communicating assignment results in a fraudulent or misleading manner, as well as using or communicating a misleading or fraudulent report.

36. (d) The review appraiser may be asked to develop his or her own opinion of value, but the primary purpose of appraisal review is to form an opinion about the quality of another appraiser's work.

37. (a) A reviewer must develop an opinion of the appropriateness of the original appraiser's analyses, opinion, and conclusions, as well as develop his or her reasons for any disagreement.

38. (c) Many of the general requirements are the same, just applied to a different methodology.

39. (d) This would be determined by an appropriate scope of work decision.

40. (b) A reviewer does not sign the original appraisal report.

41. (c) An appraisal consulting assignment must include a scope of work decision, a signed certification, and must be performed with integrity. However, advocacy is a violation of the ETHICS RULE.

42. (a) The two certifications are identical.

43. (c) All portions of STANDARD 4 are binding and departure is not permitted.

44. (a) Both STANDARDS deal with the development of assignments and use similar language.

45. (b) Both STANDARDS deal with the development of assignments and use similar language.

46. (d) An appraisal consulting assignment must include an opinion, analysis, or recommendation. The opinion of value may originate from a source other than the consulting appraiser.

47. (d) Standards Rule 5-4, concerning oral real property consulting reporting, is a specific requirement.

48. (c) The certification requires the signing appraiser to state that no one provided significant assistance, and if there are exceptions, the appraiser must provide the name of each individual who assisted.

49. (a) A hypothetical condition may be used in an appraisal consulting assignment only if its use is required for legal purposes, purposes of reasonable analysis, or for purposes of comparison; its use results in credible analysis; and if the appraiser complies with USPAP's disclosure requirements for hypothetical conditions.

50. (c) Real property appraisal consulting assignments encompass a wide variety of problems to be solved. The purpose of an assignment is to develop an analysis, recommendation, or opinion.

51. (b) The order of operation is parenthesis, exponent, multiplication, division, addition, and subtraction, therefore $17 + 24 - 5 = 36$.

52. (d) Standards Rule 3, lines 1140-1143 states "To avoid confusion between these activities, a reviewer performing an appraisal review must not sign the work under review unless he or she intends to accept the responsibility of a cosigner for that work."

53. (c) According to Standard 3 in USPAP, "Appraisal review is the act or process of developing and communicating an opinion about the quality of all or part of the work of another appraiser, including an appraisal report, appraisal review report, or appraisal consulting report." Appraisal reviews are conducted on another appraiser's work, not on the individual themselves.

54. (b) Standard 3 states "Appraisal review is the act or process of developing and communicating an opinion about the quality of all or part of the work of another appraiser...The appraiser's opinion about quality must encompass the completeness, adequacy, relevance, appropriateness, and reasonableness of the work under review, developed in the context of the requirements applicable to that work."

55. (d) An appraisal is an appropriately supported, objective, and unbiased opinion of value of a property, as of a specific date that is made by a qualified person who has no undisclosed interest in the property.

56. (b) An appraiser provides a client with adequate knowledge, experience, integrity, objectivity, and an uncompromised willingness to do the work on a timely basis for a mutually agreed upon fee. An appraiser may not offer a client advocacy.

57. (b) The appraiser must sign the certificate with each appraisal, which states that he or she has "...no (or the specified) present or prospective interest in the property that is the subject of this report and no (or the specified) personal interest with respect to the parties involved."

58. (b) The Confidentiality section of the ETHICS RULE states that an appraiser must not disclose confidential factual data obtained from a client or the results of an assignment prepared for a client to anyone other than the client and persons specifically authorized by the client.

59. (b) A feasibility analysis is a study of the cost-benefit relationship of an economic endeavor.

60. (d) According to Standards Rule 2-1, each written or oral real property appraisal report must clearly and accurately set forth the appraisal in a manner that will not be misleading, contain sufficient information to enable the users of the appraisal to understand the report properly, and clearly and accurately disclose any extraordinary assumption, hypothetical condition, or limiting condition that directly affects the appraisal and indicate its impact on value.

61. (a) According to Standards Rule 2-2, each style of written appraisal report must define the value to be estimated, and state the purpose of the appraisal (SR 2-2 a, b, and c (v)). All written appraisal reports must also identify the real estate being appraised (SR 2-2 a, b, and c (iii)).

62. (a) According to the Management section of the COMPETENCY RULE, advertising for or soliciting appraisal assignments in a manner that is false, misleading, or exaggerated is unethical.

63. (a) Departure is never permitted from a binding requirement. Departure is permitted from a specific requirement under certain limited conditions.

64. (b) The purpose of USPAP is to promote and maintain a high level of public trust in appraisal practice by establishing requirements for appraisers.

65. (b) An appraiser must disclose any fees, commissions, or things of value connected to the procurement of an assignment in the certification and in any transmittal letter in which conclusions are stated.

66. (c) It is unethical for an appraiser to accept an assignment or arrange compensation for an assignment on the attainment of a stipulated result. The securing of a loan or the closing of a real estate transaction may be a stipulated result.

67. (c) An appraiser must not disclose confidential information or assignment results prepared for a client to anyone other than the client, anyone specifically authorized by the client, state enforcement agencies, or a professional peer review committee

68. (a) An appraiser must retain a workfile for at least five years after preparation, or at least two years after final disposition of any judicial proceeding in which the appraiser provided testimony related to the assignment, whichever expires last.

69. (c) An appraiser must keep a workfile for at least five years after its preparation. The DEPARTURE RULE does not apply to the ETHICS RULE, so there are no exceptions for client requests.

70. (b) Standards Rule 2-2 (a) (iii) requires the appraiser to describe information that is sufficient to identify the real estate involved in the appraisal, including the physical and economic property characteristics that are relevant to the assignment.

71. (a) The level of detail in the presentation of information found in the URAR form is consistent with the requirements for a Summary Appraisal Report.

72. (c) Compliance with USPAP is required any time an appraiser represents that he or she is performing a service as an appraiser. Whether or not the appraiser charges a fee has no bearing on USPAP compliance.

73. (b) An appraiser's workfile must contain the name of the client and the identity of any intended users, true copies of written reports, summaries of oral reports or testimony, and any other information that supports the appraiser's opinions and compliance with USPAP. However, the workfile does not need to contain a legal description of the subject property.

74. (d) In order to perform a limited appraisal, an appraiser must determine that the process to be performed produces results that are credible, advise the client that the assignment calls for a limited appraisal, and be sure the client agrees that a limited appraisal is appropriate, given the intended use.

75. (a) An appraiser may invoke the JURISDICTIONAL EXCEPTION RULE if any part of USPAP is contrary to the law or public policy of any jurisdiction. However, only that part of USPAP that is contrary will be void.

76. (d) A hypothetical condition assumes something about the subject property that is contrary to known facts about its physical, legal, or economic characteristics; or external factors such as market conditions or trends; or about the integrity of the data used in analysis.

77. (c) An extraordinary assumption presumes as fact uncertain information about the subject property's physical, legal, or economic characteristics; conditions external to the property; or about the integrity of the data used in analysis.

78. (b) The Appraisal Foundation is a non-profit, private organization created for educational and scientific purposes.

79. (c) The definition of a complete appraisal is one in which the appraiser did not invoke the DEPARTURE RULE. An appraiser is not required to use all three approaches to value, only the approach(es) that are most appropriate to the assignment.

80. (c) The definition of a limited appraisal is one in which the appraiser invokes the DEPARTURE RULE.

81. (d) An appraiser and client must decide whether any published standards in addition to the Uniform Standards apply to the assignment being considered.

82. (c) Standard 1 deals with real property appraisal development, Standard 6 deals with mass appraisal development and reporting, Standard 7 deals with personal property development, and Standard 9 deals with business appraisal development.

83. (a) A hypothetical condition assumes something about the subject property that is contrary to its actual physical, legal, or economic characteristics; external conditions such as market conditions or trends; or the integrity of the data used in analysis. Proposed improvements have not been constructed, but the appraiser would assume their construction to complete the appraisal.

84. (b) Standard 2 deals with reporting a real property appraisal, Standard 6 deals with developing and reporting a mass appraisal, Standard 8 deals with reporting a personal property appraisal, and Standard 10 deals with reporting a business appraisal.

85. (c) An appraisal review can focus on all or part of a report, workfile, or a combination, and it may be related to an appraisal review, or appraisal consulting assignment.

86. (d) An appraiser must comply with USPAP when obligated by law, regulation, agreement with client or intended users, or by choice.

87. (a) The ETHICS RULE prohibits an appraiser from communicating assignment results in a misleading or fraudulent manner.

88. (c) An appraiser must comply with USPAP any time he or she represents that they are performing a service as an appraiser.

89. (c) An appraiser must have custody of his or her workfile, or make appropriate workfile retention, access, and retrieval arrangements with the party having custody of the workfile.

90. (a) Standards Rule 1-4 (g) requires an appraiser to analyze the effect on value of any personal property, trade fixtures, or intangible items that are not real property but are included in the appraisal.

91. (c) Standards Rule 1-5 states that an appraiser must analyze all current sales, options, and listings on the subject property, as well as all sales that have occurred in the previous three years.

92. (d) The PREAMBLE describes the overall structure of USPAP.

93. (a) The terms that comprise the DEFINITIONS section of USPAP have meanings that are specific to appraisals and that may differ from their usual meanings.

94. (d) The Appraisal Standards Board exercises authority over the subject, style, content, and substance of USPAP and establishes, improves, and promulgates USPAP.

95. (b) The Appraiser Qualifications Board exercises authority over the establishment of education, experience, and other criteria for licensing, certification, and recertification of appraisers. It defines, issues, promotes, and disseminates qualification criteria to states, governmental entities, and others.

96. (a) The Appraisal Subcommittee has authority from Title XI to oversee the activities of The Appraisal Foundation, including the ASB and the AQB.

97. (a) The purpose of USPAP is to establish requirements for professional appraisal practice, which includes appraisal, appraisal review, and appraisal consulting.

98. (c) The intent of USPAP is to promote and maintain a high level of public trust in professional appraisal practice.

99. (d) USPAP is intended for appraisers and users of appraisal services.

100. (c) An appraiser must communicate assignment results in a manner that is meaningful and not misleading or fraudulent.

101. (c) An appraiser must perform assignments with impartiality, objectivity, and independence, and without accommodating personal interests.

102. (a) Prior to accepting an assignment or entering into an agreement to perform an assignment, an appraiser must properly identify the problem to be addressed and have the knowledge and experience to complete the assignment competently.

103. (d) The two types of requirements found in USPAP are binding and specific requirements. Departure is not permitted from binding requirements. Departure is permitted from specific requirements, under certain limited conditions.

104. (a) Departure is not permitted from binding requirements. Departure is permitted from specific requirements, under certain limited conditions.

105. (a) Departure is not permitted from binding requirements. Departure is permitted from specific requirements, under certain limited conditions.

106. (c) The structure of the requirements established by USPAP complements the appraisal process.

107. (a) Standard 1 deals with the development of a real property appraisal and Standard 2 deals with the reporting of a real property appraisal.

108. (d) Standard 3 and Standard 6 are both stand-alones. Standard 3 deals with appraisal review, development, and reporting; and Standard 6 deals with mass appraisals, development, and reporting.

109. (b) Statements clarify, interpret, explain, or elaborate on USPAP. Advisory Opinions offer advice and are not part of USPAP.

110. (a) Comments are an integral part and extension of USPAP. They have the full force and effect of a Rule or Standards Rule.

111. (b) When the law and USPAP are in conflict, the appraiser must adhere to the law and invoke the JURISDICTIONAL EXCEPTION RULE.

112. (d) Prior to accepting an assignment or entering into an agreement to perform an assignment, an appraiser must properly identify the problem to be addressed and have the knowledge and experience to complete the assignment competently. Or, the appraiser must: 1) disclose the lack of knowledge and/or experience to the client before accepting the assignment; 2) take all steps necessary or appropriate to complete the assignment competently; and 3) describe the lack of knowledge and/or experience and the steps taken to complete the assignment competently in the report.

113. (a) The SUPPLEMENTAL STANDARDS RULE augments USPAP with requirements that add to those requirements established by USPAP.

114. (b) A limited appraisal is the act or process of developing an opinion of value while invoking the DEPARTURE RULE.

115. (a) A complete appraisal is the act or process of developing an opinion of value without invoking the DEPARTURE RULE.

116. (d) You cannot disclose confidential information or assignment results that were prepared for a client to anyone other than the client and anyone specifically authorized by the client. You cannot distribute copies of the appraisal unless you are authorized by the client to do so.

117. (a) An appraiser must not accept an assignment that includes the reporting of a predetermined opinion and conclusion.

118. (c) An appraiser who signs any portion of a report is also required to sign the certification, and in doing so is completely responsible for the appraisal and its contents.

119. (a) The Competency Rule requires an appraiser to have both the knowledge and the experience to perform an appraisal service competently.

120. (d) An appraiser must keep work files for at least 5 years from the date of creation or 2 years after deposition, whichever is longer. This applies to appraisals, appraisal reviews, and appraisal consulting assignments.

121. (a) An appraiser cannot let the opinions or value desired by the client, lender, owner, or any other individual influence the appraisal.

122. (b) Appraiser fees are determined by the amount of time required to complete the appraisal process and report the conclusions. The appraiser and the client may also negotiate a fee.

123. (d) Standard 10 states that appraiser guidelines and standards are issued by Federal Deposit Insurance Corporation (FDIC), Federal Reserve Board (FRB), Office of the Comptroller of the Currency (OCC), and Office of Thrift Supervision (OTS). Standard 10 also states that USPAP considers these guidelines and standards as SUPPLEMENTAL STANDARDS when they supplement USPAP requirements.

124. (a) If the specific requirement is not applicable, departure is not needed. The appraisal is still complete if the specific requirement is not applied.

125. (a) If the specific requirement is applicable and necessary, departure is not permitted.

126. (a) Departure is permitted. Advise the client prior to accepting the assignment that the appraisal calls for something less than what is required by USPAP and that this will be noted in the report. This is a limited appraisal.

127. (c) An appraiser evaluates the assignment and decides which valuation approach to use during the scope of work phase.

128. (a) An appraiser who is also a real estate broker must be careful not to mislead clients. The appraiser must make clear to clients what capacity he or she is performing in.

129. (d) An appraiser may never let bias influence his or her opinion of value. An appraiser must perform assignments with impartiality, objectivity, independence, and without accommodating personal interests.

130. (c) It is unethical for an appraiser to accept compensation for performing an assignment when the compensation is contingent upon the reporting of a predetermined result, a direction in assignment results that favors the client's cause, the amount of value opinion, the attainment of a stipulated result, or the occurrence of a subsequent event that is directly related to the appraiser's opinions and specific to the assignment.

131. (c) It is unethical for an appraiser to accept compensation for performing an assignment when the compensation is contingent upon the reporting of a predetermined result; a direction in assignment results that favors the client's cause; the amount of value opinion; the attainment of a stipulated result; or the occurrence of a subsequent event that is directly related to the appraiser's opinions and specific to the assignment.

132. (a) An appraiser must perform assignments with impartiality, objectivity, independence, and without accommodating personal interests.

133. (d) Advocacy is only permitted in non-appraisal practice such as brokerage, listing, selling, etc. An appraiser must maintain objectivity and impartiality while performing appraisal practice.

134. (b) An appraiser must disclose any fees, commissions, or things of value connected to an assignment in the certification and any transmittal letter that states the assignment conclusions.

135. (c) An appraiser must keep a workfile for at least 5 years after preparation, or at least 2 years after final disposition of any judicial proceeding in which testimony was given, whichever period expires last.

136. (c) According to Standards Rule 2-2 (vi), the appraiser must state the effective date of the appraisal and the date of the report.

137. (a) Standard 3 deals with the development and reporting of an appraisal review.

138. (c) The purpose of an appraisal consulting assignment is to develop an analysis, recommendation, or opinion where an opinion of value is a component of the analysis leading to the assignment results.

139. (d) An appraiser is one who is expected to perform valuation services competently and in a manner that is independent, impartial, and objective.

140. (b) Appraisal practice is defined as valuation services performed by an individual acting as an appraiser, including but not limited to appraisal, appraisal review, or appraisal consulting.

141. (c) Valuation services are services that pertain to all aspects of property value that are performed by appraisers and by others.

142. (b) It is unethical to base an appraiser's compensation on the value estimate of the appraisal.

143. (c) An appraiser must analyze prior sales of the subject property that occurred in the previous three years for all property types.

144. (d) Standards Rule 2-5 in USPAP requires an appraiser who signs an appraisal report to accept full responsibility for the appraisal and the contents of the report.

145. (b) An appraiser must keep records for at least five years following preparation or two years after final disposition, whichever period expires last.

146. (c) The certification statement deals with the appraiser's compensation.

147. (a) USPAP does not require the appraiser to disclose his or her actual compensation anywhere in the appraisal report. The appraiser must only state that the compensation is not contingent on the estimate of value.

148. (a) The effective date establishes the context of the value estimate. The effective date may be before, on, or after the date of appraisal.

149. (b) The certification does not require a statement regarding the effective date and the date of the report.

150. (b) Bias is a preference or inclination used in the development or communication of an assignment that prevents the appraiser's impartiality.

151. (c) Advocacy is representing the cause or interest of another, even if that cause or interest is not necessarily in line with one's own beliefs, opinions, conclusions, or recommendations.

152. (d) An appraiser's peers are other appraisers who have expertise and competency in the same or a similar type of appraisal assignment.

153. (a) A report is any written or oral communication of an appraisal, appraisal review, or consulting service that is transmitted to the client upon completion of an assignment.

154. (b) A signature can be a handwritten mark, a digitized image controlled by a personalized identification number, or other media. The appraiser must have sole personalized control of affixing the signature.

155. (b) The Fair Housing Amendments Act of 1988 prohibits discrimination in the selling, brokering, or appraising of residential real property because of race, color, religion, sex, handicap, familial status, or national origin.

156. (a) A broker may give an opinion of value at any time. If the broker is also an appraiser, he must not mislead the client into thinking he is acting as an appraiser when he gives his opinion. With this clear understanding, brokers, property managers, agents, and others may offer their opinion of value since their price opinion is not an appraisal because they are not expected to be an unbiased or disinterested party.

157. (d) The results of an appraisal may be disclosed to the client or anyone authorized by the client, state enforcement agencies, and an authorized professional peer review committee.

158. (c) An extraordinary assumption is directly related to a specific assignment, which, if found to be false, could alter the appraiser's opinions or conclusions.

159. (a) The tax assessor's number is for assessment purposes only and is issued as an aid to the county and state governments. The legal description as recorded in the title identifies the property on a legal basis for legal purposes.

160. (b) Appraise the property in an impartial and unbiased manner and tell the lender that you cannot base your appraisal on a predetermined or desired value.

161. (c) A hypothetical condition is something that is contrary to what exists, but is supposed for the purpose of analysis.

162. (b) The appraiser must comply with the COMPETENCY RULE. The appraiser must be able to research data associated with the retrospective date and to analyze the data in light of market conditions as of that date. It is not necessary for the appraiser to be, or to have been, a competent appraiser as of the effective date of value.

163. (b) STANDARD 2 addresses the reporting of real property appraisals.

164. (a) STANDARD 1 addresses the development of real property appraisals.

165. (c) The zoning used for the analysis is contrary to what actually exists. This is the definition of a hypothetical condition.

166. (a) A feasibility study is an analysis of the cost-benefit relationship of an economic endeavor.

167. (b) A market analysis is a study of market conditions for a specific type of property.

168. (c) A cash flow analysis is a study of the anticipated movement of cash into or out of an investment.

169. (a) When the only intended user of an appraisal is the client, a Restricted Use Appraisal report may be used.

170. (b) The scope of work is the amount and type of information researched and the analysis applied in an assignment.

171. (a) An intended user is the client and any other party identified as a user of the appraisal by the appraiser on the basis of communication with the client at the time of the assignment.

172. (d) An appraiser who lacks the knowledge and experience to competently complete an appraisal must disclose his or her lack of knowledge before accepting the assignment. The appraiser must also take steps to become knowledgeable about the local market. This is not accomplished by simply looking at recent sales prices, demographics, costs, or rental rates.

173. (c) Standards Rule 2-1 (c), SR 10-1 (c), and SR 6-7 (c) all state that the appraiser must accurately disclose any extraordinary assumption, hypothetical condition, or limiting condition that affects the appraisal and explain its impact on value. The Comment specifies that atypical financing is one of these that should be disclosed and explained.

174. (b) The difference between the three appraisal reports is the content and the level of detail presented in the report.

175. (a) Each written appraisal report must contain a signed certification.

176. (c) An appraiser cannot depart from a binding requirement.

177. (a) An appraiser may depart from a specific requirement if it is applicable to an assignment, but not necessary in order to result in a credible opinion or conclusion.

178. (d) A valuation service is any service that pertains to aspects of property value, and may be performed by appraisers or non-appraisers.

179. (b) A real estate broker has a fiduciary duty to his or her client, requiring the broker to act as the client's advocate. An appraiser acting as an advocate violates USPAP.

180. (a) An appraiser identifies any hypothetical conditions, extraordinary assumptions, or limiting conditions that will be used in an assignment when he or she defines the problem, which is a component of the scope of work.

181. (a) Exposure time is always presumed to precede the appraisal's effective date and is the opinion of the appraiser.

182. (d) A hypothetical condition and an extraordinary assumption both must be disclosed, their affect on value must be analyzed, and the appraiser decides whether to use one during the scope of work.

183. (d) An appraiser must disclose in the appraisal report certification any interest in the property being appraised or the parties involved in the appraisal assignment.

184. (d) "Supplemental standards are the set of requirements that are issued by government agencies, government sponsored enterprises, or other entities and establish public policy. This adds to the purpose, intent, and content of the requirements in USPAP, and have a material effect on the development and reporting of assignment results."

185. (d) "Supplemental standards are the set of requirements that are issued by government agencies, government sponsored enterprises, or other entities and establish public policy. This adds to the purpose, intent, and content of the requirements in USPAP, and have a material effect on the development and reporting of assignment results."

186. (c) Many relevant characteristics can affect property value. These include financing, legal, economic, on-site and off-site improvements, and physical characteristics. If an appraiser does not consider their affect on value, he or she is violating the COMPETENCY RULE. Failing to consider the future use of the property and the market's reaction to the future use is such a violation.

187. (b) An appraiser must disclose any present or prospective interest in the subject property in every certification.

188. (c) When a client requests a more current value or analysis of a property that was the subject of a prior appraisal assignment, it is considered a new assignment.

189. (c) Confidential information is identified by the client as confidential when he or she provides it to the appraiser and it is not available from any other source, or it is classified as confidential or private by law or regulation.

190. (d) An appraiser must disclose any fees, commissions, or things of value that are connected to the procurement of an assignment in the certification and in any transmittal letter in which the conclusions are stated.

191. (b) Appraisal consulting is the act or process of developing an analysis, recommendation, or opinion to solve a problem where an opinion of value is a component of the analysis leading to the assignment results.

192. (c) The COMPETENCY RULE requires an appraiser to be knowledgeable and experienced to perform the assignment competently, or take any necessary steps to complete the assignment competently. The appraiser must also disclose the lack of knowledge and steps taken to become knowledgeable to the client.

Practice Exam 1

1. Which of the following terms is defined as any party identified by the appraiser based on communication with the client at the time of the assignment?

   a. An intended user
   b. An associate of the client
   c. A member of a peer review committee
   d. An attorney representing the client

2. Which of the following may prevent a site from reaching its highest and best use?

   a. Deed restrictions, government regulations, and zoning
   b. Easements, zoning, and license
   c. Deed restrictions, easements, and license
   d. Government regulations, license, and right-of-ways

3. Which of the following affect market value most?

   a. Land, labor, capital, and management
   b. Progression, regression, conformity, and contribution
   c. Supply and demand, substitution, surplus, and highest and best use
   d. Government, escheat, eminent domain, and police power

4. Locational data collected during the valuation process would include information on which of the following?

   a. Interest rates
   b. Neighborhood
   c. Deed restrictions
   d. Listings

5. Which study examines an environment of buyers/sellers or landlords/tenants?

   a. Feasibility study
   b. Market study
   c. Marketability study
   d. Trade area analysis

6. The primary purpose of USPAP is to:

    a. promote and maintain the public trust.
    b. create absolute standards and rules that appraisers must follow in all appraisal assignments.
    c. provide minimum standards that appraisers must follow in performing valuation services.
    d. improve the quality of valuation services.

7. Improvements that are outside the confines of the site are called:

    a. onsite improvements.
    b. over improvements.
    c. offsite improvements.
    d. owner improvements.

8. An appraiser who has never appraised a commercial property is asked to appraise a small commercial property. She wants to keep the assignment. She should:

    a. accept the assignment and disclose her lack of experience in the final report.
    b. accept the assignment and perform the appraisal to the best of her ability.
    c. disclose the lack of experience to the client; describe the lack of experience and the steps taken to competently complete the assignment in the report.
    d. accept the assignment and invoke the DEPARTURE RULE, which releases her from any requirement to disclose her incompetence.

9. All of the following are functions of an appraiser who reviews appraisals **except**:

    a. form an opinion about the competency of the original appraiser.
    b. provide an opinion on the data and adjustments.
    c. identify the property being reviewed.
    d. identify the type of review being done.

10. A local tax is levied against a property owner to pay for the paving of a road directly in front of her property. What is this tax called?

    a. Implied easement tax
    b. Special assessment tax
    c. Road improvement tax
    d. Homeowners' tax

11. Which of the following adjustments can not be made using percentage adjustments?

    a. Time
    b. Location
    c. Special conditions
    d. Ownership

12. A two-story office building rents for $16 per square foot. The first floor measures 80 feet by 100 feet. The second story measures 80 feet by 80 feet. What is the annual rent?

    a. $160,000
    b. $124,200
    c. $230,400
    d. $260,800

13. Functional utility is:

    a. the ability of a component or item to perform its intended task.
    b. the test of a shower's water pressure.
    c. more of an issue in dining rooms than in bathrooms.
    d. increased if more expensive equipment is used.

14. Which method of site valuation is rarely used?

    a. Allocation
    b. Land residual
    c. Sales comparison
    d. Ground rent capitalization

15. Which of the following is considered an on-site improvement?

    a. The sidewalk
    b. Landscaping
    c. The street
    d. A connecting utility line

16. The economic principle of _____ states that land and improvements should not be valued on the basis of different uses.

    a. change
    b. conformity
    c. consistent use
    d. contribution

17. Which approach to value should be used when appraising excess land?

    a. Cost approach only
    b. Sales comparison and income approach
    c. Sales comparison and income approach
    d. None of the approaches are appropriate for determining the value of excess land

18. Scarcity, utility, effective purchasing power, and desire relate to:

    a. agents of production.
    b. highest and best use.
    c. supply and demand.
    d. factors that create value.

19. Which of the following property characteristics is important when selecting a comparable to use?

    a. Similar views
    b. Recent sale
    c. Located closest to the subject property
    d. All of the above are important

20. A buyer who is applying for a mortgage asks an appraiser to appraise his property. The appraiser should not concern himself with the:

    a. client's opinions.
    b. tax rate of the subject property.
    c. amount of financing necessary.
    d. evidence that supports constructions costs.

21. Data that the appraiser personally gathers is called:

    a. general data.
    b. specific data.
    c. secondary data.
    d. primary data.

22. An appraiser asks a title company to confirm a sale. The title company confirms the sale as a full value transaction using documentary transfer stamps. The stamps were issued at a rate of $.55 per $500 in value, and they total $308.55. The loan-to-value ratio is 80%, and the buyer didn't assume any pre-existing loans. What was the sales price?

    a. $280,000
    b. $350,000
    c. $561,000
    d. $701,250

23. Which adjustment converts the transaction price of a comparable into a cash equivalent?

    a. Property rights conveyed
    b. Location
    c. Condition of sale
    d. Financing terms

24. Which economic principle normally influences how an improvement, such as a house, should be placed on a site?

    a. Conformity
    b. Allocation
    c. Anticipation
    d. Substitution

25. The concept of consistent use means:

    a. land cannot be used for more than one use.
    b. land must be valued using the values of similar land types.
    c. land cannot be valued based on a use that is different from the improvements.
    d. improvements must be built in a manner that is consistent with those of the surrounding sites.

26. In a highest and best use analysis, the economic principle of _____ would influence the most profitable use of a property.

    a. substitution
    b. supply and demand
    c. change
    d. anticipation

27. Which of the following is true regarding comparables?

    a. They should be located near the subject property
    b. They should be the most similar to the subject property
    c. They may only need a time adjustment
    d. They should have sales prices within 10% of the sales price of the subject property

28. You are appraising an income-producing property and need to estimate its replacement allowance. You should be careful to avoid duplicating replacement items that you may also have included in:

    a. property management fees.
    b. repair and maintenance.
    c. fixed expenses.
    d. insurance accounts.

29. A borrower pays an amount to the lender at the time the loan is created. The payment accounts for the difference between the market interest rate and the lower face rate of the loan. This amount is called the:

    a. loan fee.
    b. discount points.
    c. discount rate.
    d. interest rate fee.

30. Any increase in value that results from a legal non-conforming use is:

    a. directly related to the improvements.
    b. directly related to the marketplace in which the property is located.
    c. directly related to the zoning ordinances.
    d. not considered in a valuation since it does not conform.

31. Why are income and expenses annualized for non-residential properties when using the income approach?

    a. The cap rate is an annual figure
    b. They allow a more accurate estimate of a stabilized income stream to be calculated.
    c. Long term leases are for a period not less than 1 year
    d. Property taxes are always based on an annual figure

32. Which of the following is not the responsibility of a condominium's Homeowners' Association?

    a. Providing a lifeguard at the pool
    b. Landscaping and maintenance
    c. Establishing a private school for residents' children
    d. Providing grounds security

33. Which of the following statements about drainage is **true**?

    a. A swale may be used to channel surface water into a natural drainage area.
    b. Drainage is not necessary if the lot has no slope.
    c. A swale can only be used with homes that are built on hillsides, as swales keep the surface water near the sides of the house to control the flow of water better.
    d. All of the above

34. Excessiveness and inadequacy are both items of:

    a. physical deterioration.
    b. functional inutility.
    c. external obsolescence.
    d. superstructure.

35. The purpose of USPAP is to:

    a. establish requirements for professional appraisal practice.
    b. develop and promulgate new appraisal techniques.
    c. adhere to local laws.
    d. uniformly develop and enforce state appraisal laws.

36. When _____, an alternative use will usually become the highest and best use of a property.

    a. the improvements represent a negative value to the property
    b. the improvements reach a specified chronological age
    c. the alternate provides a greater return on the investment
    d. the alternative uses a greater percentage of the usable land

37. In a net lease, the lessee is normally not responsible for:

    a. property taxes.
    b. insurance.
    c. regular maintenance expenses.
    d. mortgage debt service.

38. What is term for the difference between the present value of an improvement and its reproduction cost new?

    a. Accumulated deterioration
    b. Accrued depreciation
    c. Physical deterioration
    d. Value of the improvement

39. Which of the following factors is most influential in determining which approach(es) to value should be given the greatest weight during the reconciliation step of the appraisal process?

    a. The approach the appraiser is most familiar with
    b. The quantity of primary and secondary data gathered by the appraiser
    c. The nature of the assignment and the quality of available data
    d. The type of property being appraised and the quantity of available data

40. A house burns down and you must determine the replacement cost for the physical items that were lost. What type of value do you need to find?

    a. Salvage value
    b. Value in exchange
    c. Market value
    d. Insurance value

41. The definition of market value includes which of the following?

    a. The highest price
    b. The lowest price
    c. The average price
    d. The most probable price

42. Which of the following factors does an appraiser rely on most when deciding which approach(es) should be given the most weight during the reconciliation step of the appraisal process?

    a. The time it took to finish the assignment and the quantity of data available
    b. The compensation paid by the client and the client's overall importance
    c. The definition of value sought and the quality of available data
    d. The amount of outstanding debt against the property and the value of the surrounding properties

43. When should a highest and best use analysis include both as vacant and as improved statements of value?

    a. When the purpose of the appraisal is highest and best use analysis
    b. Whenever there are two or more possible uses
    c. When the land is valued separately from the improvements
    d. When zoning will change in the future

44. Which of the following is likely to result in an increase in value?

    a. Increase in supply
    b. Decrease in demand
    c. Downzoning
    d. Decrease in interent rates

45. What is the fundamental economic principle that underlies the sales comparison approach?

    a. Contribution
    b. Balance
    c. Surplus productivity
    d. Substitution

46. What is *primary data*?

    a. Data about the property when it was first constructed
    b. Data collected by the appraiser that is not available in published sources
    c. Data that the appraiser relies on most
    d. Data found in publications and other sources

47. An office building sells for $100,000. Its annual straight-line depreciation is $2,500. What will the accumulated depreciation be in three years?

    a. $3,500
    b. $5,250
    c. $7,500
    d. $12,250

48. The only access to a parcel of land is through a back alley. This will most likely cause the property value to:

    a. increase.
    b. decrease.
    c. increase or decrease, depending on the market.
    d. the value would not be impacted by this sort of information.

49. A written instrument that conveys property to a trustee and creates a lien on the real estate that is used as security for the repayment of a debt is called a:

   a. deed of trust.
   b. mortgage.
   c. grant.
   d. easement.

50. An appraiser must consider and analyze any prior sales of the subject property that occurred within what period of time?

   a. Three years for all property types
   b. Two years for one-to-four family residential property and five years for all other property types
   c. One year for one-to-four-family residential property and three years for all other property types
   d. One year for one-to-four family residential property and two years for all other property types

51. When developing an opinion of highest and best use, land is appraised:

   a. as if it is improved.
   b. according to its current use.
   c. as though it is vacant and available for development to its highest and best use.
   d. based on market area trends.

52. Use the following information to answer the question.

   Property A sold six months ago for $80,000, which is 10% above market value.
   Property B sold 3 months ago for $83,000. The buyer paid cash and absorbed a $5,000 tax lien.
   Property C sold 1 year ago for $72,000, which is 10% under market value due to foreclosure on the property.
   Residential property is currently increasing 8% per year

   The current market value for Property B is:

   a. $74,736.
   b. $75,636.
   c. $76,410.
   d. $79,560.

53. Which of the following is a combined supply and demand factor used in market analysis?

   a. Absorption rate
   b. Depreciation rate
   c. Raw land development cost
   d. Financing conditions

54. Which of the following is **not** a description of an appraisal?

   a. supported opinion
   b. objective opinion
   c. unbiased opinion
   d. statement of fact

55. All of the following economic factors affect the value of a property **except**:

   a. the prices of nearby lots.
   b. its tax burden compared to comparable properties.
   c. its utility costs.
   d. easements on the property.

56. What is the formula for calculating *effective gross income*?

   a. Total income less operating expenses
   b. Gross potential income less an allowance for vacancy and collection loss
   c. Total income plus appreciation
   d. Total income if all rentable space is leased

57. The term *plottage* means the:

   a. incremental value created by combining two or more sites to produce greater utility.
   b. value created by subdividing land, surveying it, and mapping it on a plat map.
   c. value of land according to the assessor's office plat maps.
   d. partial value of a piece of land that has been subdivided.

58. What was the original purchase price of a home if the buyer took out an 80% loan-to-value loan with monthly payments of $1,000, an interest rate of 9%, and the loan amortized over 30 years?

   a. $124,282
   b. $155,352
   c. $180,000
   d. $200,000

59. Use the following information to answer the question:

    Comparable 1 1 acre   2 car garage $51,000
    Comparable 2 0.5 acre   1 car garage $46,000
    Comparable 3 0.5 acre   2 car garage $49,000
    Subject 1 acre 1 car garage $

    What is the value of the subject property?

    a. $45,000
    b. $47,000
    c. $48,000
    d. $50,000

60. USPAP contains _____ RULES.

    a. three
    b. five
    c. six
    d. seven

61. Incentive zoning:

    a. controls density and avoids overcrowding by regulating setbacks, building heights, and open space requirements.
    b. permits higher uses to exist on land zoned for lower uses, but not vice versa.
    c. is used as a planning tool to ensure that land is used at its highest and best use.
    d. requires the street-level floors of office buildings to be used for retail establishments.

62. An area has excellent mountain vistas. Which force would it exhibit?

    a. Physical
    b. Social
    c. Economic
    d. Governmental

63. The cost approach is least reliable when appraising:

    a. new construction.
    b. an old structure with severe functional obsolescence.
    c. a single-family residence.
    d. a library.

64. What does interim use refer to?

    a. The original land use
    b. The highest and best use
    c. A temporary use until the property transitions to its highest and best use
    d. A change in a specific zoning area that allows a use that is inconsistent with the zoning classification

65. In considering the highest and best use of a property, the appraiser:

    a. chooses among the different uses determined through his analysis.
    b. selects only one general use that meets the criteria for highest and best use.
    c. never considers the highest and best use of the property as if vacant if there is a structure on the land.
    d. both a and b

66. The mean of a group of values is the same as:

    a. the average.
    b. the middle.
    c. the most common.
    d. the difference between the high and low numbers.

67. The value to a particular investor is known as:

    a. assessed value.
    b. investment value.
    c. going concern value.
    d. liquidation value.

68. An appraiser must retain a workfile for at least:

    a. 5 years after preparation or at least 2 years after final disposition of judicial proceedings in which testimony was given, whichever period expires last.
    b. 3 years after preparation or at least 1 year after final disposition of judicial proceedings in which testimony was given, whichever period expires last.
    c. 3 years after preparation or at least 5 years after final disposition of judicial proceedings in which testimony was given, whichever period expires last.
    d. 5 years, regardless of the result of the report or any testimony for a judicial proceeding.

69. Which standard of USPAP deals with real property appraisal reporting?

    a. STANDARD 1
    b. STANDARD 2
    c. STANDARD 3
    d. none of the above

70. The condition of the subject property affects which of the following?

    a. Actual age
    b. Effective age
    c. The cost approach
    d. Both b and c

71. A mortgage in which the interest rate moves with an indexed rate is called a(n):

    a. package mortgage.
    b. adjustable rate mortgage.
    c. fixed rate mortgage.
    d. reverse mortgage.

72. A lease creates two interests, one of which is the leased fee estate. Which party to the lease holds the leased fee estate?

    a. Lessor
    b. Lessee
    c. Mortgagee
    d. Fiduciary

73. Does USPAP require every appraisal report to include a complete legal description of the subject property?

    a. Yes, Standards Rule 2-1 requires a complete and accurate legal description
    b. No, USPAP Rule 2-2 requires sufficient information to identify the real estate
    c. Yes, if the report does not include a complete legal description of the subject property, the report is considered an incomplete appraisal
    d. It depends on the intended use of the appraisal report

74. The data collected for an appraisal that encompasses all of the four forces would be:

    a. general data.
    b. specific data.
    c. secondary data.
    d. primary data.

75. According to the ETHICS RULE, an appraiser may accept a referral fee, management fee, commission, or anything of value in connection with obtaining an assignment as long as the appraiser:

    a. arrives at the desired opinion of value.
    b. adheres to all other requirements of the ETHICS RULE.
    c. does not tell anyone about the fee.
    d. discloses the fee in the appraisal report.

76. The economic principle that is associated with receiving future benefits from owning or leasing land is:

    a. anticipation.
    b. contribution.
    c. change.
    d. competition.

77. Which adjustment takes into account the differences in ownership between the subject property and the comparable?

    a. location
    b. financing terms
    c. property rights conveyed
    d. physical characteristics

78. What is the value to a specific owner or occupant?

    a. Value in use
    b. Market value
    c. Going concern value
    d. Liquidation value

79. An investor requires a 10% rate of return to invest in a building. The building is expected to have a remaining economic life of 25 years. What is the appropriate building capitalization rate, using the straight-line method?

    a. 11%
    b. 11.4%
    c. 13%
    d. 14%

80. What is the term for income from a property or business, after deducting operating expenses, but before deducting income taxes and financing expenses?

    a. Net effective income
    b. Cash flow
    c. Effective gross income
    d. Net operating income

81. Which of the following will most affect the marketability of a property?

    a. Economic potential of the community
    b. Income potential of the property
    c. Economic history of the community
    d. Financing available to the property owner

82. Appraisers use _____ to determine the age of improvements.

   a. tax assessor's records
   b. the age-life method
   c. the owner's assertion
   d. the legal description of the property

83. Which of the following is an example of an involuntary conveyance of title?

   a. A will
   b. An encumbrance
   c. A mortgage
   d. A condemnation

84. What is the area of a right triangle if its hypotenuse is 5 feet and one leg is 4 feet?

   a. 6 square feet
   b. 10 square feet
   c. 20 square feet
   d. Not enough information is given to solve the problem

85. Which of the following is **true** of a fixed expense?

   a. It varies with vacancy.
   b. It varies with gross income.
   c. It varies with effective gross income.
   d. It is not affected by income or other expense factors.

86. An appraiser is determining if a property suffers from functional obsolescence. She should:

   a. determine the age-life ratio of the improvements.
   b. consider the remaining life of the short lived improvements.
   c. use the comparative unit method.
   d. compare the utility and function of the subject property with that of other properties in the neighborhood.

87. A subject property has a pool and a comparable does not: On what does an appraiser base his adjustments for the pool?

   a. The appraiser's opinion
   b. The lender's rate
   c. The market's reaction
   d. The builder's cost

88. An old, run-down house with a limited economic life stands on a site that is zoned for commercial use. This is an example of:

    a. adverse use.
    b. variance.
    c. interim use.
    d. exception.

89. What is the term for a single mortgage that is obtained for more than one parcel of real estate?

    a. Blanket mortgage
    b. Dual mortgage
    c. Wraparound mortgage
    d. Transferable mortgage

90. When an appraiser is reviewing data, he does not need to verify:

    a. the reported price and terms.
    b. the old mortgage information.
    c. the rate of depreciation.
    d. the physical measurements.

91. Which of the following is **true** of construction materials and techniques?

    a. They change over the years
    b. They vary based on the builder's mood
    c. They remain the same
    d. They don't impact the value of the property

92. How many acres are in one section?

    a. 1 acre
    b. 43,560 acres
    c. 640 acres
    d. 36 acres

93. An appraiser considers all of the following when analyzing the physical characteristics of a lot **except**:

    a. whether it is an inside lot or a corner lot.
    b. whether it is a rectangular lot or an odd-shaped lot.
    c. the presence of storm sewers.
    d. the extent of landscaping.

94. The Appraisal Subcommittee's activities are funded by:

    a. the U.S. Government.
    b. The Appraisal Foundation.
    c. a collection of registry fees from state licensed and certified appraisers.
    d. fines paid by appraisers who violate USPAP.

95. Which of the following is normally true of houses that are listed substantially above market price?

    a. They will sell before other competing properties.
    b. They will eventually sell given enough time on the open market.
    c. They will not be subject to the principle of substitution.
    d. They will not sell despite adequate market exposure and time.

96. The URAR is most appropriately used for which of the following?

    a. An individual condo in an urban area
    b. A school in an inner-city area
    c. An office complex in a suburban area
    d. A museum

97. Which of the following often requires more than one adjustment?

    a. Financing terms
    b. Special conditions
    c. Physical characteristics
    d. Location

98. Dollar or percentage adjustments should reflect:

    a. previous sales.
    b. similarities.
    c. differences.
    d. market trends.

99. Which of the following is an economic factor that influences value?

    a. Employment trends
    b. Birth rates
    c. Attitudes towards education
    d. Population change

100. Land should be appraised:

   a. as though fully developed.
   b. as if available for development to its highest and best use.
   c. such that any improvements are valued based on their contribution to the site.
   d. both b and c

101. Which element of value requires the presence of financial ability as well as the need or desire for a product or service?

   a. Demand
   b. Competition
   c. Increasing and decreasing returns
   d. Balance

102. The Department of Defense developed the King's Bay Submarine Base in southeastern Georgia to build nuclear submarines. Which of the four forces does this represent?

   a. Environmental
   b. Economic
   c. Governmental
   d. Social

103. What is the term for improvements to a site that extend over the site's property line onto an adjacent property?

   a. A license
   b. An encumbrance
   c. An easement
   d. An encroachment

104. Some areas in Southern California have been adversely affected by civil disobedience, crime, and illegal immigration. Which of the four forces are these part of?

   a. Environmental
   b. Economic
   c. Governmental
   d. Social

105. Which of the following is not considered general data?

   a. Comparable sales
   b. Environmental regulations
   c. Zoning ordinances
   d. Consumer price index

106. Matched pair analysis is typically used in which appraisal method?

    a. Allocation
    b. Extraction
    c. Sales comparison
    d. Subdivision method

107. What is the term for a quality or feature of a property that brings its owner satisfaction and non-monetary benefits?

    a. Amenity
    b. Improvement
    c. Asset
    d. Annuity

108. When making a series of adjustments in sequence, the appraiser adjusts for which of the following first?

    a. Special conditions
    b. Special financing
    c. Location
    d. Physical characteristics

109. A below-grade site needs $1,000 of repairs to bring it up to grade, as well as a sidewalk that will cost $900. Three properties that had similar repairs sold 5 months ago for $18,000 each. If the annual inflation rate is 6%, what is the subject property's value?

    a. $16,500
    b. $16,550
    c. $18,500
    d. $19,950

110. If a 30 year $100,000 straight note mortgage has an interest rate of 8%, what will the loan balance be after five years?

    a. $36,190
    b. $83,333
    c. $95,074
    d. $100,000

Practice Exam 1

Score Chart

Category	Questions	Score
Influences on Real Estate Value	44, 62, 99, 102, 104	
Legal Considerations in Appraisal	10, 37, 61, 72, 83	
Types of Value	40, 41, 49, 67, 78	
Economic Principles	2, 16, 18, 24, 45, 76, 101	
Real Estate Markets and Analysis	3, 5, 21, 29, 53, 74, 85, 105	
Valuation Process	4, 9, 17, 39, 42, 46, 96, 100	
Property Description	13, 15, 33, 34, 48, 55, 71, 91, 92, 103, 107	
Highest and Best Use Analysis	25, 26, 30, 36, 43, 64, 65, 88	
Appraisal Statistical Concepts	22, 52, 58, 66, 84, 109, 110	
Sales Comparison Approach	11, 19, 23, 27, 59, 77, 87, 89, 90, 95, 97, 98	
Site Value	7, 14, 57, 93, 106, 108	
Cost Approach	38, 47, 63, 70, 82, 86	
Income Approach	12, 28, 31, 56, 79, 80, 85	
Valuation of Partial Interests	32	
Appraisal Standards and Ethics	1, 6, 8, 20, 35, 50, 51, 54, 60, 68, 69, 73, 75, 94	

070804

Answers

1. (a) An intended user is the client and any other party identified as a user of the appraisal by the appraiser on the basis of communication with the client at the time of the assignment.

2. (a) Deed restrictions, zoning, and government regulations may not conform to current market requirements, so the site may remain undeveloped to its highest and best use.

3. (c) Supply and demand, substitution, surplus, and highest and best use are all basic principles of value. Land, labor, capital, and management are the four agents of production, not value. Progression, regression, conformity, and contribution have to do with how the type and quality of a surrounding neighborhood can affect the value of a house. Government, escheat, eminent domain, and police power are all types or aspects of the government's right to take land.

4. (b) Locational data includes information about the region, community, and neighborhood. This includes information on population characteristics, price levels, and employment opportunities.

5. (b) By definition.

6. (a) The primary objective of USPAP is to promote and maintain a high level of public trust in professional appraisal practice.

7. (c) By definition.

8. (c) The COMPTENCY RULE requires an appraiser who lacks sufficient knowledge or experience to competently complete an assignment to disclose the lack of knowledge and/or experience to the client before accepting the assignment. The appraiser must also take the steps necessary or appropriate to complete the assignment competently, and describe in the appraisal report the lack of knowledge and/or experience and the steps taken to complete the assignment competently.

9. (a) According to Standards Rule 3-1, a reviewer may form an opinion of the completeness of the report, the quality of work, and the adequacy of the report, but not on the competency of the appraiser.

10. (b) A special assessment tax is imposed only against those parcels of property that will benefit from a proposed public improvement.

11. (d) Percentages are often used to express the differences between a subject property and a comparable sale. This is especially true for time, special conditions, and location adjustments. Residential appraisals use sales price as the unit of comparison, and the adjustments are made in dollars, not percentages.

12. (c) [(80 x 100) + (80 x 80)] x 16 = 230,400

13. (a) By definition.

14. (b) By definition.

15. (b) Off-site improvements are located outside the confines of the site and include streets, curbs, gutters, sidewalks, storm sewer drains, and connecting utility lines. On-site improvements include landscaping, paving, utility lines, grading, etc. [Property Description]

16. (c) The principle of consistent use states that land may not be valued on the basis of one use while the improvements are valued on the basis of a different use.

17. (b) Both the sales comparison approach and the income approach can be used for considering the value of excess land. The cost approach cannot be used to obtain a value for land.

18. (d) By definition.

19. (d) All of the above characteristics are important to consider when selecting comparables.

20. (a) An appraiser cannot let the opinions or value desired by the client, lender, owner, or any other individual influence the appraisal.

21. (d) By definition.

22. (a) The stamps are calculated as $0.55 per $500 of new money. 561 x 0.55 = $280,000. It represents the entire transaction amount and not just the loan amount-- there were no loans assumed.

23. (d) The financing terms adjustment converts the transaction price of the comparable into its cash equivalent or modifies it to match the financing terms of the subject property.

24. (a) The principle of conformity states that residential houses should be similar in design, construction, age, condition, and market appeal. A property's conformity influences its value. Non-conformity may be an advantage or disadvantage to the property owner.

25. (c) According to the concept of consistent use, land cannot be valued based on a use that is different from its improvements. When an appraiser is analyzing a property's highest and best use, the improvements must contribute to the land value in order to have a value themselves. Improvements that do not contribute to land value may have an interim use or a negative value.

26. (c) Change impacts the most profitable use of a property because land use is constantly changing.

27. (b) Regardless of the other factors, the comps should be the most similar.

28. (b) Replacement allowances may often be mistakenly placed in with the repair and maintenance category. An appraiser must analyze all expenses carefully to avoid duplicating certain items or not counting them at all.

29. (b) Discount points are fees paid to a lender to compensate for the difference between the market interest rate and the contract or face rate of a loan.

30. (a) Usually, any benefit that a non-conforming use may bring to a property's value is directly related to the improvements.

31. (b) Residential properties are appraised using monthly income and expenses. Non-residential properties are appraised using annualized expenses. This is done to calculate a more accurate estimate of a stabilized income stream, regardless of seasonal variations in occupancy and one-time expenses such as major repairs or tax bills. These expenses could affect a single month's income.

32. (c) A Homeowners' Association is responsible for the governance of the condominium and maintenance of the common areas. Establishing private schools is not one of its responsibilities.

33. (a) Surface and storm water must be drained from property in some way. A swale that channels water off the surface of the lot to the street or into some natural drainage is a common and effective solution.

34. (b) By definition. Gold faucets in the bathroom or too few bathrooms in the house could both be examples of functional inutility.

35. (a) The purpose of USPAP is to establish requirements for professional appraisal practice, which includes appraisal, appraisal review, and appraisal consulting.

36. (a) When no value may be attributed to a property's improvements or they represent a negative value to the property, an alternative use will usually become the highest and best use.

Practice Exam 1 - Answers

37. (d) Under a net lease, the lessee is usually not responsible for the mortgage debt service. The landlord usually pays this.

38. (b) Accrued depreciation is the difference between the present value of an improvement and its reproduction cost new.

39. (c) An appraiser must consider both the nature of the assignment and the quality of the available data when determining which approach or approaches to value must be given the greatest weight.

40. (d) The insurance carrier will pay whatever the insurable value (amount on the policy) is, regardless of the market value.

41. (d) Market value is defined as the most probable price real estate should bring in a sale occurring under normal market conditions.

42. (c) When reconciling, the appraiser reviews his or her work and considers at least four factors: 1) the definition of value sought, 2) the amount and reliability of the data collected in each approach, 3) the inherent strengths and weaknesses of each approach, and 4) the relevance of each approach to the subject property and market behavior.

43. (c) Each parcel of real estate may have one highest and best use of the land or site as though vacant and a different highest and best use of the property as improved.

44. (d) Reduction in interest rates lowers payments and enables more sebt service, which in turn enables higher prices at the same payment cost.

45. (d) According to the principle of substitution, the maximum value of an item is established by determining the cost of acquiring an equally desirable substitute. This is the basis for the sales comparison approach.

46. (b) Primary data is any data the appraiser collects or compiles himself, even if the data does not directly affect the property's value. Data that was prepared by someone other than the appraiser, such as information in publications and other sources, is called secondary data.

47. (c) 3 x $2,500 per year = $7,500.

48. (c) Access via a back alley or a special service road may add to or detract from value, depending on the market.

49. (a) A deed of trust legally conveys property to a trustee who holds it as security for the repayment of a debt.

50. (c) An appraiser must analyze prior sales of the subject property that occurred in the previous three years for all property types.

51. (c) When developing an opinion of highest and best use, the appraiser must appraise the land as though vacant and available for development to its highest and best use.

52. (d) Subtract the tax lien from the price of the property to get the market value 3 months ago. $83,000 − $5,000 = $78,000. Add 2% to the old market value to get the current market value (8% per year divided by 1/4 year). $78,000 × 1.02 = $79,560.

53. (d) The combined supply and demand factors that are used in market analysis include business, employment, income, and financing conditions.

54. (d) An appraisal is an appropriately supported, objective, and unbiased opinion of value of a property, as of a specific date that is made by a qualified person who has no undisclosed interest in the property.

55. (d) The value of a property might be affected by prices of nearby properties, its tax burden compared to comparable lots, its utility costs, and service costs. Easements may impact the property value, but they are not an economic factor.

56. (b) Effective gross income is calculated by subtracting vacancy and collection loss from gross potential income.

57. (a) Plottage refers to the incremental value created by combining two or more sites to produce greater utility. The joining of the sites does not necessarily produce incremental value, it must also create greater utility.

58. (b) Using the 9% monthly table for a 30 year loan from column 5, since this is an annuity to the lender, the factor is 124.281866. Multiplying the factor by the payment amount of $1,000 equals $124,281.86. This, however, is the loan amount, which is only 80% of the purchase price, so 124,281.86 divided by 0.8 equals $155,352.

59. (c) A matched pair analysis between Comp 2 and Comp 3 shows a $3,000 adjustment for the garage space; which is then applied to Comp 1 to result in an adjusted value for the Subject Property of $48,000. An analysis of Comp 1 and Comp 3 shows a $2,000 adjustment for the difference in site area. When applied to Comp 2 this also indicates an adjusted value for the Subject Property of $48,000.

60. (b) USPAP contains five RULES: the ETHICS RULE, the COMPETENCY RULE, the DEPARTURE RULE, the JURISDICTIONAL EXCEPTION RULE, and the SUPPLEMENTAL STANDARDS RULE.

Practice Exam 1 - Answers

61. (d) Incentive zoning requires the street-level floors of office buildings to be used for retail establishments. It often allows a developer to exceed zoning restrictions in exchange for the additional retail space.

62. (a) By definition.

63. (b) An old structure with a lot of functional obsolescence requires the appraiser to estimate of a significant amount of depreciation. This produces a large margin of error and decreased reliability.

64. (c) Interim use refers to a temporary use of a property until that property transitions to its highest and best use. A good example is vacant land that is awaiting development.

65. (d) There may be more than one highest and best use that yields a similar net return.

66. (a) The mean is the same as the average. The units are added and divided by the number of units.

67. (b) By definition

68. (a) An appraiser must retain a workfile for at least five years after preparation, or at least two years after final disposition of any judicial proceeding in which the appraiser provided testimony related to the assignment, whichever expires last.

69. (b) STANDARD 2 addresses the reporting of real property appraisals.

70. (d) When the property's condition affects the effective age, it also impacts the cost approach because it impacts depreciation.

71. (b) By definition.

72. (a) The lessor, or owner, holds the leased fee estate and conveys the leasehold estate to the tenant.

73. (b) Standards Rule 2-2 (a) (iii) requires the appraiser to describe information that is sufficient to identify the real estate involved in the appraisal, including the physical and economic property characteristics that are relevant to the assignment.

74. (a) By definition.

75. (d) An appraiser must disclose any fees, commissions, or things of value that are connected to the procurement of an assignment in the certification and in any transmittal letter in which the conclusions are stated.

76. (a) According to the principle of anticipation, value is created by the expectation of benefits to be derived in the future.

77. (c) The adjustment for the property rights conveyed takes into account the differences in legal estate between the subject property and the comparable.

78. (a) By definition

79. (d) First you need to find the recapture rate using the formula: 100%/years of useful life = annual recapture rate. 100/25 = 4% recapture rate. Add this to the required return on investment of 10% to equal 14%.

80. (d) Net operating income = gross income − operating expenses.

81. (a) A major limiting factor affecting the market value of real estate is the economic potential of the community where it is located.

82. (a) Tax assessors' records are the best source of information to determine the age of improvements.

83. (d) The government has the right to force an involuntary conveyance or take title of private land for public benefit. This process is called condemnation. Just compensation is due to the property owner. All of the other choices are voluntary conveyances.

84. (a) The area of a triangle is half of the product of the sides. One side is 4 feet. The other side is 3 since it is the square root of the difference between the hypotenuse squared (25) and one leg squared (16), or 9. 3 x 4 = 12 / 2 = 6.

85. (d) Fixed expenses do not vary according to the vacancy rate or other factors.

86. (d) Functional obsolescence is a feature or improvement that is undesirable or unnecessary, or one that is desirable in the marketplace, but the property lacks. To determine functional obsolescence, the appraiser should compare the subject property's improvements and features against those of other properties in the surrounding or comparable area.

87. (c) An adjustment for differences between the subject property and a comparable is based on a typical buyer's reaction to the difference.

88. (c) Interim use is a temporary use of a property while it awaits transition to its highest and best use. Since the current use is not legally permitted due to the zoning classification, it cannot qualify as the property's highest and best use. Once the home is demolished, a commercial property must be constructed there.

Practice Exam 1 - Answers

89. (a) A blanket mortgage covers more than one parcel of real estate. It is often used for subdivisions and condominiums.

90. (b) The appraiser must verify facts concerning the comparables, such as depreciation, measurements, and reported price and terms.

91. (a) Construction materials and techniques change along with new discoveries and technology. They are also affected by changing consumer preferences.

92. (c) One section contains 640 acres.

93. (d) When analyzing the physical characteristics of a lot, the items an appraiser considers include whether it is an inside lot or a corner lot, rectangular lot or an odd-shaped lot, the if there is storm water disposal, and whether it is a flat lot or a sloping lot or one that drops off significantly. However, landscaping is not considered.

94. (c) The Appraisal Subcommittee is funded by the registration fees paid by certified or licensed appraisers.

95. (d) Houses that are listed substantially above market value usually do not sell, regardless of how long they are offered for sale.

96. (a) The URAR is most appropriate for residential properties.

97. (c) There is often more than one physical characteristic that requires adjustment.

98. (c) Adjustments may be made to reflect the dollar or percentage value of the noted differences.

99. (a) While employment trends are economic factors that influence value, all of the others are social factors that influence value.

100. (d) According to Standards Rule 1-3 (b), an appraiser must develop an opinion of highest and best use of the real estate. He or she must appraise the property as though vacant and available for development to its highest and best use, and that the appraisal of improvements is based on their actual contribution to the site.

101. (a) Demand is defined as the desire for a good or service, accompanied by the financial ability to purchase it.

102. (c) By definition.

103. (d) An encroachment is an improvement that extends over the property line onto an adjacent property.

104. (d) By definition.

105. (a) General data helps an appraiser understand the influence of the four forces of value (social, economic, governmental, and environmental) on a property's value. The forces all originate outside the property. Comparable sales fall under specific data, which includes details about the property being appraised, comparable sales and rental properties, and relevant local market characteristics.

106. (c) By definition.

107. (a) An amenity is a quality of a property, which may be tangible or intangible, that brings the owner satisfaction and non-monetary benefits, such as a view, location, or recreational facilities.

108. (b) Adjustments are made in the following order: special financing, special conditions, market conditions, location, and physical characteristics.

109. (b) To find the inflation rate, divide 6% by 12 (months in a year) and multiply the result by 5 (months since the comps were sold). 0.06 ÷ 12) × 5 = 0.025. Multiply the comparable price of $18,000 by 0.025 to get $450. This is the inflation rate for the comparables' sales price. Add the inflation rate to the comparables' sales price: 450 + 18,000 = $18,450. Finally, to determine the property's value, subtract the costs incurred to bring the subject up to grade: $18,450 − $1,900 = $16,550.

110. (d) A straight note calls for the periodic payment of interest only. At any time in the mortgage, the balance is the original loan amount.

Practice Exam 2

1. An appraiser should include a complete legal description of the property in which of the following sections of an appraisal report?

    a. Addenda
    b. Definition of the problem
    c. Highest and best use analysis
    d. Site identification

2. Which term is defined as land that is not necessary for the principal improvements on a parcel of land?

    a. Excess land
    b. Superadequacy
    c. Residual land
    d. Plottage

3. In order for a use to be considered highest and best, it must:

    a. reduce ad valorem taxes.
    b. use the largest percentage of the available land.
    c. be a profitable and legal use.
    d. result in a high gross potential income.

4. A feasibility analysis is:

    a. a study of the cost-benefit relationship of an economic endeavor.
    b. a detailed study of the asset depreciation of a development.
    c. an analysis of a site's zoning and topography.
    d. none of the above

5. What is directive zoning?

    a. Zoning that controls density and avoids overcrowding by regulating setbacks, building heights, and open space requirements
    b. A change in the local zoning ordinance permitting a particular use that is inconsistent with the zoning classification of the area
    c. Zoning used as a planning tool to ensure that land is used at its highest and best use
    d. Zoning that permits higher uses to exist on land zoned for lower uses, but not vice versa

6. Which type of entity is created to hold title to property in cooperative interest ownership?

    a. Corporation
    b. Partnership
    c. Condominium association
    d. Board of trustees

7. What element(s) must be present for value to exist?

    a. Utility alone
    b. Scarcity alone
    c. Both utility and scarcity
    d. None of the above

8. In 1986, the Tax Reform Act eliminated many of the tax advantages for passive real estate investors. Which of the four forces does this represent?

    a. Environmental
    b. Economic
    c. Governmental
    d. Social

9. What is unique about joint tenancy?

    a. Each owner has equal possession
    b. Each owner may will their interest
    c. Right of survivorship
    d. Each joint tenant may sell their interest

10. An appraiser who is determining property value may not base it on the principle of:

    a. supply and demand.
    b. surplus productivity.
    c. increasing and decreasing returns.
    d. balance.

11. Which of the following roof types slopes on four sides?

    a. Gable
    b. Gambrel
    c. Hip
    d. Mansard

12. For a commercial business, a corner lot provides:

    a. more sunlight.
    b. greater privacy.
    c. better access and exposure.
    d. increased site depth.

13. Insurable value is based on:

    a. replacement or reproduction cost.
    b. tax potential.
    c. market behavior.
    d. investment potential.

14. Which of the following is considered an off-site improvement?

    a. A detached garage
    b. A swimming pool off the back deck
    c. Landscaping, grading, and paving
    d. Curbs, gutters, and storm sewer drains

15. Which of the following types of zoning is used as a planning tool?

    a. Bulk
    b. Directive
    c. Incentive
    d. Aesthetic

16. Which organization has final authority over USPAP and any changes to USPAP?

    a. The Appraisal Subcommittee
    b. The Appraisal Qualifications Board
    c. FNMA
    d. The Appraisal Standards Board

17. By using the income approach, an appraiser can estimate value by applying an overall capitalization rate to:

    a. net operating expenses.
    b. net operating income.
    c. effective gross income.
    d. gross income.

18. If applicable, during which step of the appraisal process is income capitalization performed?

    a. Scope of work
    b. Data collection
    c. Application of approaches to value
    d. Reconciliation

19. The highest and best use of _____ is a future use.

    a. non-conforming land
    b. subdivided land
    c. special purpose property
    d. commercial property

20. An appraiser is using the sales comparison approach and is searching for comparables. Which of the following is least important?

    a. Square footage
    b. Lot size
    c. Room count
    d. Sales price

21. An appraiser's compensation must not be influenced by:

    a. the amount of effort required to complete the assignment.
    b. the value estimated in the appraisal.
    c. the expenses paid by the appraiser to complete the assignment.
    d. the time required to complete the appraisal.

22. A special purpose property's highest and best use is probably:

    a. a projected future use.
    b. as developed.
    c. its present use.
    d. a different zoning classification.

23. Is an appraiser performing a review appraisal required to explain why he or she disagrees with the original appraiser?

    a. Yes
    b. Only if the original appraiser failed to invoke the DEPARTURE RULE
    c. No, because the reviewer is expected to find flaws in the original appraisal
    d. There is no such requirement

24. In a neighborhood full of well maintained homes, a poorly maintained home is an example of:

    a. substitution.
    b. progression.
    c. regression.
    d. competition.

25. Special purpose properties should be valued based on which two highest and best uses?

    a. Value in use and value in exchange
    b. Value in use and investment value
    c. Value in exchange and investment value
    d. Interim use and speculative use

26. If an appraiser describes the process of collecting, confirming, and reporting data, he is completing which of the following?

    a. A restricted appraisal report
    b. A self-contained appraisal report
    c. A summary appraisal report
    d. None of the above

27. The term *plottage* means the:

    a. incremental value created by combining two or more sites to produce greater utility.
    b. value created by subdividing land, surveying it, and mapping it on a plat map.
    c. value of land according to the assessor's office plat maps.
    d. partial value of a piece of land that has been subdivided.

28. What does an appraiser need in order to obtain an accurate view of the marketplace and its activity?

    a. To locate a sufficient number of sales to determine a market pattern
    b. To know the standard deviation
    c. To know the sales history of the neighborhood in order to determine a market pattern
    d. To determine the sales average of surrounding properties

29. Which RULE is violated by a misleading or fraudulent appraisal review report?

    a. SUPPLEMENTAL STANDARDS RULE
    b. JURISDICTIONAL EXCEPTION RULE
    c. COMPETENCY RULE
    d. ETHICS RULE

30. Which of the following will decrease as a result of excess competition?

    a. Market interest
    b. Utility
    c. Profit
    d. Demand

31. The term GIM refers to:

    a. gross income modifier.
    b. gross income multiplier.
    c. general income multiplier.
    d. general investment manager.

32. What is the term for a series of equal periodic payments or receipts on an investment?

    a. Debt service
    b. Annuity
    c. Interest
    d. Capitalization

33. In most definitions of market value, adjustments must be made to comparable properties for:

    a. special types of financing.
    b. closing fees paid by the buyer.
    c. costs the seller is required to pay.
    d. all of the above

34. An appraiser should review the appraisal objective and the legal interests being appraised during reconciliation because:

    a. the three approaches may result in greatly varying conclusions, which indicates an error in the appraisal process.
    b. the market value will vary depending on the investor.
    c. the value may vary greatly depending on the interest being appraised or the definition of use.
    d. the appraiser should tailor the conclusion of value on the financing needs of the client.

35. An appraiser uses the abstraction method to determine the average annual amount of depreciation, which is indicated by the comparable properties sold. To find this information, the appraiser:

    a. multiplies the total depreciation by economic life.
    b. divides the average annual amount of depreciation by physical life.
    c. divides the total depreciation by effective age.
    d. multiplies the chronological age by total depreciation.

36. Use the following information to answer the question:

    Comparable 1 1 acre   2 car garage $51,000
    Comparable 2 0.5 acre   1 car garage $46,000
    Comparable 3 0.5 acre   2 car garage $49,000
    Subject   1 acre   1 car garage $

    If an appraiser performed a matched pairs analysis, what would she adjust for?

    a. + $2,000 for garage, − $3,000 for lot size
    b. − $2,000 for garage, + $3,000 for lot size
    c. + $2,000 for lot size, − $3,000 for garage
    d. − $2,000 for garage, + $3,000 for lot size

37. Which form of legal description is based on a recorded map or survey?

    a. government survey
    b. metes and bounds
    c. lot and block system
    d. geodetic survey

38. An appraiser who conducts a review appraisal and signs an appraisal report prepared by another:

    a. is not responsible for the contents of the report.
    b. must have written at least 35% of the report.
    c. must have physically inspected the property.
    d. is fully responsible for the contents of the report.

39. An appraiser may use _____ to estimate the value of a finished lot.

    a. the developer's estimates of sales price
    b. appropriate comparables from existing subdivisions
    c. sales prices from unadjusted raw land
    d. current interest rates

40. Which of the following roof types is double pitched on two sides?

    a. Gable
    b. Gambrel
    c. Hip
    d. Mansard

41. What is the definition of 'capitalization' as it is used in appraising?

    a. The initial funds invested in a project
    b. The process of converting net income into an estimate of value
    c. The value resulting from any one of the three approaches
    d. The process of calculating the amount of capital available for investment

42. A comparable property was sold subject to a special assessment. The subject property is not subject to such an assessment. What should the appraiser do?

    a. Make no adjustment.
    b. Make an adjustment to the comparable property.
    c. Make an adjustment if the assessment is greater than $5,000.
    d. Make an adjustment if the assessment is greater than $10,000.

43. The cost approach is most reliable when used on:

    a. new or newer structures.
    b. older, seasoned properties.
    c. income properties.
    d. vacant land.

44. A comparable sold 1 year ago for $300,000. Since then, values have declined 8%. The comparable had creative financing that is recognized in the market and in favor of the buyer by 5%.

    > Time Adjustment: –8%
    > Financing Adjustment: –5%

    What is the adjusted sales price of this comparable?

    a. $262,200
    b. $289,800
    c. $307,800
    d. $340,200

45. Trisha deposits $6,707 annually and accumulates $117,700 over 10 years. What was her interest rate?

   a. 10.6%
   b. 12.0%
   c. 12.4%
   d. 13.0%

46. If an area is known to have a high crime rate, it is an example of a(n):

   a. social force.
   b. governmental force.
   c. economic force.
   d. environmental force.

47. Reinforced concrete is concrete that:

   a. contains additional mortar.
   b. contains less water.
   c. contains steel.
   d. is thicker.

48. Which of the following is considered the key to the sales comparison approach?

   a. Market abstraction of the adjustments
   b. Accurate physical measurements
   c. Accurate adjustments
   d. Selection of appropriate comparables

49. Which term refers to the lump sum that an investor receives at the termination of an investment?

   a. Return
   b. Reversion
   c. Rate
   d. Capital

50. In the straight-line method of estimating depreciation, the appraiser:

   a. calculates the economic obsolescence.
   b. disregards the economic life of the property.
   c. compares the structure's effective age with its total economic life.
   d. provides for the recapture of depreciation by allowing for accruals.

51. Regression analysis may solve which of the following problems for an appraiser?

    a. Doubling up on adjustments
    b. Missing information or data
    c. Excessive adjustments
    d. Inaccurate adjustments

52. Appraisal practice is best described as:

    a. performed only by an appraiser.
    b. valuation services performed by an individual acting as an appraiser, but not limited to appraisal, appraisal review, or appraisal consulting.
    c. valuation services performed by an individual acting as an appraiser.
    d. valuation services performed only by an appraiser and limited to appraisal review or appraisal consulting.

53. Which of the following is correct regarding the reconciliation process?

    a. The appraiser should average all the approaches to value to reach his conclusion of value.
    b. The appraiser should only use the results from the approaches that provide the most favorable conclusions of value.
    c. The appraiser should consider the relationship between the final value estimate and market expectations.
    d. The appraiser should consider the relationship between the market data and market perceptions.

54. What does the term *ad valorem* mean?

    a. Additional value
    b. According to value
    c. According to sales price
    d. Additional tax

55. When performing an appraisal review, an appraiser may evaluate all of the following **except**:

    a. the quality of another appraiser's work.
    b. the analysis in an appraisal consulting report.
    c. the relevance of another appraiser's work.
    d. the competency of another appraiser.

56. San Diego is known for its mild climate and beautiful beaches on the Pacific Coast. Which of the four forces are these part of?

   a. Environmental
   b. Economic
   c. Governmental
   d. Social

57. Which of the following is general data that an appraiser should consider when performing an appraisal?

   a. Economic influences
   b. Gross potential income
   c. Comparable sales
   d. Building cost history

58. When an appraiser describes his opinion of the highest and best use of the real estate he is completing which of the following?

   a. A restricted appraisal report
   b. A self-contained appraisal report
   c. A summary appraisal report
   d. A letter report

59. When speaking of statistics, a *population* is:

   a. the number of people who live in a specific city.
   b. the number of people who live in a region.
   c. a complete data set.
   d. a portion of a data set.

60. Of the following, which is one of the four criteria of highest and best use?

   a. Cost
   b. Functionally feasible
   c. Effective purchasing power
   d. Financially feasible

61. Which study examines the profitability of a proposed property?

   a. Feasibility study
   b. Market study
   c. Marketability study
   d. Trade area analysis

62. An appraiser might include all of the following as part of a site's cost **except**:

    a. cost of grading.
    b. cost of maintenance.
    c. cost of utility connections.
    d. cost of landscaping.

63. The process of compounding interest is the opposite of the process of:

    a. calculating simple interest.
    b. discounting interest.
    c. adjusting interest.
    d. annualizing interest.

64. What is the fundamental economic principle that underlies the sales comparison approach?

    a. Contribution
    b. Balance
    c. Surplus productivity
    d. Substitution

65. An office building is valued at $100,000 and has a net income of $10,000. If the net income remains the same, but the capitalization rate increases by one full percentage point, what would the estimate of value be?

    a. $19,111
    b. $90,909
    c. $91,019
    d. $190,010

66. Which section of USPAP describes the overall structure of USPAP?

    a. Advisory Opinions
    b. DEPARTURE RULE
    c. DEFINITIONS
    d. PREAMBLE

67. Which of the following is a consideration when determining highest and best use?

    a. Physically possible
    b. Legally permissible
    c. Financially feasible
    d. All of the above

68. A children's boutique located in a neighborhood shopping center leases for $500 per month, plus 2% of the gross sales over $50,000. What were the gross sales for the year if the total rent paid for the year is $8,000?

    a. $100,000
    b. $150,000
    c. $175,000
    d. $200,000

69. What is the definition of highest and best use?

    a. The legally permissible, physically possible, economically feasible, and maximally productive use
    b. The legally permissible, environmentally sound, maximally productive, and most profitable use
    c. The current use
    d. The future, fully developed use of the property

70. What should an appraiser do to obtain necessary information about comparables?

    a. Make accurate physical measurements.
    b. Inspect the comparables and verify the data.
    c. Rely on the recorded facts of the sale and analyze the data.
    d. Inspect the comparables and interview the lender.

71. In statistical analysis, the _____ measures the dispersion of numbers in a data set.

    a. mean
    b. mode
    c. standard deviation
    d. range

72. All of the following are used to analyze a property's highest and best use **except**:

    a. direct zoning.
    b. aesthetic value.
    c. incentive.
    d. bulk zoning.

73. When appraising a new house based on plans provided by the builder, what should the appraiser do regarding upgrades such as flooring and security systems?

   a. Ask the salesperson how much the buyer paid for the upgrades and use that figure as the adjustment for those items.
   b. Do not consider the upgrades because upgrades do not impact market value.
   c. Note the upgrades but do not adjust for them because all of the comparables should be new homes from the same development.
   d. Reconcile these upgrades in the identifiable market and determine the impact, if any, on value.

74. A property is currently valued at $53,280 and sold 2 years ago for $36,000. What is the monthly rate of appreciation?

   a. 2%
   b. 3%
   c. 4%
   d. 10%

75. What is primary data?

   a. Data about the property when it was first constructed
   b. Data collected by the appraiser that is not available in published sources
   c. Data that the appraiser relies on most
   d. Data found in publications and other sources

76. Four houses have sales prices of $200,000, $260,000, $238,000, and $224,000. What is the mean?

   a. $60,000
   b. $230,000
   c. $230,500
   d. $249,000

77. The unit-in-place method:

   a. estimates the cost of labor and materials for each component of a building.
   b. estimates the cost of the current improvement as is.
   c. compares the construction cost with another building that has recently sold.
   d. includes units of land as part of the cost of construction.

78. What is the term for the legally and physically possible use that, at the time of appraisal, is most likely to produce the greatest land value?

    a. Highest and best use
    b. Vacant
    c. Improved use
    d. Fully developed

79. An appraiser does not use one of the usual approaches to value. In the Summary Appraisal Report, this exclusion must be:

    a. stated and explained.
    b. stated in the certification.
    c. included if requested by the client.
    d. referred to as irrelevant.

80. The economic life of an improvement has expired when:

    a. the improvements no longer contribute to the property value.
    b. the improvements no longer earn sufficient income to justify their continued operation.
    c. the property value as improved is no longer greater than the value as vacant.
    d. all of the above

81. What does the term *amortization* refer to?

    a. The periodic repayment of debt
    b. The accumulation of interest
    c. The increase in value of real estate over time
    d. The decrease in value of real estate over time

82. What characteristics must an item have to have value?

    a. Scarcity, utility, desirability, and transferability
    b. Scarcity, utility, desirability, and entrepreneurship
    c. Scarcity, utility, desirability, and effective purchasing power
    d. Desirability, labor, utility, and entrepreneurship

83. Which of the following terms refers to the *mortgagor*?

    a. Trustor
    b. Trustee
    c. Broker
    d. Borrower

84. What is the length of one side of 1/16th of a square section?

    a. 1/2 mile
    b. 1/4 mile
    c. 1/8th mile
    d. 1/16th mile

85. According to USPAP, who usually sets the supplemental appraisal standards for commercial banks that are insured by the federal government?

    a. The Federal Reserve Districts
    b. The Appraisal Standards Board
    c. The appraiser
    d. The FDIC

86. When may an appraiser invoke the JURISDICTIONAL EXCEPTION RULE?

    a. When there is a conflict between the requirements of USPAP and the applicable law or public policy requirements of a jurisdiction
    b. When there is a conflict between the appraiser's knowledge and the scope of work required by the appraisal assignment
    c. When there is a conflict between the client's desired estimate of value and the appraiser's professional opinion of value
    d. When there is a conflict between the appraiser's competency in a given area and the public policy requirements of a jurisdiction

87. The Gramm-Leach-Bliley Act (GLB):

    a. made illegal lender discrimination based on age, gender, national origin, marital status, religion, and race.
    b. guaranteed a worker's right to be paid fairly by establishing a 40-hour work week, minimum wage, and restrictions on child labor.
    c. established the Office of Thrift Supervision to ensure another savings and loan disaster does not happen.
    d. ensured consumer privacy is protected, and prohibited financial institutions from releasing non-public and personal consumer information.

88. Which of the following defines *plottage value*?

    a. The incremental value created by combining two or more sites to create greater utility
    b. The value of the land on which the improvement is built
    c. The value of a parcel of land according to tax rolls
    d. The total value of a parcel of land that has been subdivided to create greater utility

89. Which of the following statements is **correct** regarding the sales comparison approach?

    a. When selecting comparable sales, the appraiser does not consider the age of the property.
    b. When using the sales comparison approach, the appraiser adjusts the comparable properties to the subject property.
    c. An appraiser should never use comparable sales that are more than six months old.
    d. The sales prices of comparables are always conclusive evidence of market value in the area.

90. When valuing a site, which appraisal method deducts the value of site improvements from the overall sales price of a property?

    a. Allocation
    b. Extraction
    c. Ground rent capitalization
    d. Sales comparison

91. A $100,000 loan has monthly payments of $908.70. The first month's interest totals $833.33 and the principal is $75.37. What is the annual mortgage constant?

    a. 0.03
    b. 0.09
    c. 0.11
    d. 0.13

92. The primary strength of the Sales Comparison Approach is that:

    a. it is the most mathematically accurate.
    b. it is always the easiest approach to use.
    c. it is a direct reflection of buyers and sellers in the marketplace.
    d. it considers the cost to reproduce improvements.

93. What is a factor that expresses a relationship between value and a particular property feature?

    a. Element of comparison
    b. Unit of measure
    c. Unit of comparison
    d. Essential element

94. More people recycle their bottles, aluminum cans, and paper than ever before. Which of the four forces does this represent?

    a. Environmental
    b. Economic
    c. Governmental
    d. Social

95. 250,000 square feet is equivalent to:

    a. 390.63 acres
    b. 5.74 acres
    c. 25,000 square yards
    d. 1 section

96. Which of the following is not part of an appraiser's concept of land?

    a. Ethnic
    b. Social
    c. Geographic
    d. Legal

97. Public regulations determine what types of materials may be used to construct improvements. These regulations are:

    a. easements.
    b. building codes.
    c. setback requirements.
    d. zoning ordinances.

98. A developer purchased a parcel of land that she plans to subdivide. She determines that 10% of the parcel is unusable, and another 5% will be set aside for streets and common areas. She divides the remainder of the parcel into lots to be sold off. If she sells 23 acres, how many acres did she originally purchase?

    a. 17.5 acres
    b. 20 acres
    c. 27 acres
    d. 30 acres

99. An appraiser needs to determine the optimal building-to-land ratio for a site that will be improved with an office building. Which of the following economic principles will she use?

    a. Conformity
    b. Balance
    c. Contribution
    d. Change

100. *Surplus productivity* refers to:

    a. the income that is generated above the current market rate for a specific type of property.
    b. the income that remains after costs for labor, capital, and coordination have been deducted.
    c. the income attributable to land rent that remains after operating expenses, taxes, and debt service have been deducted.
    d. the income generated in excess of the average level of productivity.

101. All of the following are used to calculate effective gross income **except**:

    a. other income (e.g., vending machines).
    b. vacancy.
    c. operating expenses.
    d. collection loss.

102. All of the following are acceptable methods of estimating building costs **except**:

    a. unit-in-place method
    b. quantity survey method
    c. breakdown method
    d. comparative unit method

103. An appraisal's effective date:

    a. establishes the context of the value estimate.
    b. is always the same date as the appraisal report.
    c. must not be later than the date of the appraisal report.
    d. must not be prior to the date of the appraisal report.

104. When using the sales comparison approach, what is the proper sequence for making adjustments?

   a. Property rights, conditions of sale, market conditions, financing, location, and physical characteristics.
   b. Financing, conditions of sale, market conditions, property rights, location, and physical characteristics.
   c. Property rights, financing terms, conditions of sale, market conditions, location, and physical characteristics.
   d. Physical characteristics, location, property rights, financing, conditions of sale, market conditions.

105. A property's value to a specific user is called:

   a. assessed value.
   b. value-in-use.
   c. insurable value.
   d. value-in-exchange.

106. Which method of site valuation is most commonly used?

   a. Allocation
   b. Land residual
   c. Sales comparison
   d. Ground rent capitalization

107. A property with a gross income of $24,000 sells for $210,000. What is the gross income multiplier?

   a. 5.64
   b. 7.33
   c. 8.75
   d. 11.97

108. An apartment building contains 260 units, which rent out at a rate of 10 per month. What is the annual absorption rate?

   a. 2.17%
   b. 46.15%
   c. 3.85%
   d. 26%

109. When estimating the net operating income of a property, an appraiser considers all of the following expenses **except**:

   a. property insurance.
   b. mortgage payments.
   c. decorating expenses.
   d. real estate taxes.

110. A developer offers 50 single-family homes for sale at $350,000 with special financing. However, he is also offering the same homes for $340,000 if the buyers secure their own financing. What should an appraiser do with this information?

   a. It depends on whether the client is concerned about financing.
   b. Nothing because the buyer makes the financing decision, not the appraiser.
   c. Discuss the special financing in the report and give his or her opinion about the value it adds or detracts.
   d. Complete the appraisal "as is".

Score Chart 2

Category	Questions	Score
Influences on Real Estate Value	8, 12, 46, 56, 94	
Legal Considerations in Appraisal	5, 9, 15, 37, 42, 96	
Types of Value	7, 13, 33, 54, 105	
Economic Principles	24, 30, 60, 64, 82, 99, 100	
Real Estate Markets and Analysis	32, 49, 61, 63, 75, 81, 83, 87, 91, 108	
Valuation Process	1, 18, 26, 34, 53, 57, 58, 73	
Property Description	2, 11, 14, 40, 47, 62, 84, 95, 97	
Highest and Best Use Analysis	3, 19, 22, 25, 67, 69, 72, 78	
Appraisal Statistical Concepts	45, 59, 68, 71, 74, 76, 98	
Sales Comparison Approach	20, 27, 28, 36, 44, 48, 51, 70, 89, 92, 104	
Site Value	10, 39, 88, 90, 93, 106	
Cost Approach	35, 43, 50, 77, 80, 102	
Income Approach	17, 31, 41, 65, 101, 107, 109	
Valuation of Partial Interests	6	
Appraisal Standards and Ethics	4, 16, 21, 23, 29, 38, 52, 55, 66, 79, 85, 86, 103, 110	

Answers

1. (a) A complete legal description of the property should be included in the addenda.

2. (a) When a building site is larger than is necessary for the improvements, the extra land is called excess land. Vacant sites may also have excess land if the area is larger than is necessary for its highest and best use.

3. (c) Highest and best use is defined as the physically possible, legally permissible, economically feasible, and maximally productive use.

4. (a) A feasibility study is an analysis of the cost-benefit relationship of an economic endeavor.

5. (c) Directive zoning is used as a planning tool to ensure property is used at its highest and best use.

6. (a) Cooperative ownership is a form of ownership in which a corporation is created to hold title to the entire property.

7. (c) Utility is basic to value, but it does not establish value by itself. Scarcity must also be present. No object can have value unless it possesses some degree of utility as well as scarcity.

8. (c) By definition.

9. (c) The most important and unique quality of joint tenancy is the right if survivorship. A joint tenant cannot transfer title to his or her share through a will.

10. (a) An appraiser may base the value of a site on the principles of balance, contribution, surplus productivity, and increasing and decreasing returns.

11. (c) A hip roof slopes evenly on all four sides.

12. (c) Corner locations are exposed to more automobile and pedestrian traffic than interior lots.

13. (a) Insurable value is based on the replacement or reproduction cost of physical items that are subject to destruction or loss.

14. (d) Off-site improvements are located outside the confines of the site and include streets, curbs, gutters, sidewalks, storm sewer drains, and connecting utility lines. On-site improvements include landscaping, paving, utility lines, grading, etc.

15. (b) Bulk zoning controls density by regulating setbacks, building heights, and percentage of open area. Incentive zoning requires that street floors of office buildings be used for retail establishments. Aesthetic zoning requires buildings to conform to certain types of architecture.

16. (d) The Appraisal Standards Board exercises authority over the subject, style, content, and substance of USPAP and establishes, improves, and promulgates USPAP.

17. (a) The overall capitalization rate can be applied only to the net operating income. The formula used in the income approach is value = income ÷ overall capitalization rate.

18. (c) Capitalizing income is part of the income approach to value. It is performed as part of the approaches to value.

19. (b) Subdivided land is awaiting development and its highest and best use is its future, fully developed use.

20. (d) The goal of any approach to value is to seek the value indication. Using sales price as a search parameter is like seeking a predetermined result.

21. (b) It is unethical to base an appraiser's compensation on the value estimate of the appraisal.

22. (c) The highest and best use of a special purpose property as improved is probably its current use.

23. (a) A reviewer must develop an opinion of the appropriateness of the original appraiser's analyses, opinion, and conclusions, as well as develop his or her reasons for any disagreement.

24. (b) A home that is poorly maintained will benefit from its location in a neighborhood of well-maintained homes. Conversely, a well maintained home that suffers from its location in a neighborhood of poorly-maintained homes is an example of regression.

25. (a) Special use properties should be valued on the basis of their value in use and value in exchange. Value in use is based on the current use of the property. Value in exchange is based on an alternative use. Because special use properties may have a limited number of uses or only one use, the appraiser may have to value them based on an alternative use.

26. (b) According to USPAP, the operative word in a restricted appraisal report is state (Standards Rule 2-2 (c) ix); the operative word in a summary appraisal report is summarize (Standards Rule 2-2 (b) ix); and the operative work in a self-contained appraisal report is describe (Standards Rule 2-2 (a) ix).

27. (a) Plottage refers to the incremental value created by combining two or more sites to produce greater utility. The joining of the sites does not necessarily produce incremental value, it must also create greater utility.

28. (a) The value of a property is generally accurate when the sales comparison approach is based on a sufficient number of sales similar to the subject property with appropriate adjustments.

29. (d) The ETHICS RULE prohibits an appraiser from communicating assignment results in a fraudulent or misleading manner, as well as using or communicating a misleading or fraudulent report.

30. (c) Reasonable competition stimulates further creative contribution, but in excess it can destroy profits.

31. (b) GIM stands for gross income multiplier. The GIM equals the value of the property divided by the gross annual income.

32. (b) An annuity is a series of equal payments or receipts on an investment. Annuity tables calculate present and future values of annuities.

33. (a) Adjustments to comparables must be made for special or creative financing or sales concessions.

34. (c) The interest being appraised and the definition of use can influence the final conclusion of value. The value will probably vary slightly depending on which approach was used, due to the natural variations in data.

35. (c) When using the abstraction method, an appraiser divides the total depreciation by the effective age in order to determine the average amount of depreciation indicated by each of the sold properties.

36. (c) Find the two comparables that are exactly the same, except for the adjustment you are trying to determine. The difference in price between the two comps will equal the value of the adjustment. For example, Comp 1 and 3 are identical except for the lot size. Comp 3 is ½ acre smaller and $2,000 less expensive. Therefore, ½ acre is equal to $2,000.

37. (c) The lot and block system is based on a recorded map or survey. The rectangular survey is based on townships, sections, ranges, and acres. The metes and bounds system measures property by describing the property's boundaries.

38. (d) Standards Rule 3, lines 1140-1143 states "To avoid confusion between these activities, a reviewer performing an appraisal review must not sign the work under review unless he or she intends to accept the responsibility of a cosigner for that work."

39. (b) An appraiser can determine the estimated value of a finished lot by analyzing appropriate comparables from existing, competitive subdivisions that have recently been developed.

40. (b) A gambrel roof is double pitched on two sides and is most often seen on barns.

41. (b) Capitalization refers to the process of converting net income into an estimate of value.

42. (b) An appraiser must always adjust the comparable(s), never the subject property.

43. (a) Older structures have a lot of depreciation to estimate, making the cost approach less reliable. Income properties are appraised using the income capitalization approach. The cost approach does not apply to vacant land.

44. (a) Since the comp is superior in both regards, adjust it negatively for the financing and time differences. $300,000 x (1 – 0.05) x (1 – 0.08). Cash equivalency is always adjusted first, then time.

45. (b) You will need to use either a financial calculator or a compound interest table to solve this problem. To use the annual compound interest tables, look up the factor in Column 2: Future Value Annuity of $1 Per Year; Row: 10 years. Usually, you multiply that factor by the amount you are investing annually ($6,707) to determine how much you will have accumulated by the end of 10 years. However, in this case we already know the result is $117,700, but we need to know the interest rate that gets us there. To do this, work backwards. Divide $117,700 by $6,707. This equals 17.548829. Look in the compound interest tables for the factor that is closest to 17.548829. The 12% compound interest table contains the factor closest to 17.548829.

46. (a) By definition.

47. (c) Reinforced concrete is structural concrete reinforced with steel.

48. (d) Appropriate comparables are essential to the sales comparison approach. The best comparables require no or very minimal adjustment.

49. (b) Reversion is the lump sum an investor receives at the termination of an investment.

50. (c) The straight-line, or age-life method of calculating depreciation is the easiest to understand and use. The formula is effective age/total economic life = accrued depreciation.

51. (a) Doubling up on adjustments exists when more than one set of matched pairs is used and some comparison elements may interact. Regression analysis may help measure the interaction of data.

52. (b) Appraisal practice is defined as valuation services performed by an individual acting as an appraiser, including but not limited to appraisal, appraisal review, or appraisal consulting.

53. (d) The appraiser should always consider market data and perceptions. The appraiser will need to use subjective judgments when reconciling alternate conclusions, since some differences in value will occur between the approaches.

54. (b) Ad valorem is Latin for "according to value."

55. (d) An appraisal review is the development of an opinion about the quality of another appraiser's work, including the appraisal report, appraisal review report, or an appraisal consulting report. The reviewer considers the completeness, adequacy, relevance, appropriateness, and reasonableness of the work under review.

56. (a) By definition.

57. (a) General data includes the social, economic, governmental, and environmental influences that affect property values in the region.

58. (b) In USPAP, Standards Rule 2-2 (a) (x), requires the appraiser to describe the support and rationale for the appraiser's opinion of the highest and best use of the real estate as part of a self-contained appraisal report.

59. (c) A population is a complete data set or all the data in a certain group.

60. (d) The four criteria are: physically possible, legally permissible, financially feasible, and maximally productive.

61. (a) By definition.

62. (b) Appraisers include such items as the cost of clearing a site, grading, and landscaping, drainage, water and sewer connections, electric and gas service, private access streets, alleys, drives, and sidewalks as part of the site analysis.

63. (b) The process of compounding interest increases the amount of money. The process of discounting decreases the amount of money. Future value = principal + interest (compounding); present value = principal − discount (discounting).

64. (d) According to the principle of substitution, the maximum value of an item is established by determining the cost of acquiring an equally desirable substitute. This is the basis for the sales comparison approach.

65. (b) Net income/value = capitalization rate. $10,000/$100,000 = 0.10 or 10%. If the capitalization rate increases by 1%, then $10,000/0.11 = $90,909.

66. (d) The PREAMBLE describes the overall structure of USPAP. [Appraisal Standards and Ethics]

67. (d) The four tests used to determine highest and best use are: physically possible, legally permitted, economically feasible, and maximally productive.

68. (b) $500 x 12 months = $6,000 minimum rent. $8,000 − $6,000 = $2,000 rent due from gross sales. $2,000 ÷ 0.02 = $100,000 gross sales over $50,000. $100,000 + $50,000 = $150,000 total gross sales for the year.

69. (a) A property's highest and best use is determined using four tests. In order for a use to be highest and best, it must be legally permissible, physically possible, economically feasible, and maximally productive.

70. (b) In order to obtain all of the information needed to use a comparable sale, the appraiser should inspect each comparable property and verify the nature of the sale with the buyer, seller, or broker.

71. (c) The standard deviation measures the differences between individual variates, or numbers, and the entire population. To find the standard deviation, determine the mean of all the variates in the population. Then find the deviation of each individual variate from the mean. Square the deviation of each variate. Add all the squared deviations and find the square root of that sum. Finally, divide that number by the number of variates in the population.

72. (c) Direct, aesthetic value, and bulk are all types of zoning. Zoning is one of the primary considerations in determining if a property's use is legally permitted, the second requirement for a highest and best use.

73. (d) "A" assumes that cost equals value; "B" ignores upgrades; "C" assumes all comps have upgrades; "D" searches for the contributory value, if any.

74. (a) The difference between the two values is $53,280 − $36,000 = $17,280. Divide the difference by the original sales price to determine the amount of change: $17,280 ÷ $36,000 = 0.48 or 48%. Divide 48% by 24 (the number of months in two years) to get the monthly rate of increase: 2%.

75. (b) Primary data is any data the appraiser collects or compiles himself, even if the data does not directly affect the property's value. Data that was prepared by someone other than the appraiser, such as information in publications and other sources, is called secondary data.

76. (c) The mean is the average.

77. (a) The unit-in-place cost estimate is calculated by breaking up a building into components and estimating the cost of the material and labor required to construct that unit, on the date of appraisal.

78. (a) The highest and best use of land is the physically possible, legally permitted, economically feasible, and maximally productive use.

79. (a) In a Summary Appraisal Report, an appraiser must state and explain the reason for excluding any of the usual appraisal approaches and any permitted departures from the specific requirements of Standard 1.

80. (d) All of these answer choices indicate that the improvements no longer contribute to value and it's time to demolish them.

81. (a) Amortization is the periodic repayment of a debt, such as a mortgage, over time.

82. (c) By definition.

83. (d) The person or company who takes out the loan is the mortgagor.

84. (d) A section is a mile square; ¼ mile x ¼ mile = 1/16 mile.

85. (d) Standard 10 states that appraiser guidelines and standards are issued by Federal Deposit Insurance Corporation (FDIC), Federal Reserve Board (FRB), Office of the Comptroller of the Currency (OCC), and Office of Thrift Supervision (OTS). Standard 10 also states that USPAP considers these guidelines and standards as SUPPLEMENTAL STANDARDS when they supplement USPAP requirements.

86. (a) An appraiser may invoke the JURISDICTIONAL EXCEPTION RULE if any part of USPAP is contrary to the law or public policy of any jurisdiction. However, only that part of USPAP that is contrary will be void.

87. (d) The Gramm-Leach-Bliley Act implemented the most sweeping overhaul of financial services regulation in the United States in over 60 years. Also known as The Financial Modernization Act of 1999, it includes privacy provisions to protect consumer information held by financial institutions.

88. (a) Plottage value is the increase in value that results when two or more adjacent sites are combined to create greater utility.

89. (b) Comparable properties are always adjusted to the subject property, never the subject property to the comparables.

90. (a) By definition.

91. (c) The annual debt service is $10,904.40 ($908.70 x 12 months). Divide the annual debt service by $100,000 = 0.109 rounded to 0.11. The principal and interest figures are irrelevant.

92. (c) The sales comparison approach is easily understood and directly reflects the actions of buyers and sellers in the marketplace.

93. (c) By definition.

94. (d) By definition.

95. (b) 250,000 divided by the number of square feet in 1 acre (43,560) = 5.74 acres.

96. (a) An appraiser recognizes the geographic, legal, social, and economic concepts of land.

97. (b) Building codes control the design of permitted buildings and the types of materials that may be used.

98. (c) To solve this problem, work backwards. She sold 23 acres. To determine how many acres she had before she set aside the unusable portion and the percentage for streets and common areas, divide 23 acres by 85% (100% − 15%). This equals 27.06, rounded to 27 acres.

99. (b) The principle of balance states that there is an ideal equilibrium in assembling and using the factors of production. In this example, the appraiser needs to determine the balance between the land and the building.

100. (b) Surplus income is the remainder after the costs of labor, capital, and coordination have been deducted from the total income. Residual valuation techniques are based on the concept of surplus productivity.

101. (c) Effective gross income is calculated before deducting operating expenses. Effective gross income less operating expenses equals net operating income.

102. (c) The breakdown method is used to estimate accrued depreciation.

103. (a) The effective date establishes the context of the value estimate. The effective date may be before, on, or after the date of appraisal.

104. (c) Adjustments should be made in this order: property rights conveyed, financing, conditions of sale, market conditions (time), location, and physical characteristics.

105. (b) Value-in-use is the value of a good to a specific user, based on its productivity (in the form of income, utility or amenity).

106. (c) When adequate comparable data is available, this method is the one most frequently used.

107. (c) The formula to find the gross income multiplier is: sales price/gross income = gross income multiplier. $210,000/$24,000 = 8.75.

108. (b) The annual rental rate is divided by the total supply: (10x12) ÷ 260.

109. (b) Mortgage payments are not a factor in determining net operating income.

110. (c) Standards Rule 2-1 (c), SR 10-1 (c), and SR 6-7 (c) all state that the appraiser must accurately disclose any extraordinary assumption, hypothetical condition, or limiting condition that affects the appraisal and explain its impact on value. The Comment specifies that atypical financing is one of these that should be disclosed and explained.

Monthly Compound Interest Tables

		1	2	3	4	5	6
Annual Interest Rate	Years	Future Value of $1	Future Value Annuity of $1 per Month	Sinking Fund Factor	Present Value of $1 (Reversion)	Present Value Annuity of $1 per Month	Payment to Amoritize
8	30	10.935730	1490.359449	0.000671	0.091443	136.283494	0.007338
9	30	14.730576	1830.743483	0.000546	0.067886	124.281866	0.008046

Annual Compound Interest Tables

		1	2	3	4	5	6
Annual Interest Rate	Years	Future Value of $1	Future Value Annuity of $1 per Month	Sinking Fund Factor	Present Value of $1 (Reversion)	Present Value Annuity of $1 per Month	Payment to Amoritize
8	5	1.469328	5.866601	0.170456	0.680583	3.992710	0.250456
9	30	10.062657	113.283211	0.008827	0.099377	11.257783	0.088827